The International Monetary System

Richard N. Cooper. 1985. *Economic Policy in an Interdependent World: Essays in World Economics.* Cambridge, Massachusetts: The MIT Press.

Richard N. Cooper. 1987. *The International Monetary System: Essays in World Economics.* Cambridge, Massachusetts: The MIT Press.

The International Monetary System

Essays in World Economics

Richard N. Cooper

The MIT Press
Cambridge, Massachusetts
London, England

This book was set in Palatino by Asco Trade Typesetting Ltd., Hong Kong, and printed and bound by Halliday Lithograph in the United States of America.

Library of Congress Cataloging-in-Publication Data

Cooper, Richard N.
  The international monetary system.

  Includes bibliographies and index.
  1. International finance.   I. Title.
HG3881.C6733   1987   332.4'5   86-7400
ISBN 0-262-03124-8

Contents

Introduction

I first became interested in the international monetary system as a graduate student at the London School of Economics in the late 1950s. A leading problem at that time was large foreign-held balances of sterling and whether Britain should "fund" them to reduce the possibility of raids on the Bank of England's limited reserves. I felt then that the issue as posed was badly oversimplified, that the main problem was private sterling balances that would be difficult to fund, and that the official balances which were the main focus of attention, far from being a major problem, had been largely stabilizing in their effect on the British currency. These views were developed, with supporting evidence, some years later during my participation in a Brookings Institution study of the British economy (R. E. Caves, ed., *Britain's Economic Prospects*, 1968).

This interest in international monetary questions was revived, reinforced, and extended during my stint as an economist on President Kennedy's Council of Economic Advisers (CEA). The new Council was concerned with the "gold problem," as John F. Kennedy called it—because there had recently been extensive foreign official conversions of dollars into gold—but the wide international role of the dollar made it difficult to consider the gold problem comprehensively without addressing the fundamental characteristics of the international monetary system itself. Under the direction of James Tobin, the council undertook a study of the international monetary system. Tobin's colleague at Yale, Robert Triffin, had just published his critique of the international monetary system and pointed to its fundamental long-run instability (*Gold and the Dollar Crisis*, 1960). But Kennedy's Secretary of Treasury, Douglas Dillon, and Under-Secretary for Monetary Affairs, Robert Roosa, were not interested in fundamental changes in the monetary system. They preferred to deal with the immediate pressures on the dollar through such measures as "operation twist" on the structure of interest rates to deter the outflow of US capital without discouraging domestic investment, the issuance of foreign currency–guaranteed Roosa bonds to foreign central banks, the promulgation of a "gold budget" to reduce U.S. government expenditures overseas, and in time the introduction of an interest equalization tax and other direct controls on outflows of capital from the United States.

Secretary Dillon was succeeded by Henry H. Fowler, who, with strong encouragement and assistance from Francis Bator on the staff of the National Security Council, took a more lively interest in the monetary system as a whole and urged a detailed examination of what might be done to solve Triffin's dilemma: The world economy could not thrive without a continuing increase in official dollar balances, but such an increase would gradually undermine the credibility of the gold convertibility, which foreign monetary authorities took for granted as they added to their dollar balances. The main technical discussions within the US government took place in an interagency group chaired by Under-Secretary of Treasury Fred Deming. The group included Francis Bator, Arthur Okun from CEA, and Dewey Daane and Robert Solomon from the Federal Reserve Board. Anthony Solomon and I represented the State Department. What finally emerged from these discussions and their international counterparts was the SDR, dubbed "paper gold" by financial journalists, which was negotiated in 1967, installed in 1968, and first issued as a genuine international fiat money in January 1970. (Robert Solomon has written an excellent history of the creation of the SDR in his *The International Monetary System: 1945–1981.*)

In the meantime, there had been a large increase in US government expenditures associated with the rapid buildup of US forces in Vietnam. Lyndon Johnson had delayed asking for and getting a tax increase to finance this buildup, and that in turn led, via domestic inflationary pressures, to an overvalued dollar. In some respects the situation in the late 1960s was similar to the situation in the early 1980s, with a rise in the real value of the US dollar financed by inflows of capital from the rest of the world. But the mechanisms differed sharply between the two periods; the appreciation of the dollar occurred in the late 1960s because of domestic inflation, whereas in the early 1980s the inflow of capital drawn by high US interest rates led to an appreciation of the dollar and downward pressure on domestic prices.

By the late 1960s there was much concern about how to introduce greater exchange rate flexibility into the monetary system. The growing international mobility of capital produced large-scale currency speculation in anticipation of the discrete changes in exchange rates that the Bretton

Woods system envisaged. Moreover, the US government was disturbed by the fact that the United States could not control its nominal exchange rate, because in practice other countries determined the rate between their currencies and the dollar. Both these considerations heightened interest in various forms of greater flexibility, with a number of academic economists recommending that exchange rates be allowed to float freely, determined by market forces without official intervention.

The new Nixon administration was faced with these complex issues in 1969. Henry Kissinger, newly appointed as the Assistant to the President for National Security Affairs, had been told by a friend that the first foreign policy crisis he might face would be an international monetary crisis. I was asked to brief Kissinger on these questions in December 1968 and early January 1969, and agreed to monitor them for him on a part-time basis after the inauguration if he would agree to hire Fred Bergsten as a full-time assistant, which he did. Ernest Johnston, from the State Department, and Robert Hormats, fresh from the Fletcher School, rounded out the small economics group on the staff of the National Security Council. I was involved throughout 1969. Kissinger had a heavy agenda and by his own admission did not take great interest either in trade or in monetary issues; rather, he adopted a "watching brief," as he later put it in *The White House Years* (p. 950). It was not until the large oil price increases of 1973–74 that economic issues caught his eye as possibly being important components of foreign affairs.

But Paul Volcker as the new Under-Secretary of Treasury for Monetary Affairs could not ignore them. Tight money in the United States drew in funds from the rest of the world in 1969, thereby to some extent concealing the fundamental difficulties. When the American economy went into recession in 1970 and interest rates dropped sharply, that exposed a large payments deficit. In the meantime, John Connally had succeeded David Kennedy as Secretary of the Treasury, and his unsubtle technique for dealing with the problem was to urge President Nixon to impose an import surcharge and cease convertibility of the dollar into gold. Nixon acted in August 1971, in a program that also included price controls in the United States. After a turbulent autumn, the Smithsonian Agreement of December 1971 resulted in an agreed devaluation of the dollar against the major European currencies and the Japanese yen. But the international monetary system remained unsettled, and various countries abandoned fixed parities and allowed their currencies to float in the marketplace. In March 1973 floating became generalized, as all the major countries ceased to fix their currencies to the US dollar. In 1972 a formal exercise in international monetary reform was undertaken under the auspices of the International Monetary Fund (IMF) by the Committee of Twenty. The United States put forward a "reserve indicator" proposal for guiding exchange rate movements. This proposal bears some similarity to a proposal I put forward in 1969 (reprinted here as chapter 3). The US proposal was reported in the CEA's Economic Report for January 1973. But rapidly moving events overtook systematic deliberation, and each country was left to fend for itself. Belatedly, the Committee of Twenty recognized what was happening and in the spring of 1974 endorsed a high degree of national choice in determining exchange rate arrangements.

Agreement was reached in Jamaica in January 1976 to legitimize exchange rate flexibility by amending the IMF articles of agreement. The new Article 4 pays obeisance to exchange rate stability and even envisages a time when fixed parities might be reestablished "on the basis of the underlying stability of the world economy." But the language was chosen carefully. Countries pledge themselves "to promote a stable system of exchange rates," not a system of stable exchange rates. And they "seek to promote stability by fostering orderly underlying economic and financial conditions and a monetary system that does not intend to produce erratic eruptions," thus implying that "unstable" exchange rates are a consequence of unstable underlying conditions rather than a failure to fix the rates. The new article in effect allows each country to have any regime of exchange rates that it wants, subject only to the two conditions that it notify the IMF of its arrangements and that it "avoid manipulating the exchange rates or the international monetary system in order to prevent effective balance-of- payments adjustment or to gain an unfair competitive advantage over other members." But this agreement left open all the difficult practical problems of actually managing a system of flexible exchange rates.

After 1974 the world's attention shifted from the international monetary system to the problems of adjusting to much higher oil prices and the deep recession associated with them. Reform of the monetary system dropped into the background, or rather became a secondary component of a North-South debate on reform of the world economic system as a whole, a component that was overshadowed by commodity policy, energy policy, trade issues, and foreign assistance, although the decision-making procedures of the International Monetary Fund came in for strong attack by some developing countries.

One component of the international monetary system that was actively discussed in the late 1970s concerned the role of the US dollar in official reserves and the possible need for a "substitution account" to absorb some of those dollars in exchange for some other asset that did not depend for its issuance on an individual country. As with sterling twenty years earlier, I was skeptical that the large officially held dollar balances were in fact a serious problem for the stability for the international monetary system. In my view, official dollar holdings were overwhelmed both in volume and in potentially destabilizing movement by large private dollar holdings, and I feared that a preoccupation with official balances and the creation of a substitution account would simply be a diversion of thought and official energy from more important issues. And indeed technical discussions among finance ministry officials and with the IMF quickly bogged down over the third-rate issue of who should bear the ultimate exchange risk of the substitution account in the event of certain contingencies.

Interest in the monetary system as a whole revived in the early 1980s, when several politically prominent Americans pressed for a revival of a monetary role for gold. The French and some other Europeans would have been delighted at this American initiative twenty years earlier but yawned in indifference in the 1980s. The interest in monetary gold was an American peculiarity that attracted some high-level attention for a variety of reasons, ranging from a search for effective discipline against inflation of the type that had plagued nations in the preceding decade to, it must be said, pure nostalgia. My view was that it would be impossible to revive gold in a monetary role that would provide effective discipline over national governments. The argument is developed in chapter 2 of this volume.

I thought that a constructive role for official IMF gold could be found by selling it into the private market at prices well above its book value, the capital gains to be used for agreed international purposes, such as foreign assistance to developing countries. These ideas were put forward in 1973 in *Toward A Renovated World Monetary System*, written with Motoo Kaji and Claudio Segre. I proposed this idea again to Henry Kissinger in 1974 to help deal with what was then called the "recycling" problem following the emergence of large balance-of-payments surpluses of oil-exporting countries. In addition to agreeing on amending the IMF articles of agreement, the 1976 Jamaica meeting also agreed that the IMF should sell one-sixth of its substantial gold holdings onto the private market and devote the capital gains from such sales to helping the poorest countries that had been hard hit by the increase in oil prices and the 1975 world recession.

Concern also arose in the early 1980s over the substantial misalignment among major currencies and what rules of the system might avoid such misalignments in future. It was in this period too that European monetary cooperation was revived, and the European monetary system was established, under which a number of European currencies established fixed parities among themselves and defined bands within which these currencies would be allowed to fluctuate against one another in the marketplace.

This, then, was the general background against which the essays in this volume were written. Something more can be said about the specific context of each essay here. With the exception of minor corrections they are published here as they were originally published or issued, so the context is important. They have been grouped in this volume under broad headings of common interest rather than in chronological order.

The first essay serves as an introduction to the volume as a whole. It attempts to lay out the major features of any international monetary system and the considerations that go into the choices among those features. It was written for a Brookings Institution conference of economists and political scientists, to bring the two disciplines into communication on matters of international economic policy. It adopts a much wider scope than the Committee of Twenty, which was just completing its deliberations. The key point of the article for political scientists and diplomats is that in designing the rules for a world economic system, political will alone is not sufficient to make the system work. Certain technical conditions of feasibility must also be met. The point is obvious to engineers. They cannot and do not try to build bridges in violation of the laws of physics. But the frequency of references to political will when it comes to international economic reform suggests that the point is not obvious to those preoccupied with the exercise of power, either as wielders or as students of those who are wielders, and demonstrates their great reluctance to consider the behavior of households and firms as a force that has to be reckoned with in considering the design of any economic system.

The next three articles discuss three different monetary systems: the gold standard, a system of exchange rate parities that are allowed and indeed encouraged to "glide" or crawl against one another, and experience under floating exchange rates.

The paper on the gold standard (chapter 2) was written in 1981, while the US Gold Commission was examining the possibilities for restoring some monetary role to gold. William Brainard and George Perry suggested that it would be useful to have a review of experience and issues for the Brookings Panel on Economic Activity. I felt that devoting time and space to the issue represented a misallocation of BPEA time, for there were more urgent issues of economic analysis and policy, but agreed to do it if they insisted on going ahead with this low priority project. In retrospect I believe they were right. The historical gold standard has been idealized out of recognition through years of teaching a highly stylized version of it in economics courses. Many of those who lived through it were dissatisfied with the performance of the gold standard in its brief heyday in the late nineteenth century, and today's publics would have found it intolerable. It is useful to set the historical record straight. The second half of the paper addresses several proposals for reviving a monetary role for gold in the late twentieth century and finds all of them flawed, basically for one fundamental reason. The dollar price of gold is no longer historically and immutably given, so it can be altered at will, and it very likely would be altered if conditions under a revived gold standard became too uncomfortable. That fact alters enormously the expectational environment of a gold standard and would weaken decisively any disciplinary role which gold could play.

Chapter 3 was written in 1969 in an attempt to suggest a method for introducing more flexibility into a system of fixed exchange rates while still retaining some of the advantages of fixed exchange rates. It is a variant of a proposal made a few years earlier by John Williamson, but with less emphasis on automaticity and greater linkage to reserve movements. As noted above, the US government later espoused a weaker reserve indicator proposal in 1972, but it was overtaken by the move to generalized floating in 1973.

Chapter 4 reviews the experience of the first eight years of floating exchange rates. It was written for a Festschrift for Robert Triffin, one of the most persistent and perceptive analysts of the international monetary system over the years, and a most agreeable colleague during my fourteen years at Yale University. The timing of this article was magnificently bad. It was written in late 1980, and it argued that, while floating exchange rates did not satisfy all the claims of its advocates, on the whole the world under floating exchange rates had performed reasonably well and roughly according to expectations, given the severe shocks to which the world economy had been subjected during that period. Movements in effective exchange rates of the major countries were not great, and they behaved broadly as required to adjust for inflation differentials and to imbalances in the current account. This article did not foresee the huge increase in the value of the dollar that would occur in the period from 1981 to 1984 in response to the macroeconomic policy mix adopted by the United States and by other major countries. A combination of tight monetary policy and expansionary fiscal policy in the United States with contractionary fiscal policy in Britain, Germany, Japan, and (later) France resulted in high US interest rates relative to those abroad. That in turn resulted in huge flows of capital into the United States, which sharply bid up the value of the dollar, so that by late 1984 the dollar was over 30 percent stronger in real terms than it had been in 1980 with respect to other major currencies weighted by trade with the United States. This pattern of events had important consequences for the performance of the world economy as a whole and in particular for the level and distribution of investment. I would thus render a somewhat less generous view of experience under floating exchange rates today than I did in 1980. I return to this issue in the final chapter of this volume.

Chapter 5 was written for the Committee for Economic Development in 1972 as a background exposition of alternative mechanisms of adjustment to disturbances in international payments, a central feature of any international monetary system. It examines in general terms a number of proposals for introducing greater exchange rate flexibility into the monetary system, of the type that were then being urged on a reluctant Committee of Twenty. As noted, these issues were soon to be overtaken by generalized floating of exchange rates in March 1973. The article does not address what has since become standard fare in recent treatment of balance-of-payments questions, namely the difference between temporary and permanent disturbances. This question used to be taken up under the heading of the "liquidity" which was to be available to countries to cover temporary disturbances to the current account. Present practice is to derive results from a two or more period optimizing model, typically with well-defined utility functions, as though a country can be treated as an enlarged household that makes well-considered consumption choices over time. I am dubious about whether this fashionable approach adds substantially to our knowledge about how countries do or should behave. But certainly the decision of whether to adjust or finance a disturbance to the balance of payments is a crucial one for any country, and it has been so considered for many years. All too often, however, it is difficult to know at once whether a disturbance is temporary or permanent.

The issue of adjustment is treated again in chapter 6, which addresses the guidelines the IMF should establish in a world of floating rates for official intervention in exchange markets. The essay was written in 1976 following the Jamaica agreement to permit floating subject to the two general conditions noted earlier. I suggest here that the overall guiding principle should be that countries should not take actions that avoidably hurt other countries. The chapter discusses more specific application of this principle and the role IMF guidelines might play. It again mentions the desirability of reserve targets as discussed in chapter 2.

Chapters 7 through 9 were all written in the early 1970s, and all concern the role of national currencies, especially the US dollar, in the international monetary system. The dollar at that time was under a considerable cloud. There had been large capital outflows from the United States in 1970 and 1971, the dollar was devalued in December 1971 after a stormy autumn following the Nixon-Connally shock, and it was still greatly unsettled in 1972. Moreover, President De Gaulle had complained during the 1960s of the "exorbitant privilege" of the dollar, and the complaint gained both credence and support in European and even in American circles as the Vietnam War became increasingly unpopular. So a major question for those concerned with the international monetary system was, What should be done with the large outstanding dollar balances, and how can the role of the dollar be reduced and the dollar made more symmetric to other currencies? In this setting I suggested that many observers were substituting abstract wish for operational analysis, that careful thought would suggest how difficult it would be to make the system completely symmetric with respect to all currencies, and why, if there was to be an asymmetry among currencies, the US dollar was the logical choice for the central role. In chapter 7 I develop the analytical point, and in chapter 8, written for the more general readership of *Foreign Policy*, I draw the implication that, for all the alleged weaknesses and disadvantages of the dollar, it was likely to remain the key international currency for many years because of the difficulty of dislodging a well-established currency from its position of primacy in the absence of a clear alternative.

In chapter 9 I discuss a related issue, the creation of a common European currency within the European Community. The article was written in 1971, as the members of the EEC were making their first serious attempt at close monetary cooperation and shortly after Britain had applied for entry into the European Community. I was somewhat pessimistic about the impact of British entry on the British currency, but I also argued that, if this pessimism proved to be unwarranted, sterling would provide the most natural basis for a new European currency, for reasons similar to those that accounted for the entrenched position of the dollar on the world scene, namely a strong and efficient financial market.

In chapter 10 I consider the future role of the SDR, which was by official agreement of the mid-1970s to become "the principal reserve asset" of the international monetary system. This article is a comment on a long, fine paper by Peter Kenen, of Princeton University, in which he argues the desirability and the technical feasibility of extending the use of the SDR to private markets. Kenen argued, and I agree fully, that this extension is necessary for moving the SDR into a central place as a reserve asset. Furthermore, success in that endeavor could ultimately permit some formal symmetry among currencies, with much less reliance on the US dollar or indeed any other national currency. I argue here that the original (1967) rationale for creation of the SDR remains valid in today's world, despite the presence of exchange rate flexibility among major currencies and despite the vast growth of international money and capital markets. I also argue that it is in the interest of the United States to keep the SDR alive, because in the course of time—two decades from now, say—Americans will find the international role of the dollar a more burdensome inhibition on the pursuit of domestic economic policy than they do now. If properly nurtured, the SDR could relieve the United States of that greater burden. But it will require active cultivation of a plant that will not grow from infancy by itself in the present inhospitable environment.

Chapter 11 is an expository article that attempts to cover briefly all aspects of the international monetary system for the benefit of non-specialists. It was written in early 1982 for a conference at the Chinese Academy of Social Sciences to serve as a general introduction to the subject for the Chinese, who had begun to take a lively interest in how the international economic system functions.

Chapter 12 was written in the spring of 1983 for the British Commonwealth Conference on the possibilities for the evolution of the IMF into a world central bank. This paper points out that the evolution of national central banks was gradual: They did not always have the authorities and the responsibilities that they have today. It also points out that the IMF has already evolved part way toward a world central bank, but that it lacks some of the key powers of a central bank; in particular, it is not a true lender of last resort because it cannot create fiat money at its own volition.

The last chapter, after offering a brief survey of the evolution of the international monetary system since 1945, concludes that present arrangements are not sustainable indefinitely. Contrary to the implication of chapter 4, it argues that movements in real exchange rates are too great to be tolerable in conjunction with relatively free trade and capital movements and therefore foresees growing restrictions both on trade and on capital movements unless the world moves consciously toward a system that reduces real exchange rate uncertainty. In the article I then offer a bold—some would say utopian—proposal for eliminating exchange rate uncertainty by creating a common currency for the industrial democracies and a common system for management of that currency. Needless to say, this is not a politically feasible proposal in the near future. But it is not too early to begin thinking about where we ultimately want to end up if dissatisfaction with the present system remains as high as it has become in recent years.

The debt crisis and the exceedingly strong dollar in 1984 and early 1985 have drawn attention to the possibility of defects in the international monetary system. The recent official view, as expressed in a Group of Ten report in September 1985, is that the system itself is satisfactory and that the problems we observe arise mainly from poor national economic policies. Even if the official view is correct, it raises the question of whether a system of rules more sharply defined than those currently prevailing can impose some constructive discipline on national economic policies. That, after all, was the strong underlying assumption of the Bretton Woods system designed over forty years ago. That remains a central issue in thinking about the international monetary system of the future.

1

Prolegomena to the Choice of an International Monetary System

The international monetary system—the rules and conventions that govern financial relations between countries—is an important component of international relations. When monetary relations go well, other relations have a better chance of going well; when they go badly, other areas are likely to suffer too. Monetary relations have a pervasive influence on both domestic and international economic developments, and history is strewn with examples of monetary failure leading subsequently to economic and political upheaval. Recent years have seen considerable turmoil in international monetary relations, and a marked deterioration in relations between Europe, Japan, and America. Ideally, monetary relations should be inconspicuous, part of the background in a well-functioning system, taken for granted. Once they become visible and uncertain, something is wrong.

As a consequence of this recent turmoil, intense official discussions on the nature and the future of the monetary system were belatedly begun in late 1972, under the auspices of the International Monetary Fund (IMF). A year later, little real progress in these discussions could be recorded (official press releases to the contrary notwithstanding). De facto monetary relations between countries were on a radically different course from the official discussions.

Many intricate details attend consideration of alternative monetary arrangements, and the details are often vitally important. It is not possible, however, to discuss them all in an essay charged with covering a broad spectrum of possible monetary arrangements and the broad implications of alternative monetary arrangements for the world as a whole, for groups of particular countries, and for particular groups within countries.

This essay has a somewhat more limited purpose. It attempts to survey systematically various possible types of international monetary regime,

International Organization 29, no. 1 (1975): 63–97. Reprinted by permission.

to identify criteria for choice between alternative monetary regimes, and to discover the reasons for disagreement between nations and between groups within nations on the choice of an international monetary regime. It draws on recent monetary history and on current discussions of reform of the monetary system for illustrations, and tries to suggest why cost-benefit analysis, while an appropriate framework in principle, is in practice so difficult to execute in this area. If the essay carries any principal message, it is that sources of disagreement do not generally derive from divergent interests, but rather from diverse perspectives and hence different conjectures about the consequences of one regime as compared with another. In short, disagreement arises mainly from ignorance about the true effects, so that we must use reasoned conjecture rather than solid fact to guide our choices, and reasonable people may and do differ with respect to their conjectures. The essay concludes with some brief observations on the appropriate role of international organizations in the international monetary arena and on the broad directions I believe the international monetary system should take.

I define a *regime* as any particular set of rules or conventions governing monetary and financial relations between countries. *Regime* seems preferable to *system* or *order*, both of which are sometimes used in this context, since it encompasses arrangements that are neither orderly nor systematic. A monetary regime specifies which instruments of policy may be used and which targets of policy are regarded as legitimate, including of course the limiting cases in which there are no restrictions on either.[1] I propose here to outline a number of international monetary regimes in terms of their major features, and to offer some brief comments on their costs and benefits. Each regime has many variants, variants that may either aggravate or mitigate the disadvantages, so that the distinctions between them are not in fact as sharp as I sometimes make it appear. Moreover, each regime may operate in many different ways, and a given regime may either be resoundingly successful or totally stymied, depending on how the participants operate within it. Some regimes lack the technical requisites for success and are bound to fail; others, internally consistent, can work effectively in one political milieu but not in another. Students of international relations too often focus on the political milieu to the neglect of requirements of internal consistency and technical proficiency; economists are prone to the opposite error.

One possible regime would be to have no rules or conventions at all—to allow each country to do what it thinks best, without any form of coordination. This may be called a free-for-all regime, with the understanding that in international monetary affairs governments and central banks are principal actors, so that the term *free-for-all* refers primarily to their actions, not merely to those of private transactors. In contrast, a regime of freely floating exchange rates and no controls on private international transactions, that is, a regime in which governments agree not to interfere either with transactions or with the foreign exchange market in any way, is definitely not a system without rules; indeed, it involves extraordinarily stringent proscriptions.

A free-for-all regime does not commend itself. It would allow large nations to try to exploit their power at the expense of smaller nations. It would give rise to attempts by individual nations to pursue objectives that were not consistent with one another (e.g., inconsistent aims with regard to a single exchange rate between two currencies), with resulting disorganization of markets. Even if things finally settled down, the pattern would very likely be far from optimal from the viewpoint of all the participants.

A well-analyzed sequence from the realm of trade policy that encompasses all three of these disadvantages illustrates the possibilities. A large nation attempts to exploit its monopolistic position at the expense of other nations by imposing an optimum tariff. Other things being equal, it can gain by imposition of a tariff, the appropriate size of which depends on the monopoly position of the country. But other things do not generally remain equal, for other countries can also gain through the imposition of tariffs. Such retaliation creates a new situation for the first country, which should then alter its tariff, perhaps by raising it, to exploit fully its monopoly position. And so the tariff war goes, creating much turmoil with trade during the process, until a point is reached at which no country can gain further through unilateral action. Furthermore, the resulting pattern of tariffs will almost certainly leave all countries worse off than they would have been if the first country had not attempted to exploit its advantage.[2] A regime that prohibits or limits tariff warfare would be mutually beneficial.

Similar examples can be found in the monetary realm. For instance, a general shortage of liquidity under a gold standard regime might lead various countries to devalue their currencies in terms of gold in order to improve their payments positions for the purpose of adding to their stocks of money. This behavior would lead to competitive depreciation all around, with an ultimate write-up in the value of gold in terms of all currencies and possibly some stimulation of new gold production, but only after a painful and acrimonious transition. It would be far better to agree together on a "uniform change in par values" (in the language of the Bretton Woods

Agreement) of currencies against gold, thus avoiding the needless change in relative currency values and the disruptions to national economies that would obtain under the hypothesized circumstances. It would be better still to abandon reliance on a commodity in short supply and create, by agreement, some form of fiduciary asset, such as domestic paper money within economies and special drawing rights at the international level.

Moreover, a free-for-all regime ignores the vital point that money, including international money, is a social convention, a collective human contrivance of the highest order. One after another during the nineteenth and early twentieth centuries, nations evolved domestic monies and then endowed them with legal tender status. At the international level, some kind of international money has also evolved. First came the commodity monies, silver and gold, then the national monies, sterling and the dollar. All served better than nothing but all fell short of an optimal solution. International agreement is required to do better.

Types of International Monetary Regimes

Perceiving that some form of order is necessary does not determine *what* kind of order. Many are possible, indeed, too many to discuss comprehensively. I thus confine the following discussion to three broad features, or dimensions, of a monetary regime, and to various possible stopping points along each dimension. The choice of these particular dimensions among many is influenced by the fact that they are the most prominent in current discussions of reform of the monetary system. The dimensions are (1) the role of exchange rates, (2) the nature of the reserve asset(s), and (3) the degree of control of international capital movements.

These features can be viewed as varying along a continuum, but for purposes of discussion it is perhaps more useful to specify particular points in each of these dimensions. Thus table 1.1 sets out an array of possible monetary regimes, drawing one element from each of the columns. Logically there would be 45 regimes (5 × 3 × 3) on the basis of the elements in table 1, but *freely* floating exchange rates strictly would require no reserve asset, so that in fact only 39 different regimes are described there—still too many to discuss comfortably, even before allowing for the many variants of each.

The textbook gold standard, which still provides the historical basis for comparison in many discussions of the international monetary system, is entry I.A.1. in table 1.1: fixed exchange rates (except for modest variation within the gold points), gold reserves, and full freedom of capital move-

Table 1.1
Several possible international monetary regimes (choose one from each column).

Role of exchange rates in balance-of-payments adjustment	Reserve asset	Degree of market convertibility for capital movements
I. Fixed exchange rate	A. Gold	1. Full
II. Adjustable parities	B. SDRs*	2. Dual market
III. Gliding parities	C. US dollars and other national currencies	3. Controlled
IV. Managed float		
V. Free float		

*Refers to special drawing rights, first created in 1970 by the International Monetary Fund.

ments. The original Bretton Woods system is entry II.A.3. in table 1.1, although the requirement that capital movements be controlled was implicit rather than explicit in that agreement. During the 1950s and again since 1970, Canada adopted the system IV.C.1., that is, a regime of managed flexibility in exchange rates and reliance on the United States dollar as its principal reserve asset.

The last example illustrates the important point that not all countries need abide by the same conventions within a given international monetary regime. Thus the European Community countries have set themselves the objective of adopting I.D.1. (where D stands for the as yet undetermined new European reserve asset), regardless of the practices that obtain in the rest of the world. Many small countries may prefer II.C.1. with respect to a "mother country" (e.g., the Sterling Area) even though large countries are on a different regime. But to function, the mixed international regime must still meet certain consistency requirements: the different components must be compatible with one another.

Just specifying a regime in these gross dimensions does not indicate how well it will work. That depends, among other things, on how countries behave *within* the rules and conventions of a particular regime, not merely on the choice of regime. This fact greatly complicates the choice of a regime, since how countries will behave once it is adopted cannot be forecast with certainty. However, some regimes do have technical weaknesses as compared with others. An adjustable peg regime with uncontrolled capital movements will evoke large movements of funds whenever a change in exchange rates is in prospect, for example, and a gold standard requires balance-of-payments adjustment to take place through variations in domestic employment. To point to these difficulties shifts the discussion from *possible* regimes to the desirability of alternative regimes.

Criteria for Choosing a Monetary Regime

Choice between alternative regimes requires a specification of objectives, with relative weights to indicate which ones must govern when a conflict arises between them. It is the liberal Western tradition to place as the ultimate objective the well-being of individual members of society (rather than the power of the state, the wealth of the ruling autocracy, etc.). Individual well-being has both an economic dimension, taken in its broadest terms, and a security dimension, also taken in its broadest terms. The first involves the economic capacity of an individual to pursue his own aims, and the second involves his liberty to do so without unnecessary interference from the state or from other individuals.

At this high level of generalization, there is little dispute between major participating countries over objectives of the international monetary system or over any other set of conventions governing relations among nations or men. Disputes, rather, arise over the best way to obtain these objectives, over means rather than over ends. It is nonetheless useful to state the ultimate objectives from time to time, for it frequently happens that means become proximate ends, and in the pursuit of these proximate or inter-mediate objectives in ever greater technical detail, actors may lose sight of the ultimate objectives and even compromise them for the sake of achieving some instrumental objective. Restrictive balance-of-payments measures by all major nations during the 1960s illustrate the point all too vividly.

By what criteria should we judge an international monetary system, having in mind its ultimate purpose of improving the economic well-being and the security of mankind? Four come to mind: (1) economic efficiency, (2) its scope for accommodating local diversity in objectives, (3) its contri-bution to harmony in international relations beyond monetary relations, and (4) its ability to achieve a desired distribution of the gains, both between countries and within countries, that arise from one regime over another. Economists have tended to focus their attention on the first of these criteria, with some attention to the second and the fourth. They have also devoted considerable attention to the technical workability of the numerous variants of alternative regimes.

Economic efficiency concerns the effectiveness with which we use the world's limited natural and human resources to make possible the improve-ment of economic well-being. The single most frequently used measure is per capita national product, although economists recognize that the figures they actually use to represent this concept can be misleading if not appropriately interpreted. In the context of international monetary reform, economic efficiency has been considered under three broad categories: (1) macroeconomic management, or the degree to which the international monetary system facilities or impedes the full employment of resources and the attainment of price stability; (2) microeconomic efficiency in the use of resources, especially as it is influenced by exchange rates as prices that guide the allocation of resources; and (3) microeconomic efficiency in the use of money as a lubricant for efficient resource allocation. The last of these categories has received the least systematic attention (partly because it cannot now be handled by conventional economic theory) yet, as I discuss below, represents an important area of reservation about a regime of flexible exchange rates.

Controversy over the Choice of a Monetary Regime

Simply stating the criteria by which alternative international monetary regimes should be judged is not the same as determining which one dominates the others, even if the criteria could be fully quantified. Controversy over the choice of an international monetary regime arises in five separately identifiable categories: (1) understandably different preferences over the different distributional implications, actual or perceived, of alternative regimes, (2) different weights attached to the various criteria when compromises must be made between them, (3) different national economic circumstances, even when preferences regarding the criteria are similar, (4) disagreement over the effectiveness of alternative means to achieve agreed ends, and (5) uncertainty about the trustworthiness of other countries with regard to their behavior within any chosen regime. Each of these sources of controversy deserves extended comment, but it is only possible to touch on them lightly here.

Distribution

Disagreements arising from different distributional implications are perhaps the most straightforward source of controversy, although even here there is much disagreement about what actually are the distributional implications of alternative regimes. Several kinds of gain arising from alternative monetary regimes can be identified.

First, there is the question of seigniorage. Traditionally, seigniorage is the gain that accrues to the mint arising from any difference between the commodity value of the materials going into a coin and the monetary value of the minted coin. Strictly speaking, seigniorage is the difference *net* of the costs of minting, and under a competitive regime of free access to the mint seigniorage will be zero. In the course of time, governments asserted a monopoly over the power to coin money and restricted coinage, and seigniorage—in effect, monopoly rents—accrued to national governments.

By analogy, we can ask what happens to the seigniorage, if any, arising from the use of a particular reserve asset under alternative international monetary regimes.[3] The seigniorage under a gold standard regime accrues to the owners of gold mines, in the form of greater intramarginal rents on the production of gold than would be the case in the absence of monetary demand for that metal. Not surprisingly, among nations the Union of South Africa and the Soviet Union have been the two most consistent supporters of returning to gold as the principal international reserve asset; these two countries are the first and second largest producers of gold in the world, and stand to gain the most in seigniorage from reliance on gold.

The seigniorage question has recently been raised in connection with the use of national currencies, mainly the US dollar, as international reserve assets. It has been alleged that the United States gains substantial seigniorage by virtue of international use of the dollar, and that this particular distribution of the gains from a monetary system to the world's richest country is perverse.

The debate is too complicated to explore thoroughly here, but the presence of seigniorage in this case is not in fact self-evident. It is undeniably true that international use of the dollar is a convenience to the American traveler, who does not always have to buy foreign money because his dollars are widely acceptable. In that respect, international use of a national currency is like international use of a national language: it confers benefits of convenience on the residents of the home country. But that is not seigniorage. And in any case, utilitarian calculation would suggest that international use of both the dollar and of English as the money and the language of convenience is optimal, since Americans represent by far the largest group of world travelers. (Where, as in southern Europe, Germans or others are the dominant group, their currency is similarly usable.)

Foreign holdings of US currency notes represent an inconsequential portion of foreign dollar holdings. Most *official* dollar holdings, those that constitute international reserves, are held as interest-bearing securities, such as Treasury bills and certificates of deposit. To the extent that the markets in these securities are competitive, and in fact financial markets for large transactors are among the most competitive markets anywhere, no seigniorage exists, i.e., no special gains arise from a privilege of currency issue. The gains from financial specialization are of course present, but they are diffused widely to all users of the financial system, foreign as well as domestic, partly in the form of interest payments. It simply represents another form of international specialization, such as that associated with commodity trade, leading to mutual gain. This is true even when it is observed that overall the United States has borrowed short and lent long, earning the difference in yield between short-term and long-term assets. Under competitive conditions, this difference merely represents the costs and risks associated with financial intermediation; again no special gain arises, and again it represents just another form of mutually beneficial specialization.[4]

Finally, it has been suggested that the United States has reaped a special gain by "borrowing" extensively abroad (international use of the dollar, looked at from the other side of the transaction, represents borrowing by the United States from the rest of the world, just as a checking account represents borrowing by the bank from the depositor) and then depreciating the real value of its extensive debt by generating inflation. Thus the United States can allegedly impose an inflation tax on the rest of the world. But this assertion presupposes that interest rates do not adjust fully to compensate for the expected rate of inflation. The fact that US Treasury bill rates carried an average yield of 7.02 percent in 1973 compared with only 3.95 percent in 1965, both boom years, is surely explainable largely by an expectation in the latter period of more rapid inflation. If the adjustment in interest rates is complete, the inflation tax can be levied only on non–interest-bearing dollar assets, of which central banks hold relatively little. A gain of course can arise during a period of *changing* expectations when interest rates have not adjusted fully to the new situation, and during such a period this version of the seigniorage argument has some merit. But otherwise it is not compelling.

The seigniorage question arises most explicitly in a regime with an international fiduciary asset such as the IMF's special drawing rights (SDRs), for they represent a form of costless money that carries purchasing power. How they are allocated seems to confer real benefits directly on the recipients, and the complaint has been voiced that allocation according to the present IMF quotas, over 70 percent of which are assigned to the industrial countries, represents an undesirable and even an unfair system of distribution. The issue has been brought forward in current discussions of international monetary reform as a proposal to link SDR creation and development assistance by shifting the allocation of new SDRs heavily toward the less developed countries. Indeed, the latter countries as a group have all but made some movement in this direction a precondition for their approval of any monetary reform. (Again the issues are too complicated to be discussed fully here.[5]) Many observers fear that such a link would undermine the success of the SDR as a reserve asset, and thereby nullify its principal purpose, which most countries, at least at the level of rhetoric, purport to share, for the sake of a secondary distributional objective. Moreover, even the issue of whether there is true seigniorage here at least requires some further analysis, since the IMF quota formula for allocating SDRs purports to measure, with admitted imperfection, the liquidity needs of different nations; to the extent that it does so accurately, allocation of SDRs results in no net transfer of resources over time, and thus in no real seigniorage (i.e., no greater consumption or investment than otherwise).

Seigniorage as a source of distributional gain has drawn the greatest attention from economists, although in practice it is perhaps the least important of the distributional effects. Several other distributional effects arising from a reserve currency standard based on some national currency (formerly the pound sterling, more recently the dollar) can be mentioned. First, it has been claimed that the dollar exchange standard gave the United States much wider scope to pursue its preferred domestic economic and other policies, even its foreign policies, than was available to other countries. The United States could simply cover any resultant balance-of-payments deficit by issuing more IOUs, which other countries would add to their reserves, whereas other countries would be sharply limited by the amount of reserves they had available.

This contention, which has adherents in the United States as well as abroad, is interesting for its implicit acceptance of a regime of fixed exchange rates, or alternatively its implicit assumption that a depreciation of the currency of a country pursuing expansionist economic or high-spending foreign policies would be unacceptable to the public and would compel retrenchment of those policies. The latter assumption is exceedingly doubtful, at least as applied to the United States. Indeed, the improvement in international competitiveness resulting from devaluation of the dollar is more likely to be welcomed in our still mercantilistic world, and was indeed even hailed as a victory when the Nixon administration achieved a devaluation in late 1971. And the assumption of fixed exchange rates is of course unwarranted in today's world.

It is arguable that far from gaining greater room for maneuver for its policies, the United States in the 1960s was, if anything, inhibited in its policies by the reserve currency role of the dollar, for the government ruled out devaluation as an acceptable measure (partly on grounds that because of the reserve currency role of the dollar, an effective devaluation could not be achieved, since other countries would simply devalue their currencies as well) and instead took a number of steps to protect the dollar that actually ran against its domestic economic or foreign policy aims. This was true of such measures as maintaining relatively high interest rates during the 1960–61 recession, reducing and tying foreign aid, and restricting outflows of capital from the United States.[6] This much can be conceded to the point, however: the reserve currency country can never find itself in the financially desperate straits that other countries can, with no alternative but to cut expenditures abroad quickly and drastically; it always has automatic access to short-term credit.

A more subtle distributional effect arises under a reserve currency regime, with possibly powerful effects *inside* the reserve currency country as well as inside other countries. With foreign acquisitions of the dollar, the United States could run a larger balance-of-payments deficit (measured in conventional terms) than would otherwise be the case. Or to put the same point a different way, the dollar could command more units of foreign currency than would otherwise be the case. By the standards of any alternative regime, the dollar would be overvalued and other currencies would be undervalued. Overvaluation of the dollar means that American exports are less competitive (and imports more competitive) than they would otherwise be, and this in turn implies that factors of production heavily engaged in the foreign trade sector would experience a smaller demand for their services than would otherwise be the case. The factors used relatively intensively to produce nontraded goods and services, on the other hand, would be relatively better off, assuming that conditions of full employment are maintained. For an economy as complex as the American one, it is not entirely clear which segments of society constitute these different groups. But it is a fair conjecture that an overvaluation of the dollar would penalize American farmers and the skilled workers in American manufacturing. It is no coincidence that organized labor in the United States became more protectionist during the period of growing deficits (financed by foreign "lending" to the United States through the acquisition of dollars) around 1970, and that this protectionist sentiment diminished somewhat after two devaluations of the dollar.

By the same token, a reserve currency regime with fixed exchange rates permits other currencies to be undervalued and thus permits other countries to enjoy export-led growth.[7] For the same reason as that given above, those factors of production engaged relatively heavily in the foreign trade sector, both producing exports and producing goods that compete with imports, will benefit from this arrangement, while others will suffer. Little can be said in general about this, except that the owners of land from which primary products are produced in exporting countries will generally benefit from such undervaluation of their currency.

Yet another distributional effect arising under a reserve currency regime involves the special status it is thought to confer upon the reserve currency country. Considerations of status leave economists somewhat baffled, since it is not clear what tangible or intangible benefits flow from it, apart from the feeling of high status itself.[8] But there is little doubt that the reluctance of some Britons to shed the reserve currency role of sterling arose from status considerations as well as from the business they thought sterling brought to the City of London, and President de Gaulle and his followers both coveted and resented the special status they thought the international role of the dollar conferred upon the United States.[9]

Other regimes also have distributional effects, but it is not always clear what they are. For example, inflation tends to redistribute real income away from those whose incomes do not respond fully to the rate of inflation, so that any influence of an international monetary regime on the rate of world inflation would have distributional effects, at least in the medium run. But there is no general agreement on whether a regime of fixed or of flexible rates is likely to be more conducive to inflation, or even on whether the substitution of SDRs for gold as international reserve assets will in practice be more conducive to inflation. Thus little specific can be said about these effects.

Different Preferences

The second broad source of controversy involves different preferences between objectives where some compromise is necessary, because articulation of the objectives leads to some conflict between them. The classic trade-off in economic analysis is between efficiency and distributional considerations.[10] Different parties may disagree on the desirable lines of compromise. Actually, this type of disagreement has been relatively absent in the debate on international reform. But it can be found lurking below the surface in several areas. Discussion of the link between SDRs and development assistance has so far given full preference to efficiency considerations in the generation of international liquidity. But some opponents of the link suspect that in a regime in which dependence on SDR creation as a source of development assistance has become heavy, it would be exceedingly difficult to sustain a negligible increase in SDRs even when that is what liquidity requirements dictate. That is, they worry that distributional considerations will dominate efficiency considerations when the hard choices have to be made. Similarly, in their pursuit of monetary unification, European countries have resisted the choice of a single, existing European currency as the basis for a future European currency, even though on balance that would probably be the most efficient thing to do, because of the special status and other alleged advantages this would confer on the country whose currency was chosen. The drive for a system of multiple currency intervention at the global level reflects a similar willingness to forgo efficiency for the sake of symmetry. Surprisingly, no country seems to oppose this change, perhaps because none yet appreciates fully the operational complexities it involves.

A second, and major, area in which different preferences are a source of disagreement concerns the extent to which the international monetary system should "discipline" national economies. Since the 1940s, under the dual influence of the Great Depression and the Keynesian revolution in economic theory, democratic governments have accepted the obligation to maintain national full employment. Ideally, nations would pursue macroeconomic policy so balanced that, apart from external influences, a reasonable degree of price stability would be achieved along with full employment. In fact, however, a number of countries have a history of excessive government spending, a practice now legitimized by the desire to maintain full employment. Some experts look to the international monetary system to provide the necessary restraint on expansionist economic policies, attempting to impose this discipline through a balance-of-payments constraint. Others find the achievement of balance between domestic macroeconomic objectives difficult enough without adding an additional constraint, and they desire, therefore, an international monetary system that at a minimum is neutral as regards the domestic objectives of macroeconomic policy and preferably provides some help in reconciling them.

This difference of view, which to some extent arises from differences in national historical experience, underlies the present impasse in official discussions on the monetary system. It takes the technical form of different views on the exchange rate regime, on the degree of compulsion in the use of exchange rates, and on the severity of the requirements for settlement of deficits. I return to this issue below, and suggest an interpretation in terms of divergent views *within* countries, especially the continental European countries.

Different National Circumstances

Yet another source of disagreement on the features of the monetary regime
is the very different character of national economies, as distinguished from
differences in preferences between objectives. A single individual averse
to rain may behave quite differently in different objective environments,
always carrying his umbrella in Norway and never carrying it in Egypt.
Similarly, two countries with similar preferences among the overall objectives may elect different monetary regimes because of their different
objective environments. A small, high-income country may be highly
dependent on foreign trade for its welfare and hence be reluctant to
sanction any measures that restrict trade. It may also be extremely open, so
that it is sensitive to economic developments abroad and at the same time
has little monetary-fiscal leverage over its own macroeconomic developments because of the high leakages abroad. Under these circumstances, the
country is likely to oppose exchange rate flexibility and trade restrictions
for balance-of-payments reasons (and perhaps also restrictions on capital
movements, depending on its dependence either on foreign capital inflows
or on earnings from its own foreign investments); it will favor a regime that
imposes a moderate degree of discipline on its major trading partners
so as to minimize imported inflation or depression. A large, relatively
closed economy, in contrast, will desire to maintain the maximum freedom
of domestic monetary management and thus will oppose a system that
restrains its freedom on domestic economic policy; it will also be more
receptive to the use of trade restrictions as a balance-of-payments measure,
and more hospitable to flexible exchange rates.

The position of the small, open economy on exchange rate flexibility is
governed in part by the perception that residents under a flexible rate
regime, which exhibits a high degree of openness and has no controls on
capital movements, may hold a high proportion of their money balances in
foreign currencies (so as to stabilize the value of money balances in terms
of commodities, a high proportion of which, by assumption, come from
outside the country), thus denying the country both the seigniorage gains
arising from the creation of domestic currency and the little freedom it may
still retain to influence macroeconomic events through domestic monetary
management. It is this consideration that leads to the notion of an *optimal*
currency area, one that achieves the appropriate balance between the scale
economies of a single monetary unit, on the one hand, and the seigniorage
gains and advantages of national monetary management, on the other.[11]

A \ B	I	II
I	5(B) 3(A)	0(B) 0(A)
II	0(B) 0(A)	3(B) 5(A)

Figure 1.1
Payoffs to choice of regime.

A Game-Theoretic Formulation

The above sources of disagreement among countries on the choice of a monetary regime can be characterized in game-theoretic terms by specifying a payoff matrix (the net rewards) to each country arising from alternative choices of regime. This construction represents a necessary step if a quantitative cost-benefit analysis is to be done for alternative monetary regimes. For simplicity, consider only two countries (A and B) choosing between two international monetary regimes (I and II). Suppose, in correspondence with the arguments put earlier about the disadvantages of a free-for-all regime, that both countries gain substantially by agreeing on a regime: *some* rules of behavior are better than none, and we suppose that no agreement leads to a free-for-all regime.[12] A hypothetical "payoff" to each of the countries under the four possible configurations of regime is shown in figure 1.1. Each box represents a choice of regime by each country. Thus the southeast box represents the choice of regime II by both countries. Each box contains two numbers, one representing the net gain (after allowance for disadvantages) to country A, and the other representing the net gain to country B. Thus, in the southeast box A gains 5 and B gains 3.[13]

As the payoff matrix is constructed, both countries gain by reaching agreement, whether the gain be subjective or objective. Country A clearly prefers that both countries agree on regime II, while B prefers that both countries agree on regime I. The differences in reward may arise from any of the three broad sources of disagreement discussed above—straight distribution of system gains, different preferences between objectives that are differentially served by the alternative regimes, and different environmental circumstances in the two countries. The first and third of these sources of difference may be commensurable (e.g., measurable by impact on

GNP), while the second clearly is not. For this reason alone, it would be virtually impossible to construct such payoff matrices corresponding to any actual set of choices. Moreover, the payoff matrix would in any case have to be enlarged (1) to allow more regimes between which to choose (no conceptual problem), (2) to enlarge the number of countries choosing regimes (much more of a conceptual problem, especially when coalitions are possible),[14] (3) to allow for uncertainty in the payoffs (one source of which is considered below), and (4) to allow for divergent factions *within* countries, which may form coalitions across national boundaries.

Allowing for all these factors would impose formidable if not insurmountable difficulties for comprehensive analysis of the negotiations on international monetary reform. But, in fact, the discussions have not gotten to the point at which these are the serious obstacles to analysis. For there remains fundamental disagreement on the relationship between particular features of a monetary regime and the costs and/or benefits associated with it. Most of the technical work aims at narrowing the still substantial differences of view on what may be called the "technology" of international monetary relations, the relationship between means and ends. Thus, it is not possible to fill in even the subcomponents of a payoff matrix to the satisfaction of most observers. This represents yet a fourth category of controversy.

Disagreement over Means-Ends Relationships

Even with similar objectives and similar circumstances, honest men may and do disagree over the best way to achieve those common objectives, especially when the relationships are as complex and indirect as they are in international monetary affairs. Based on their own training and experience, and in the face of frustratingly ambiguous evidence, accomplished technicians form their own judgments about what is the best way to do this or that. Sometimes technicians disagree among themselves. At least as often, however, they share a view that is at variance with "outsiders" who have taken a broader but less detailed look at the issue or with politicians who suspect, sometime justifiably, that technicians are really trying to influence objectives by pressing their views on a particular means-ends relationship. This last case develops not so much because technicians have ultimate objectives at sharp variance with those of society as because they have implicitly substituted in their own thinking proximate, instrumental objectives for the ultimate objectives, and thus lose sight of the latter when considering issues as broad as reform of the monetary system.

Several examples of divergent views over means-ends relationships can be cited, although they often comingle differences in objectives as well. The most fundamental difference of view in contemporary discussions on monetary reform concerns the extent to which there should be governmental controls on private economic transactions, especially capital movements between nations. By and large, the American government has taken a stance of extreme liberalism in this regard, and in this it has been joined by Germany. At the other extreme stands France, joined by a few of the smaller European countries. The French government holds that a high degree of control on international capital movements is necessary to protect national economies from capricious financial disturbance from abroad.

This difference of view stems from deeply rooted philosophical differences between the liberal Anglo-Saxon tradition and the tradition of centralized France, running from Colbert through Napoleon to the present day. To some extent it involves a difference in objectives, for the Americans place a higher value on economic freedom than do the French government and bureaucracy (though not higher than the French people, who have traditionally taken strong pride in their individualism, including their ability to thwart government directive). And to some degree it reflects a genuine difference of view, rooted in the traditions and experience of each area, concerning the best way to maximize economic well-being. Anglo-Saxons have generally accepted the competitive model of Adam Smith, who showed that under certain circumstances private pursuit of gain results in the social good, and that most of the weaknesses of the economic system arise from government interference, often for the private gain of particular individuals or groups. French thought, steeped in syndicalism, has never been deeply moved by this model of economic behavior, and French policy has never (except briefly during the nineteenth century) attempted to put it into practice.

Not surprisingly, each country tends to extend its own proclivities to the international arena. The difference becomes operational in considering the degree of flexibility that should be accorded to exchange rates (greater flexibility implying greater trust in the ability of the market to produce an acceptable result) and in the degree of freedom that should be accorded to private international capital movements. The two issues interact, in that the urgency felt by France and several other governments to control capital movements increases with the flexibility allowed to exchange rates. These governments fear that capital movements will lead to an "inappropriate" exchange rate, i.e., one that will deprive the country of employment in the export industries, or that capital movements will lead to high variability in exchange rates, with capricious consequences for domestic output and employment. The Anglo-Saxon view, to employ an inadequate shorthand for a complex issue, denies that a properly functioning market will lead to these results, and observes that the international relocation of capital guided by profitability will generally raise incomes, that is, improve economic welfare, all around.

A second area of technical disagreement concerns the efficacy of changes in exchange rates in influencing trade and service flows between nations in the modern world. Some observers contend that the highly technological nature of contemporary trade greatly reduces the sensitivity of trade and investment flows to changes in currency values, and that even when such sensitivity is present, it takes such a long time to become manifest that changes in exchange rates cannot be relied upon to equilibrate international payments. Other observers reject this elasticity pessimism and argue that changes in exchange rates (whether the adjustable parity or more flexible versions) are so far superior economically to alternative modes of correcting payments imbalances—trade controls or deflation of domestic economies—that heavy reliance should be placed on this mode of correction.

The difficulty in casting discussions of international monetary reform into a quantitative cost-benefit framework at the present time is specifically illustrated by the controversy over the merits of a regime of flexible exchange rates (free float, no reserve asset required, full convertibility for capital movements—V.1. in table 1.1). Conventional economic theory suggests that a system of freely flexible rates would be highly desirable, compared with alternatives, essentially on the grounds that under competitive conditions economic efficiency is best achieved by allowing prices, including the exchange rate, to respond to market forces. A regime of flexible exchange rates is quite consistent with the active use of macroeconomic measures to assure full employment, and it provides maximum freedom to economic transactors. Thus it would seem to dominate all alternative regimes.

This conventional view of flexible exchange rates is under challenge, although it has not yet been challenged decisively either on the theoretical or on the empirical plane. The theoretical objections that have been raised to a regime of flexible exchange rates indicate the range and complexity of argument about this particular regime, and hence implicitly about other regimes.

It is contended, first, that a regime of flexible exchange rates is subject to abuse by governments, that they will be tempted to engage in competitive depreciation in order to generate domestic employment by exporting their unemployment to other countries. Brief experience with flexible exchange rates during the 1930s supports this fear.[15] The counter-argument is that: (1) governments now have more effective instruments for influencing aggregate demand than they did in the 1930s, so that they do not have to engage in competitive depreciation; (2) competitive depreciation is a game two (or more) can try to play, and if all attempt it, none will succeed; (3) the absurdity of the above situation will quickly become apparent, and nations will cease to engage in fruitless and absurd activity; and (4) concern with competitive depreciation is a thing of the past, the problem of the present and future is world inflation, and this will lead to greater domestic opposition to currency depreciation.

Second, it is contended that a system of flexible rates will reduce the balance-of-payments discipline on national governments and thereby remove a major restraint on inflationary spending.[16] The counterargument is that inflationary policies will quickly lead to a depreciation of the currency, and that this will become evident to the public more quickly than does inflationary spending that has as its initial impact the depletion of foreign exchange reserves. Depreciation raises prices, whereas use of reserves in the short run benefits the public by temporarily permitting a rise in consumption. Thus political pressures against inflationary policies are likely to be greater, not less, under a regime of flexible exchange rates. Moreover, it is a will-of-the-wisp to suppose that a system of fixed exchange rates really imposes discipline on governments in the modern world, since they know they can devalue if it ultimately proves necessary.

It is contended, third, that flexible exchange rates do not really achieve their objective of balancing international payments, because they rely for their effect on money illusion on the part of the public, and money illusion is rapidly disappearing as publics become more sophisticated about functioning in an inflationary environment.[17] The counterargument is that while money illusion helps, the effects of changes in exchange rates are not totally vitiated in the absence of money illusion, and that in any case money illusion in all its possible forms has not yet disappeared and is not likely to.

Fourth, it is contended that money is not neutral in the economic system, as the conventional theory underlying flexible exchange rates supposes, and that too much fluctuation in the price of one money in terms of another will lead to real losses in economic efficiency that have not been reckoned in the calculation.[18] The counterargument is that this point is conjectural, and that at worst the efficiency losses will be small compared with those of alternative regimes.

It is contended, fifth, that currency speculation will not always be stabilizing, that destabilizing currency speculation may disrupt real economic activities and thereby impose efficiency losses, and that some destabilizing speculation may nonetheless become self-justifying because of exchange rate–induced changes in money wages and other factor prices.[19] The modern wage-standard economy has no natural or equilibrium price level, and arbitrary movements in the exchange rate may set off a round of disruptive cost inflation. The counterargument is that destabilizing speculation is a bugaboo and that private speculation is likely to lead the exchange rate far closer to its equilibrium than is official intervention.

Sixth, it is contended that a system of flexible exchange rates fails to promote international cooperation; by conferring greater autonomy on national governments, it removes a pressure for cooperation and introduces a divisive element into international relations. The counterargument is: What alternative is less divisive? Moreover, actually operating a system of flexible exchange rates will require a high degree of coordination of the exchange market intervention that will inevitably take place, and therefore may actually foster international cooperation.

Just to enumerate these points conveys some sense of the continuing debate—and its inconclusiveness. Until the costs of a regime of flexible exchange rates are clear, it is impossible to compare it definitively with other regimes. And the technical controversy over the costs and benefits of other regimes is only slightly less acerbic and inconclusive. We are still a long way from reaching professional—and hence official—agreement on the entries in the payoff matrix.

Lack of Trust in Other Countries

A final source of disagreement over alternative monetary regimes concerns the varying extent to which their smooth functioning depends on relations of trust among countries, and the presence or absence of such trust. In particular, a regime may be attractive to one country if other countries behave within the regime in certain ways but not if they behave in other ways. Can they be counted upon to behave in the desired ways? The resolution of this uncertainty depends upon the commitments other countries make, their past record in honoring such commitments, the extent to which failure to honor commitments automatically carries penalties, the "hostages" the first country holds over the other countries both inside and

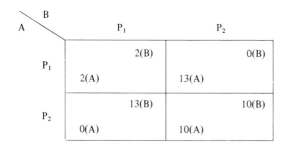

Figure 1.2
Contingent payoffs in regime I: Symmetric case.

outside the monetary arena, the general feeling of friendship and goodwill other countries have toward the first country, and a host of other factors.

The problem can be posed in terms of the type of payoff matrix introduced above. Suppose that the choice of regime I, instead of giving rise to a certain payoff to each country as shown in figure 1.1, produces benefits that depend on the particular policies adopted by each country within the framework of regime I. The payoff matrix thus might look like that shown in figure 1.2, where each country is assumed to be able to choose between two policies, P_1 and P_2, and the outcome for each country depends upon the choice of each. For simplicity, assume that regime II yields the certain payoff (5, 3) shown in figure 1.1. The payoff structure shown in figure 1.2 is that of the classical prisoner's dilemma. The joint-maximizing policy for both countries is P_2, but if either country chooses P_2, the other can do still better by choosing P_1. Unless there is a high degree of mutual trust between the countries, each country will end up choosing P_1, the loss-minimizing policy. But if that is the case, it would have been better for both to choose regime II in preference to regime I, for on the assumption in this essay, both countries would be better off than they are in the northwest corner of regime I. Without mutual trust, both countries would prefer regime II; with mutual trust, they would prefer regime I.

The payoff matrix is symmetric in figure 1.2, but of course in general it will not be. Thus the payoffs might have the asymmetry shown in figure 1.3, whereby in regime I country B loses substantially if country A chooses the first policy, P_1, but A loses only slightly if B chooses P_1 when A has chosen P_2. Under these circumstances, B's trust in A must be very high for it to prefer regime I, whereas A will always prefer regime I over regime II,

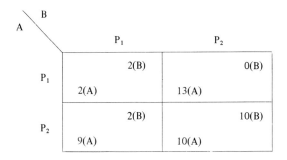

Figure 1.3
Contingent payoffs in regime I: Asymmetric case.

in contrast to the case in figure 1.2 in which mutual distrust would lead to a stable choice of regime II by both countries.

Under these kinds of circumstances, in which there is high reward for cooperation and mutual confidence but in which some distrust lingers, attempts may be made to redefine the regime, for example by ruling out P_1 as a legitimate instrument of policy in figure 1.2, or by ruling it out for A in figure 1.3 but not necessarily for B. Exemptions of less developed countries from some of the General Agreement on Tariffs and Trade (GATT) trading rules can be interpreted in this light: the damage that the less developed countries can inflict on others is negligible, while the industrial countries can inflict considerable damage on them, and on one another, through use of restrictive trade actions. Where trust is not complete, some form of international organization may be helpful to police the rules and supervise the imposition of penalties for violation of the rules. Both the GATT and the International Monetary Fund contain these features.

In the context of monetary reform, a functioning dollar standard has many positive aspects from many points of view, *provided* that the United States manages its domestic economy in such a way that it exerts a stabilizing influence on the rest of the world economy, e.g., provided that it does not inflate excessively, as it did in the late sixties.[20] But as with country A in figure 1.3, the United States has some incentive to inflate, since during the period in which expectations have not yet adjusted fully to the new situation under a regime in which dollars are extensively used as international reserves, it can in effect borrow from the rest of the world at subsidized interest rates; it imposes an inflation tax on outstanding dollar holdings. Loss of confidence in American macroeconomic management is one of the major sources (but not the only source) of dissatisfaction with the international monetary system as it had evolved by the early 1970s.

To sum up, the costs and benefits of international monetary reform must be decomposed in a number of ways: between countries, between divergent groups within countries, according to differences in preferences and in objective circumstances. Even then substantial uncertainty remains in the payoffs, for the analytical relationships between the technical features of each monetary regime and the attainment of objectives are only imperfectly understood, and there is the further uncertainty of how participating nations will actually behave within any given monetary regime. It would be nice if we could write down payoff matrices for alternative monetary regimes of the types shown in figures 1.1, 1.2, 1.3, suitably complicated to allow for the many relevant facets of the problem. But in the present state of knowledge, it simply cannot be done.[21]

The high degree of ignorance and uncertainty regarding the payoffs from alternative regimes has two consequences for discussions on international monetary reform. First, advocates of particular regimes may "fudge" the alleged payoffs to make them seem as believably attractive as possible to all parties, which is standard procedure in any advocacy process. Second, many parties simply do not know where their real interests lie; thus they pursue aggressively those few dimensions of the problem where they see their interests clearly to the neglect of what in fact may be far more important aspects of the problem, or they adopt a bargaining stance in the monetary area that may serve them well in bargaining with the same countries on quite different issues. A timely and graceful concession in the monetary arena, a concession that may in fact benefit the country making it, may be rewarded with a counterconcession by other countries in other areas of negotiation. There seems little doubt that the positions of France in international monetary discussions of the mid-sixties and of the less developed countries in the early 1970s were influenced by these considerations, for the positions they took on monetary questions were surely not in their national interests in the monetary arena alone.

A Brief History of Monetary Regimes[22]

The monetary regime reflected in the Bretton Woods Agreement of 1944 was a reaction to but also reflected deeply what had gone before it: the gold standard as it was understood; and the monetary chaos that prevailed on those occasions, immediately following the First World War and again in the Great Depression, in which the gold standard broke down.

The principal feature of the gold standard that made it unattractive to all countries following the Great Depression was that strict adherence to its canons required the domestic economy to be governed by balance-of-payments considerations, regardless of how inflationary or deflationary that might be. A secondary objection was that reliance on new gold production (minus private demand) for additions to international reserves left such additions to the caprice of technological change, new discoveries or exhaustion of mines, variations in private gold hoarding, and other irrelevant developments, which were at best inconvenient and at worst could work real hardship on the world economy. International discussion of these difficulties began in the nineteenth century, barely after the gold standard had become established, and resulted in international discussions in 1922 to economize on the use of gold by concentrating it in the hands of central banks and gradually replacing public circulation of gold money with fiduciary money.

The Bretton Woods Agreement asserted the primacy of domestic economic policy aimed at the maintenance of full employment and at the same time established the responsibility of each nation to the community of nations in the realm of international financial policy—a reaction to the self-serving, defensive, and ultimately destructive free-for-all of the 1930s. Domestic economic policies were to be protected from the strictures of the balance of payments through a double screen: *temporary* imbalances were to be financed, if necessary by drawing on lines of credit at a newly established lending institution, the International Monetary Fund (IMF); and *fundamental* imbalances were to be corrected by an alteration in the country's exchange rate. Responsibility to the community of nations was to be assured through a new set of agreed rules, policed by the IMF, that among other things (1) required each country to establish a fixed value (par value) for its currency, (2) forbade restrictions on payments for goods and services, and (3) required international approval of any change in an exchange rate that ultimately had to be made to correct a fundamental disequilibrium in the balance of payments.

In formulating the above regime, the British and American architects had to reach some balance between liberty to pursue domestic economic objectives and license to run payments deficits at the expense of the rest of the world. The final agreement was an unsatisfactory compromise between an earlier American plan to involve the IMF in closer scrutiny and even direction of each nation's domestic and exchange rate policies and a British plan to permit large-scale borrowing if necessary but which was subject to increasing penalties. The resulting IMF had too little authority for the first and too little lending capacity for the second. Thus the Bretton Woods regime could not fulfill its assignment. Moreover, the distinction between temporary and fundamental imbalance proved less sharp in practice than it was in theory, so that countries procrastinated in changing their exchange rates. When changes finally did come, their need was clear, and they were large, providing an opportunity for large profits from private speculation on a change in the exchange rate. As the mobility of capital increased over time, this last feature developed into a fatal flaw in the Bretton Woods conception. To work, the agreement implicitly required effective control of international capital movements, something that cannot be assured.

A second weakness of the system was its failure to provide in any realistic way for steady increases in international reserves, since the mechanism for this implied by the system would have called for steady increases in the price of gold, which involved both political and conceptual difficulties.

The consequence of these two weaknesses was that the regime that actually functioned during the 1950s and 1960s was rather different from the Bretton Woods system, even though the latter was formally in force. After the major devaluations of 1949, changes in exchange rates by major countries were virtually unknown until the late 1960s. This was not because imbalances in payments did not arise. Rather, it was because the alteration of a par value was fraught with both political and economic risks. Thus, alternative mechanisms were found—adjustments in domestic economic policy, and the introduction or removal of restrictions on foreign trade and other foreign transactions—both of which were sharply out of keeping with the origins and the stated objectives of the Bretton Woods Agreement. The potential pain of these measures for many countries was relieved by the undervaluation of their currencies relative to the US dollar, so that balance could be maintained during the fifties through gradual removal of the postwar trade restrictions, and the surpluses of the sixties (the counterpart of the US deficit) could be ignored so long as they remained moderate.[23]

Similarly, the problem of augmenting international liquidity was "solved" through a process whereby countries added US dollars, earned through balance-of-payments surpluses, to their international reserves, a development for which there was no real place in the Bretton Woods system. This emergence of a dollar exchange standard was fraught with difficulties of its own, however, and proved to be only modestly more durable than the

Bretton Woods system. The use of dollars as international reserves had two consequences: it permitted the United States to run deficits by borrowing from other countries to the extent of their buildup of dollar reserves; and it gradually undermined the assumption that led to a willing acquisition of dollars in the first place, viz., that the dollar was as good as gold because it was convertible into gold, the primary reserve asset of the Bretton Woods system. As the outflow of dollars associated with United States direct investment abroad and then with the war in Vietnam grew steadily, foreign restlessness at the first consequence grew correspondingly. And as the total volume of foreign-held dollars grew, the credibility of their convertibility into gold diminished, until the inevitable inconvertibility was made formal in August 1971.

Thus the Bretton Woods system had an imperfect balance-of-payments adjustment mechanism and an imperfect method for satisfying world liquidity needs. Both deficiencies were filled pragmatically through un-systematic adaptation, but the resulting regime was also unsatisfactory. Dissatisfaction mounted rapidly when in the late 1960s what had been moderate US payments deficits threatened to become, and then in 1970 actually became, insupportably large. Major countries began to adjust their exchange rates as called for by the Bretton Woods system, and this proved to be highly disruptive of financial and foreign exchange markets, as well as to general confidence in the smooth functioning of the international monetary system and the capacity of governments to manage international financial matters successfully. Finally, governments abandoned any attempt to maintain fixed exchange rates, and in March 1973 (earlier for Canada and Britain) they allowed their currencies to float in exchange markets, several European countries cooperating sufficiently so that their currencies would float together.

It is fair to say that no government willed this result, although some found it less inconvenient than others. It resulted from lack of adequate foresight among governments regarding important trends in international finance and from an inability to agree on corrective measures.

Governments perceived the difficulties of the regime regarding inter-national liquidity earlier than they saw the difficulties regarding the adjustment mechanism. After prolonged and laborious negotiation, they propounded a solution to the international liquidity problem involving special drawing rights (SDRs), which were created to relieve both gold and dollar of the burden of providing future international liquidity. The solution was in principle an adequate one, but it did not deal with the other weaknesses in either the Bretton Woods or the dollar exchange regimes.

Disaffection with the evolving international monetary system was expressed in several ways. Several European (and Latin American) countries resented what they considered to be Anglo-Saxon dominance of the International Monetary Fund. Britain and the United States together had over 50 percent of the original IMF votes, under a system of weighted voting reflecting their relative dominance of the world economy immediately before and after the Second World War; their shares diminished with the passage of time but remained large. When special arrangements to augment the resources of the IMF were established in 1961, at continental European insistence they were governed outside the IMF by the newly established Group of Ten, where the proportionate weight of continental European countries was higher. And when SDRs were established in 1969, Europeans insisted on a further shift in decision-making authority, which gave them an effective veto over all major SDR decisions (if they acted together).

Second, Gaullist France ostentatiously adopted a policy in 1964 of converting all the dollars it acquired, and previously had been willing to hold as dollars, into gold. This move was partly motivated by broader political considerations aimed at reducing general United States influence in Europe, but it was also partly motivated out of a genuine concern with the emerging weaknesses of the dollar exchange standard and an attempt to restore the original conception of the Bretton Woods system. It was, indeed, on these latter grounds that the French moves received some applause from others who did not share de Gaulle's political motivations.

Murmurs of dissatisfaction abroad became a chorus with the marked deterioration of the US trade balance in 1968 and 1969, which was generated directly and indirectly by the Vietnam War, by the masking of this deterioration in 1969 and early 1970 by very tight money in the United States, transmitted unwelcomely to European and other countries, and by the huge US payments deficits of late 1970 and of 1971. Official dissatisfaction with the evolving state of affairs grew rapidly, but agreement on a particular alternative arrangement, or even on what possible alternative arrangements there were, remained elusive. In September 1972 the Committee of Twenty, drawn from the membership of the IMF, was finally established to examine possible lines of reform and to make proposals.

Discussions by the Committee of Twenty

Work through the end of 1973 by the Committee of Twenty succeeded in clarifying the broad range of issues that required improvement and also in revealing how fundamental are the disagreements on fundamental issues. It is not possible here to dissect in detail the issues that have been considered by the Committee of Twenty, the various national positions on each of them, and the possible reasons for these divergent positions. The fundamental differences of view underlying disagreement on what seem to be mere technical details have already been discussed earlier in this essay. They revolve around the degree of autonomy countries should be permitted in pursuit of domestic economic policy, the efficacy and desirability of relying principally on exchange rates for balance-of-payments adjustment, the future role of the US dollar in the international monetary system and its relationship to freedom of action by the United States, and the possible use of the international monetary regime for the direct provision of aid to poor countries.

A number of European countries want the international monetary regime to provide a bulwark against inflation by imposing discipline on the spending and monetary policies of national governments. This is partly to correct what they perceive to be the abuses of the dollar exchange standard, under which there was little restraint on US policies, especially after gold convertibility of the dollar became tenuous. But it is partly also, I believe, to provide an external source of support (the international financial community and the international rules of the game) to domestic financial officials in their continuing struggle with pressures at home which they view as excessively expansionist. Thus, to an important extent, the international monetary negotiations, whose participants are drawn heavily from relatively conservative financial communities within each country, are being used as a piece in a competition between those urging restraint and those urging expansion within each of several important countries. To the extent that the members of the financial group can succeed in implanting *their* preferences (e.g., regarding the trade-off between inflation and unemployment) in the rules of the international monetary regime, they strengthen their hand later in the domestic debate by being able to invoke on their behalf the need to adhere to the international rules and the need to preserve harmony with other countries, considerations that rightly carry weight in any domestic debate over policy. Viewed in this way, it is a mistake to conceive the debate over international monetary reform entirely in terms of opposition of one national position to another.

The United States has taken the position that balance-of-payments adjustment should be prompt, symmetrical as between countries in deficit and surplus, relatively obligatory, and (reading between the lines) achieved if necessary, and often preferably, through changes in exchange rates. The focus on external measures (such as the exchange rate) to correct payments imbalances takes the pressure off adjustment of domestic demand, desired by some Europeans. The insistence on obligatory adjustment (backed by sanctions) is designed to deny the option to countries in surplus of simply deferring action and allowing their surpluses to continue, which the United States fears would be the case if the more discretionary, judgmental, and nonobligatory approach favored by the Europeans were adopted. Thus, in terms of the earlier discussion of distrust, the United States is fearful that under the regime favored by the Europeans, surplus countries (cast in the role of country A in figure 1.2) will elect policy P_1, no action, when the time comes for decisions, even though at the present time they verbally accept the principle that surplus countries should also take adjustment measures, P_2. The United States would like to specify the regime so as to exclude the policy of no action by surplus countries.

An analogous distrust exists on the question of settlement of balance-of-payments deficits. The United States agrees that convertibility of the dollar into some reserve asset (presumably SDRs) should be restored as a part of overall mometary reform. But some Europeans would like to go further and require that the United States settle *all* of its payments deficits in reserve assets other than the dollar, whereas the United States would have convertibility take place only at the request of the countries acquiring dollars. This would leave open the possibility, Europeans fear, that the United States would pressure countries into holding more dollars than they really desire, thereby restoring the US capacity to finance its deficits by issuing its own currency. A regime with obligatory settlement in nondollar assets would deny this possibility to the United States.

For its part, the United States points to the need in a well-functioning monetary regime for elasticity in reserve creation, which would be provided by the continued use of dollars not converted into SDRs. But the United States has supported a particular solution (among many possible solutions) to this legitimate problem that inevitably gives rise to suspicion and distrust at unexpressed US motives.

During the first year and a half of discussion in the Committee of Twenty, the eight representatives from less developed countries acted more or less as a group, having coordinated their positions ahead of time (as did the European representatives, though they broke rank more often). They strongly advocated a link between SDR creation and development assistance for understandable reasons, and in a form that had the least possible restraint on use of the funds. This form of the link was not in the interests of such major developing countries as India, Indonesia, Pakistan, and Bangladesh, which would stand to gain from channeling resources through the international lending agencies, but was necessary to maintain cohesion among the group. On other issues, such as the adjustment process, representatives of less developed countries have taken some surprising positions not obviously in their economic interests. For example, they have given strong support to restoration of a system of fixed and infrequently changed exchange rates. This was the global adjustment mechanism we had previously, and it resulted in tied aid, reduced aid, controls on capital movements, and eventually even restrictions on travel and imports, not to mention policy-induced economic recessions in some countries—all measures that have damaged the economies of developing countries.

An explanation for the position of these countries, if it is rational, must go outside the arena of economics.[24] If these countries have an economic interest in maintaining some relatively fixed currency relationship with their major trading partners (rather than let their own currencies float freely), as many of them do, then a regime involving a high degree of flexibility in exchange rates between leading currencies (even if it falls short of floating exchange rates) will compel developing countries to choose one of several currencies to which to tie their own. This choice, it may be feared, will not be devoid of political implications, even if only symbolic ones, for it smacks of the reestablishment of spheres of influence and neocolonialism. Thus they would prefer a world in which this choice can be avoided by having all the leading currencies tied to one another in a relatively fixed relationship. They then go on to attempt to safeguard the economic position of developing countries in such a regime by asserting that the regime should give special consideration to the problems of developing countries, both as regards application of the rules directly to those countries (e.g., they can float their own currencies if that seems the best thing to do) and as regards exemption from the more harmful effects of any adjustment measures (e.g., controls on capital outflows or restrictions on imports) that industrial countries feel compelled to adopt. They cannot, of course, be exempt from the deleterious effects on their exports of recessions in industrial countries induced by balance-of-payments problems. But this concern may be muted at the present time of world inflation.

Finally, the position of less developed countries on balance-of-payments adjustment may be subject to similar influences noted above for the European countries: financial officials desire the sanction of the international regime in dealing with their own more expansionist colleagues at home. But if that is the case, the possibility of their exemption from the rules should be played down.

General Observations

A clear-cut cost-benefit analysis from the viewpoint of particular nations or groups within nations is not possible for alternative monetary regimes, given our present uncertain state of knowledge about the role of money, about the effects of changes in exchange rates on expectations and on economic behavior, and about the influence of international liquidity on national policymakers. Useful observations can, however, be made about the prospects of failure of certain international monetary regimes in terms of broad, generally agreed objectives.

Some possible regimes, such as the gold standard, can readily be rejected. Others that probably ought to be rejected still command attention, however, and the grounds for attention are to be found less in a clear perception of national or sectional interest by the proponents than in a muddled and partial appreciation of the capacity of these regimes to attain the generally agreed objectives. Just as agreement on international measures of public health was not finally achieved until the technical nature of the source and transmission of diseases was fully understood, after which controversy virtually ceased, so full agreement in the monetary area is not likely to be achieved until we have much more knowledge about the technical economic relationships involved. Even after that point controversy will remain, for the objectives and national interests in the monetary arena are far more complex than was true for public health.[25] But these differences are not yet the principal obstacles to agreement.

Two further observations can be made. First, an international monetary regime, like law, should not be changed frequently. Change creates transitional uncertainty and also reopens former political compromises, even when they work satisfactorily. Expectations and economic values become keyed to a particular regime, and changes in it, or even the prospect of changes, can prove highly disruptive of normal economic intercourse. One of the confusions of 1973 was that the old regime was clearly breaking up but no new regime was yet agreed. Currencies floated in the meantime, and some of the uncertainties associated with a change in regime were erroneously attributed to the flexibility of exchange rates.

Moreover, it is difficult to alter one part of a regime without reopening discussion on many other parts, questions which were often settled earlier through agonizing negotiation. During the mid-1960s reform of the monetary system focused rather narrowly on the problem of international liquidity, but even then a condition for agreement was a host of amendments to the Bretton Woods Agreement, mainly aimed at altering the process of decision making (with the effect of giving greater weight to continental European views without the corresponding increase in quotas, which would have been the normal and appropriate way to achieve such reweighting under the original agreement) and at altering several other features that were thought to involve status. Reform of the process for generating international liquidity proved to be insufficient (as a number of analysts warned at the time), but when other dimensions of the monetary regime were opened for revision, the occasion was also taken to reopen the provision of international liquidity, especially the formula for SDR distribution.

Second, a word should be said about the relationship of the international monetary system to domestic economic policy. International finance is an arcane subject and normally attracts little attention. The public ordinarily does not have strong feelings about it, so long as things go well, although a possible exception resides in the residual public attachment to gold as a monetary metal, an attachment that is much stronger in some countries than in others and that acts as a constraint on governmental freedom of action. The public, at least in the United States, is likely to accept any reasonable sounding proposal, unlike in the area of foreign trade policy where much more is at stake for particularistic interests.

On the other hand, precisely because the public does not perceive much stake in the international monetary system, it will not be willing to make many sacrifices to preserve it once its dictates conflict sharply with the requirements of domestic economic policy. The same is true in most other major countries. During the 1950s and 1960s, it is true, the British government imposed considerable hardships on the British public for the sake of preserving the international position of sterling. But those days are over, and in any case can be interpreted as protecting a factional interest within Britain, not with preserving an international regime per se. Germany's revaluations, when they came, were made primarily for domestic (anti-inflationary) reasons; and at various times Canada, Britain, France, and the United States all abandoned the international rules when a sharp conflict with domestic interests developed. Thus it is neither realistic nor, I would add, desirable to ask of the international monetary system that it impose strong conditions on domestic economic policy. Rather, the regime should strive for harmonious diversity.

International Organizations and the Desirable Directions for Reform

This eassy has attempted to lay out in systematic fashion the possible sources of disagreement on reform of the international monetary system and some of the reasons for those disagreements. While it has here and there identified special interests that may well be expected to urge particular aspects rather than others, its general message is that the sources of disagreement are *not* to be found, by and large, in divergent interest groups of the type so often examined by political scientists. The sources of disagreement are less rooted in divergent interests than in divergent perspectives arising out of history and ideology, perspectives that economic theory and the lessons of recent experience have thus far failed to bring together. In addition to these divergent perspectives, some mutual distrust and some old-fashioned divergence of interest also contribute to the disagreements, but they are relatively minor partners.

The nature of this volume requires addressing two further issues: where international organizations fit into the picture, and how the international monetary system should be reformed. These are each large topics, they do not fit comfortably into this essay, and I have written extensively elsewhere on both these topics, especially on the second.[26] Nonetheless, it is necessary to say something about each of them.

I regard the role of international organizations as derivative from the task to be performed. Therefore, in the monetary arena, the presence and the appropriate form of international organization depends on the regime actually selected.

A different view is possible. It is that international organizations should exist to provide a sense of participation for many or all nations, not merely to perform certain tasks. Other things being equal, providing a sense of participation is a good thing. But sometimes it can be accomplished only by diminishing the efficiency with which essential tasks are performed or even by jeopardizing the performance altogether. In the international monetary arena, this possible conflict between participation and efficient task performance is perhaps more acute than it is in many other arenas, for quick and decisive action is often the key to preventing an unruly financial situation from getting out of hand.

In practice, the IMF has been one of the most proficient of the great panoply of extant international organizations. It is true that the IMF (meaning its executive board and its senior staff, not of course all staff members) has been slow to acknowledge the need for reform. It resisted for many years the notion that there was a world liquidity problem, but it eventually became an enthusiastic supporter of SDRs. It also resisted for years the notion that there was an adjustment problem requiring greater flexibility in exchange rates, and it is still not clear whether the IMF will become an enthusiastic supporter of greater flexibility of exchange rates in the international monetary system. But these observations only suggest that this international organization should not be left with the sole responsibility for initiative. By and large, it has performed well.

It is interesting to speculate on whether its good performance has been related to its almost unique decision-making apparatus among international organizations, whereby its 126 member countries are represented by only twenty individuals sitting on their behalf. There is here the beginning of representative government at the global level, with constituencies being nations rather than individuals. The twenty members of the executive board operate under a system of weighted voting (and while formal votes are rarely taken, the weights nonetheless play an informal role in the decision making), where the weights depend on IMF quotas, which in turn depend roughly on a measure of economic importance in the world economy. Twenty is a far more manageable group than 126.

Despite its relative proficiency, the IMF has had to be supplemented by other formal and informal modes of international economic cooperation. The formal economic reviews of the IMF were too far removed from responsible officials to be of immediate use in coordinating economic policies or even in allowing the actions of other countries to influence constructively each country's actions. Therefore, the Economic Policy Committee of the Organization for Economic Cooperation and Development (OECD) and its various subcommittees, especially Working Party Three with its mere ten members and top-level representation, came to play a much more important role. Moreover, because IMF machinery for making a loan was too clumsy to deal quickly with immediate flare-ups in financial markets, a series of "swap" arrangements was established between the Federal Reserve System and other central banks, and later between European central banks, to provide immediate short-term credit on a no-questions-asked basis.

Success or failure in the international monetary arena depends on agreement and cooperation between a dozen or so countries, in the important sense that other countries could violate agreements without undermining the regime. That is why this essay focuses on the main industrial countries of North America, Western Europe, and Japan. The Soviet Union and China, of great importance in the arena of national security and military strategy, are inconsequential in the international monetary arena because both are so withdrawn from the world economy in their national economic policies. Similarly, while less developed countries have a strong interest in the character and performance of the international monetary regime, their adherence to its rules is not critical to its success.

But, in fact, many of them will find it advantageous to adhere to the rules much of the time.

Relative importance, of course, changes with time, and any regime should be flexible enough to adapt to such changes. Moreover, the monetary system may be subject to shocks of a magnitude and character that were not anticipated at all. The huge drain on reserves caused by the steep increase in oil prices in late 1973 will drastically alter ownership of the world's foreign exchange reserves. But the behavior of the oil-exporting countries is not likely to be influenced much by whether they are members of the IMF. Just as they abandoned solemnly sworn contracts when they found they could gain thereby, they would certainly exempt themselves from any rules under a drastic change in circumstances.

Thus, the reasons for more universal forums than a group of ten rest on an appreciated desire for participation by most countries and on a conscious awareness of the problems of small countries, as well as on an expressed intention that they not be overlooked. The price paid for these two benefits involves greater unwieldiness in decision taking, even when all participants are of good will, plus the complications for decision taking that arise when some participants for which the stakes in this arena are or seem to be low threaten to withhold agreement here in bargaining for improvements in their position in other arenas. Bargaining across areas of interest, of course, is not limited to marginal participants, but any failure to reach agreement arising from unwillingness of the marginal participants to agree reflects a very unfavorable cost-benefit ratio for the world economy.[27]

I believe that in the monetary arena wide participation is desirable, but not so desirable as to allow it to hold up important cooperative steps between the key nations. Translated into institutional terms, discussions on reform of the monetary system are appropriately held within the framework of the IMF. But if they threaten to bog down because of that organization's (near) universalism, discussions should be withdrawn from that forum to one in which progress can be made more quickly. So far, however, progress has been blocked by fundamental disagreements between the major participants, not with the marginal ones.

Another point about international organizations especially germane in the monetary arena is that any formal organization and body of rules typically requires formal equality for the participating nations. A state is a state, large or small. Limited deviation from this principle can be found in weighted voting and in permanent as opposed to rotating membership on committees, as with the UN Security Council. But the strains toward formal symmetry between members is very strong.

Yet the world economy is very asymmetric in its functioning. For technical reasons, it is both likely and desirable that one or a few currencies will emerge with special status in market transactions.[28] Even when this fact is fully known and acceptable, it cannot always be formally acknowledged and sanctified in treaties, in part for reasons of status touched on earlier in the essay. There thus emerges a discrepancy between what governments say in formal negotiations and what they do, or are willing happily to accept, in day-to-day operations—a discrepancy between their stated preferences and their revealed preferences. In the monetary arena this discrepancy can be observed in attitudes toward the US dollar, both as an intervention currency and as a reserve currency, in attitudes toward the flexibility of exchange rates, and (within Europe) in attitudes toward European monetary unification.

Formal arrangements induce sovereign states to insist on formal symmetry in status, partly to cater to nationalist sentiment at home. Informal arrangements carry no such compulsion. To the extent that asymmetries of treatment are important for efficient functioning, informal arrangements are therefore likely to be superior to formal arrangements that emerge from a negotiating process. In the international monetary sphere, an English-style constitution, built up through a series of acceptable practices, may be both easier to attain and even superior in content to a fully negotiated American-style constitution. Indeed, precisely such informal arrangements seem to mark the current monetary regime of managed flexibility of exchange rates, which few (if any) countries are willing to accept formally but which most (if not all) fully accept in practice.

What should a renovated monetary system look like? I suggest that four major improvements must be made. First, we need greater flexibility of exchange rates than the Bretton Woods regime allowed but less than would obtain under a system of free floating. Sound economic policy calls for a greater brake on movements in exchange rates than private speculators can always be expected to provide. Thus, we need either a system of closely managed floating, with rules governing central bank intervention, or a system of exchange rate parities with strong presumptive rules for "gliding" the parities. In practice, these alternatives need not be very different, but a system of managed floating will perhaps be easier to achieve from the condition of general floating prevailing in 1974. Of course, not all countries need to float their currencies to the same degree;

small, open economies may be well advised to link their currencies somewhat more rigidly to one of the major currencies.

Second, the SDR needs to be detached from gold and its characteristics need to be altered to strengthen its role, with a view to its becoming the major medium for international reserves in the future. This change will require formal negotiations between countries; charter building through practice will not achieve this aim. Gold should be downgraded as an international monetary medium by eliminating its formal role wherever practicable. Some gold will continue to be held by governments for some time, for precautionary reasons. But they stockpile other durable commodities as well; gold should have no special monetary role.

Third, the community of nations should establish an international lender of last resort that is able to extend large amounts of credit on short notice in order to forestall major economic collapse. At present, the lending capacity of the IMF is too limited in scale, too hedged about with restrictions, to play this role. With the SDR moving into a central role, this lending function could be performed through special issues of SDRs to be repaid as quickly as possible after each crisis has passed but not more quickly than is appropriate for sound economic policy.

Fourth, closer international surveillance is required over the Eurocurrency market to ascertain whether the pyramid of credit being built there is too great or too shaky. At this stage better information is mainly required; but at some point limits on Eurocurrency expansion may become necessary.

The changes outlined here could be accomplished by the leading countries in a variety of institutional frameworks, but because it exists and has performed reasonably well, and because it has a wide membership, the IMF offers a natural starting place for these changes. With suitable (and substantial) modification in its structure and in its mode of operation, it could oversee an adjustment process based on managed exchange rate flexibility, serve as a lender of last resort—a central bank for central banks—and track developments in the Eurocurrency market to make sure that they do not get out of hand. But as suggested above, the role of institutions should be derivative, not primary. If relying on the IMF requires too much compromise with proficiency in performing these tasks, other arrangements should be made.

In terms of table 1.1, I favor the regime designated IV.B.1. or a version of III.B.1. not very different: high but not complete exchange rate flexibility subject to collective management, SDRs, and freedom of capital movements. The last stipulation requires that national governments both can and do rely to a greater extent on fiscal policy and less on monetary policy for domestic economic stabilization. Monetary policy must be regarded increasingly from a global point of view. In the possibly long transition to this state, which will require substantial alteration in domestic economic policy in many countries, it will be necessary to maintain some limits on the freedom of international capital movements, especially short-term bank lending. Without such limits, national monetary policy will lose much of its leverage over domestic economic conditions, a loss that is not acceptable so long as governments are held responsible for macroeconomic stability (as they should be) yet are denied the flexible use of fiscal measures. This stricture applies especially to Germany, Japan, and the United States, where for different reasons fiscal policy is a clumsy instrument of stabilization policy.

Notes

1. A particularly poignant example of the severe limits a given regime can impose on the use of instruments of policy, and of the psychological hold a regime of long standing can have on even well-informed observers, is the surprised anguish of Fabian socialist Sidney Webb when, in 1931, in the face of enormous unemployment, Britain abandoned the fixed price of gold and allowed the pound to float: "No one told us we could do this," (A. J. P. Taylor, *English History, 1914–1945* [New York: Oxford University Press, 1965], p. 297, cited in Fred Hirsch, *Money International* [Garden City, N.Y.: Doubleday, 1969], p. 4.)

2. Harry G. Johnson has pointed out that in the final equilibrium it is possible for one country to be left better off than in the free trade situation; but both countries taken together will certainly be worse off, and I judge that in most circumstances each country taken separately would be left worse off. See his "Optimum Tariffs and Retaliation," in his *International Trade and Economic Growth: Studies in Pure Theory* (Cambridge, Mass.: Harvard University Press, 1967).

3. Herbert G. Grubel. "The Distribution of Seigniorage from International Liquidity Creation," and Harry G. Johnson, "A Note on Seigniorage and the Social Saving from Substituting Credit for Commodity Money," in R. A. Mundell and A. K. Swoboda, eds., *Monetary Problems of the International Economy* (Chicago: University of Chicago Press, 1969), pp. 269–82, 323–29.

4. These arguments require some qualification. If competitive banks are subject to non–interest-bearing reserve requirements, as they are in the United States, then the interest rate on their certificates of deposit will be correspondingly reduced, and some seigniorage does arise. Furthermore, from 1963 to 1974, the United States imposed taxes (the Interest Equalization Tax) and other restrictions on capital outflow from the United States, with the encouragement and approval of many European countries, and such restrictions on financial intermediation would again give rise to some seigniorage.

5. For a convenient summary of the debate, with extensive references to the literature, see Y. S. Park, *The Link Between Special Drawing Rights and Development Finance*, Essays in International Finance, no. 100 (Princeton, N.J.: Princeton University, September 1973).

6. As James Tobin, writing in 1964, put it: "if the financial ship has weathered the storm [of the dollar crisis], it has done so only by jettisoning much of the valuable cargo it was supposed to deliver." See his "Europe and the Dollar," *Review of Economics and Statistics* 46 (May 1964): 123.

7. For an explanation of how this occurs, see Richard N. Cooper, "Dollar Deficits and Postwar Economic Growth," *Review of Economics and Statistics* 46 (May 1964): 155–59.

8. But see the discussion of status in a related context in Frank and Baird's essay in this volume.

9. With evident resentment, de Gaulle wrote of the "monumentally overprivileged position that the world had conceded to the American currency" (*Memoirs of Hope: Renewal and Endeavor* [New York: Simon & Shuster, 1971], p. 371).

10. In certain circumstances, these broad objectives need not conflict: social organization can be arranged to achieve maximum economic efficiency, and then the fruits of that efficiency can be distributed through lump-sum transfers to satisfy the desired distribution. But in practice lump-sum transfers are difficult to achieve, and other forms of redistribution almost inevitably impinge adversely on efficiency. Thus a trade-off arises and compromises must be made.

11. For an analytical summary of the discussion on optimal currency areas, see Herbert G. Grubel, "The Theory of Optimum Currency Areas," *Canadian Journal of Economics* 3 (May 1970): 318–24.

12. This, of course, need not actually be the case. Countries may implicitly agree on certain conventions governing behavior even when they are unable to reach explicit agreement, thus avoiding the disadvantages of a complete free-for-all.

13. Several interpretations are possible for the numbers entered in the payoff matrix. If the gains are commensurable, they can be added together according to some common unit of measurement and compared. Net increase in GNP would be an example. It is clear from the discussion above, however, that not all the advantages and disadvantages of alternative monetary regimes can be expressed in commensurable units. Status and maneuverability of action would be examples. In that case, each country must weigh for itself the various advantages and disadvantages of each configuration according to some utility index, and the entries in figure 1.1 then represent a scaling for each country according to its own utility index. But in that case, the gains to A as perceived by A, while comparable with one another, are not comparable with the gains to B as perceived by B. Entries for B in the four boxes can be compared with one another, and those for A can be compared, but entries for B cannot be compared with entries for A. Indeed, it is quite possible that country B will perceive the gains to A differently from the way

A perceives them, and vice versa. For example, on B's utility scale the entry for A in the southeast box might be 8 instead of 5. This kind of difference is especially likely if status is an important consideration for B.

The payoff matrix is also drawn showing no net gain for either country in the case of disagreement on regime. If the payoffs to each country are commensurable, the payoff need not be the same for both countries in cases of disagreement. For example, B might actually *lose* in comparison with A, so that the entries for B in the northeast and southwest boxes would be negative. B would then have a stronger incentive to reach agreement than would A. If the payoffs are not commensurable, then the possibility of loss is merely a matter of choice of scale for each country. The lowest entry for *each* country can be arbitrarily chosen to equal zero, and the other entries for that country are then scaled to it.

14. For a brilliant exploratory treatment of many similar decision units confronting binary choices, see Thomas C. Schelling, "Hockey Helmets, Concealed Weapons, and Daylight Savings: A Study of Binary Choices with Externalities," *Journal of Conflict Resolution* 17 (September 1973): 381–427.

15. The standard source is League of Nations [Ragnar Nurkse], *International Currency Experience* (New York: League of Nations, 1944).

16. Henry Wallich, "Why Fixed Rates?" Committee for Economic Development, New York, 1973. (Mimeographed.)

17. Robert A. Mundell, "Monetary Relations between Europe and America," in Charles P. Kindleberger and A. Shonfield, eds., *North American and Western European Economic Policies* (London: Macmillan & Co., 1971; New York: St. Martin's Press, 1971).

18. Charles P. Kindleberger, "The Case for Fixed Exchange Rates, 1969," in *The International Adjustment Mechanism* (Boston: Federal Reserve Bank of Boston, 1970); and Arthur Laffer, "Two Arguments for Fixed Rates," in Harry G. Johnson and A. Swoboda, eds., *The Economics of Common Currencies* (London: Allen & Unwin, 1973), pp. 25–34.

19. Richard N. Cooper, *The Economics of Interdependence* (New York: McGraw-Hill, 1968), chapter 9; and Cooper, "Issues in the Balance of Payments Adjustment Process," Committee for Economic Development, New York, 1973 [chapter 5].

20. R. I. McKinnon, *Private and Official International Money: The Case for the Dollar*, Essays in International Finance, no. 74 (Princeton, N.J.: Princeton University, April 1969); also Mundell.

21. Bold and interesting attempts for the United States have been made by Robert Z. Aliber, *Choices for the Dollar* (Washington, D.C.: National Planning Association, 1971), and C. Fred Bergsten, *The Dilemmas of the Dollar: The Economics and Politics of United States International Monetary Policy* (New York: Praeger for the Council on Foreign Relations, 1974). A more formal attempt at one component of the payoff is in K. Hamada, "Alternative Exchange-Rate Systems and the Interdependence of Monetary Policies," in Robert Z. Aliber, ed., *National Monetary Policy and the International Financial System* (Chicago: University of Chicago Press, 1974).

22. Some interpretations of postwar international monetary history can be found in Stephen D. Cohen, *International Monetary Reform, 1964–69: The Political Dimension* (New York: Praeger, 1970); Richard N. Cooper, *The Economics of Interdependence*, chapter 2; Keith Horsefield and others, *The International Monetary Fund 1945–1965*, 3 vols. (Washington, D.C.: IMF, 1969); Fritz Machlup, *Remaking the International Monetary System* (Baltimore, Md.: The Johns Hopkins Press, 1968); Bergsten, *The Dilemmas of the Dollar*, chapter 2–3.

23. Richard N. Cooper, "Dollar Deficits and Postwar Economic Growth," *Review of Economics and Statistics* 46 (May 1964): 155–59.

24. See also the views on this issue of Carlos Diaz-Alejandro in this volume.

25. John F. Kennedy feared that the gold issue could be successfully used against him by political opponents, and this view led to his conservative approach to international financial questions. See Theodore C. Sorensen, *Kennedy* (New York: Harper and Row, 1965) pp. 405–8.

26. See "Flexing the International Monetary System: The Case for Gliding Parities," in Federal Reserve Bank of Boston, *The International Adjustment Mechanism*, reprinted in Harry G. Johnson and A. K. Swoboda, eds., *The Economics of Common Currencies* (London: Allen & Unwin, 1973), pp. 229–43 [chapter 3]; US Congress, Joint Economic Committee, *International Monetary Reconstruction, Hearings before the Joint Economic Committee, February 22, 1973*, 93d Cong., 1st sess.; and *Towards a Renovated World Monetary System*, a report to the Trilateral Commission, the Triangle Papers, no. 1, New York, 1973.

27. Even without such bargaining across arenas, the attempt to achieve universalism may weaken an organization's effectiveness at task performance because its principles or procedures are diluted to accommodate the diverse circumstances of the enlarged membership. One of the factors weakening the General Agreement on Tariffs and Trade during the 1960s was the insistence by some new members that as less developed countries they were subject not only to different rules (which was generally agreed) but also were not bound by the GATT's procedures for settling disputes. No organization can maintain its function in the face of erosion of its internal procedures. The weakening of the GATT (which also has other sources) has redounded to the disadvantage of all countries, new as well as old members.

28. See Richard N. Cooper, "Eurodollars, Reserve Dollars, and Asymmetries in the International Monetary System," *Journal of International Economics* 2 (September 1972): 325–44 [chapter 7].

2   The Gold Standard: Historical Facts and Future Prospects

GOLD is a hardy perennial. It provides a psychological and material safe haven for people all around the world, and its invocation still produces deep-seated visceral reactions in many. It is not surprising, then, that when economic conditions are unfavorable, proposals to strengthen the role of gold in the monetary system find an audience much wider than the "gold bugs" who have always seen the demise of the gold standard as the negative turning point in Western civilization.

The early 1980s is one of these periods. A number of proposals have been put forward to reinstitute some monetary role for gold, varying from window dressing to a full-fledged revival of the gold standard. These proposals are being treated with a seriousness that would have been astonishing twenty, ten, or even five years ago. An official examination of the subject was undertaken by the Gold Commission, which was established by President Reagan in June 1981 and issued its contentious report in March 1982; and several bills have been submitted to Congress with the objective of reviving a monetary role for gold.[1]

This paper first offers a review, necessarily brief, of the heyday of the historical gold standard, focusing on those features that today are alleged to be the advantages of a gold standard. The paper then provides an examination of the leading proposals for reviving gold at the present time and addresses problems with and consequences of their implementation. Finally, since interest in reviving gold lies primarily in a desire to eliminate inflation and preserve a noninflationary environment—a point on which the historical gold standard offers little comfort—a final section of the paper considers other proposals for commodity standards that go beyond reliance on the single commodity, gold, to stabilize the general level of prices.

Brookings Papers on Economic Activity 1 (1982): 1–45. Reprinted by permission.

Before turning to the history of the gold standard, however, I examine briefly the stated and sometimes implicit objectives of those who advocate an important monetary role for gold. The primary emphasis, as noted above, is the restoration and maintenance of price stability; it is this motive, I believe, that gives gold such wide support. If the monetary side of the economy is somehow restrained by gold, the argument runs, the economy cannot inflate and prices will be stabilized. That is ultimately an empirical question, which can be addressed scientifically. But there seem to be other motivations as well. Some see restoration of gold as a way to reestablish fixed exchange rates among major currencies. To accomplish this result, all the relevant countries would have to restore a monetary role to gold in the required fashion. Action by the United States alone would not accomplish this objective; currencies could float against the US dollar even if it were tied to gold.

Finally, and perhaps most fundamentally, many advocates want greater automaticity in management of the economy, and especially monetary policy, as an objective in its own right even if the automaticity results in greater economic instability. Such underlying philosophical differences in preferences do not readily lend themselves to economic or other empirical analysis, although they derive in part from a supposed association of large government discretion in economic (and other) management with a loss of individual freedom. I am not aware, however, that this last association has been made in arguing for a return by the United States to a gold standard, at least since Americans have once again been permitted to buy and sell gold freely.[2] But to the extent that such philosophical views govern, historical evidence on economic performance under the gold standard is of secondary importance, if that. It is to the historical record, nonetheless, that I now turn.

History of the Gold Standard

While gold has been used as a store of value and as a means of payment since ancient times, the international gold standard proper dates only from the 1870s.[3] It lasted until 1914, and then had a brief revival in the late 1920s. Britain, it is true, was on a full legal gold standard from 1816, and on a de facto gold standard after 1717, when Sir Isaac Newton, by then a famous personage and Master of the Mint, did not depreciate gold enough when he set the official silver price of the gold guinea at 21 shillings and thereby inadvertently continued to drive the newly reminted full-bodied silver coins out of Britain—an illustration of Gresham's law—leaving only worn silver coins to circulate as means of payment along with the overvalued gold coins. This error in judgment established the gold standard in practice; it was codified into law following the Napoleonic wars in what became in the nineteenth century the world's leading economic and military power. That in turn influenced others, especially Germany and later Japan, to turn to the gold standard, which was seen as part of the syndrome of British success. So the gold standard as it has come down to us in textbooks, though not the monetary use of gold, was in a sense an accident of history.

Until the late nineteenth century most countries were on a bimetallic standard, interspersed with occasional periods of inconvertible paper (as in the United States in the 1780s and the 1862–78 period, or in Britain from 1797 to 1821). Some countries, such as China and Mexico, were on silver alone and remained so into the twentieth century. Holland and Belgium even switched from bimetallism to silver alone in 1850 on the grounds (following the California gold discoveries in 1848) that gold was too unstable to provide the basis for the currency. The United States adopted a de facto gold standard with resumption of specie payment on the Civil War greenbacks in 1879 (some would say it was formal, since the standard silver dollar was dropped from the coinage in the "crime of 1873"); it moved formally with the Gold Standard Act of 1900.

What were the features of this gold standard? Arthur Bloomfield, perhaps the leading American authority on the gold standard, characterized it in this way: "The national monetary unit was defined in terms of a given quantity of gold; the central bank or treasury stood ready to buy and sell gold at the resulting fixed price in terms of the national currency; gold was freely coined and gold coins formed a significant part of the circulating medium; and gold could be freely exported and imported."[4] These conditions in turn implied nearly fixed exchange rates between the currencies of countries on the gold standard, assured by the possibility of profitable gold arbitrage whenever exchange rates reached the gold export or import points, determined by mint charges (if any) and the costs of shipping gold.[5]

How did this system fare in terms of economic performance? The idealized gold standard as it appears in textbooks conveys a sense of automaticity and stability—a self-correcting mechanism with minimum human intervention, which assured rough stability of prices and balance in international payments.

The actual gold standard could hardly have been further from this representation. As noted above, the major countries of the world were on the gold standard proper only from the 1870s to 1914, and briefly between the two world wars. The first period went down in history as the Great Depression—until, that is, the second period came along to exceed it in depth and severity.

With a dose of nostalgia, the gold standard period looks somewhat better to us than it did to contemporaries. Economic growth during the late nineteenth century was very respectable, although in per capita terms it falls short of the 2.1 percent achieved in the United States during the thirty years between 1950 and 1980. Variability in income growth was substantially higher under the gold standard than it was after World War II, and average unemployment was also considerably higher (see table 2.1). Moreover, the last third of the nineteenth century was a period of unprecedented controversy over the monetary standard in the United States, first over the resumption of gold convertibility at a fixed rate for the Civil War greenbacks, then over the monetary role of silver. Legislation was almost constantly before Congress to change monetary relations. Some of the legislation passed into law. The Bland-Allison Act of 1878 authorized the US Department of the Treasury to buy $2 to $4 million in silver each month, and the Sherman Silver Purchase Act of 1890 raised this figure to nearly $6 million and made the purchase of nearly all US output obligatory. The Silver Purchase Act was repealed in 1893 following a sharp decline in the world price of silver and a sharp increase in calls on gold at the Treasury. The year 1896 saw the only US presidential campaign devoted to the issue of the monetary standard, following William Jennings Bryan's nomination on the basis of his famous "cross of gold" speech. A National Monetary Commission was established following the "panic of 1907," and the Federal Reserve Act passed in 1913.

Most of the attempts to alter monetary relations and to dislodge the United States from a gold standard failed. But the point is that the issue was a source of continual turmoil and uncertainty, not serene stability.[6]

There was less monetary debate in Britain during this period—that had taken place in 1815–20, surrounding the resumption of specie payment after the Napoleonic wars. But even Britain was not immune from concerns about the monetary system, and established the Royal Commission on the Depression of Trade and Industry in 1886 and the Gold and Silver Commission in 1887, to both of which Alfred Marshall gave important testimony. There were international conferences on the monetary standard (mainly an effort to preserve bimetallism) in 1878, 1881, and 1892, although Britain attended without enthusiasm.

So much for the political agitation. What about economic developments? The late nineteenth century was no doubt a period of rapid growth,

Table 2.1
Economic Variables in the United States and the United Kingdom under the Gold Standard and since World War II.

Measure	United Kingdom		United States	
	Gold standard, 1870–1913	Postwar, 1946–1979	Gold standard, 1879–1913	Postwar, 1946–1979
Average annual change in wholesale prices (percent)[a]	−0.7	5.6	0.1	2.8
Standard deviation of price change (percent)[b]	4.6	6.2[c]	5.4	4.8[c]
Average annual growth in real per capita income (percent)	1.4	2.4	1.9	2.1
Coefficient of variation of annual percentage changes in real per capita income (ratio)[d]	2.5	1.4	3.5	1.6
Average unemployment rate (percent)	4.3[e]	2.5	6.8[f]	5.0
Average annual growth in money supply (percent)[a]	1.5	5.9	6.1	5.7
Coefficient of variation of growth in money supply (ratio)[d]	1.6	1.0	0.8	0.5

Sources: Michael David Bordo, "The Classical Gold Standard: Some Lessons for Today," *Review of the St. Louis Federal Reserve Bank*, vol. 63 (May 1981), p. 14, and calculations from George F. Warren and Frank A. Pearson, *Gold and Prices* (Wiley, 1935), pp. 13–14, 87; B. R. Mitchell, *Abstract of British Historical Statistics* (Cambridge University Press, 1971), pp. 367–68; Council of Economic Advisers, *Economic Report of the President, January 1982*; and International Monetary Fund, *International Financial Statistics*, various issues.

a. Calculated as the time coefficient from a regression of the log of the variable on a time trend.

b. Calculated as the standard error of estimate of the fitted equation $\ln P_t = a \ln P_{t-1}$, where P_t is the wholesale price index in year t.

c. 1949–1979.

d. Calculated as the ratio of the standard deviation of annual percentage changes to their mean.

e. 1888–1913.

f. 1890–1913.

especially in manufacturing. There was a sharp decline in both inland and ocean transportation costs and a great increase in international trade. But it was also a period of great distress, with large-scale emigration from Europe, and one in which there was great labor strife, resulting in the formation of labor unions.[7]

Price Movements

Price stability was not attained, either in the short run or in the long run, either during the period of the gold standard proper or over a longer period during which gold held dominant influence. In fact, in the United States short-run variations in wholesale prices were higher during the prewar gold standard period than from 1949 to 1979. The standard deviation of annual movements in prices was 5.4 percent in the earlier period and only 4.8 percent in the latter period (see table 2.1).[8] It could be argued that such short-run variations are of little economic consequence— it is the long-run trend that is important for contracts and other economic transactions, and the trend was upward in the postwar period. However, current efforts to explain the costs of inflation focus inter alia on the confusion of signals that is introduced when the general level of prices is changing, so that buyers and sellers, with imperfect information, cannot clearly distinguish the relative price movements that are important for resource allocation. This argument applies with even more force to short-term fluctuations in price levels than to long-term movements.

However, the gold standard did not assure price stability in the long run either. Price "stability" in the sense of a return to earlier levels of prices was obtained over longer periods only by judicious choice of the years for comparison. If one chooses 1822, 1856, 1877, late 1915, and 1931, for instance, the US wholesale price level indeed appears unchanged. But between these dates there were great swells and troughs (see figure 2.1).

Table 2.2 shows cumulative price movements from peak to trough (excluding the US Civil War) in four countries during the century from 1816 to 1913. Although each country had its distinctive national developments, the parallelism among price movements is striking.[9] Prices declined 30 to 45 percent from the highs of the post-Napoleonic period, rose about 50 percent until the general establishment of the gold standard in the 1870s, fell about 50 percent again until the gold discoveries of the late 1890s, then rose sharply in the two decades before World War I. This is hardly a pattern of stability, even long-term stability, although there were prolonged periods of price decline as well as of price rise. But the full

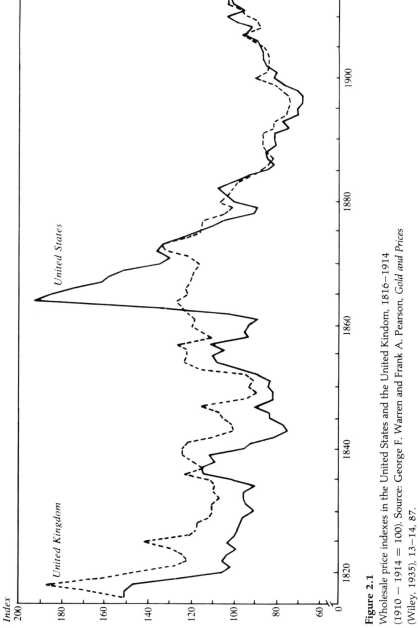

Figure 2.1
Wholesale price indexes in the United States and the United Kindom, 1816–1914
(1910 − 1914 = 100). Source: George F. Warren and Frank A. Pearson, *Gold and Prices*
(Wiley, 1935), 13–14, 87.

Table 2.2
Wholesale Price Indexes for the United States, the United Kingdom, Germany, and France, Selected Years, 1816–1913.

Year and period	United States	United Kingdom	Germany	France
Indexes (1913 = 100)				
1816	150	147	94	143
1849	82	86	67	94
1873	137	130	114	122
1896	64	72	69	69
1913	100	100	100	100
Changes (in percent)				
1816–49	−45	−41	−29	−33
1849–73	67	51	70	30
1873–96	−53	−45	−40	−45
1896–1913	56	39	45	45

Sources: Data for the United States and the United Kingdom are from Warren and Pearson, *Gold and Prices*, pp. 87–88; data for Germany and France are from B. R. Mitchell, *European Historical Statistics, 1750–1970* (Columbia University Press, 1975), pp. 736–39.

swings are so long in duration—forty to sixty years—that they can hardly have offered much comfort for any but the longest term financial contracts, and then only because of the accidents of war or discovery.

Although *we* know that the price level of 1822, during a period of secular price decline, would be restored by 1856, a period of price increase, and again by 1877, a period of decline, did the *contemporaries* know it? That is what is relevant. Two points can be made on this score, although some puzzles remain. First, even the idea of a price index was in its infancy. Laspeyres, whose name is still used on base-weighted index numbers, published his ideas in 1864. At about the same time, Stanley Jevons (credited by Irving Fisher as the originator of index numbers) was making the distinction between short-term and long-term fluctuations in the general level of prices. The idea of a general level of prices had been around for a long time, but refinement and regular measurement had not yet occurred. Jevons was certainly aware of them, and of their reciprocal, the value of gold, when he raised the question in 1875 of whether "having regard to these extreme changes in the values of the precious metals, it is desirable to employ them as the standard of value in long lasting contracts."[10] And in his testimony before the Royal Commission on the Depression of Trade and Industry in 1886, Alfred Marshall proposed that the government "should publish tables showing as closely as may be the changes in the purchasing power of gold, and should facilitate contracts for payments to be made in terms of units of fixed purchasing power." In the same evidence Marshall alludes to a "search for a better and more stable currency than our present."[11] From these remarks one may infer that there was not a generally accepted index of the purchasing power of (gold) money, and that contracts written in money terms were not stable in terms of purchasing power over goods other than gold, presumably even after allowing for adjustments in the interest rate (to which Marshall does not allude).

Second, what is perhaps more directly to the point, the financial community—both borrowers and lenders—apparently thought that the long-term price level was roughly stable from its present level, adjusted slightly on the basis of recent past experience, but they were continually fooled. Long-term interest rates in the United States, as measured by railway bonds with original maturities from twenty to one hundred years, fell steadily from 9.5 percent in 1857 (the first year of the series), to 6.6 percent in 1877, 4.3 percent in 1896, and 3.8 percent (the low point) in 1902, rising again to 4.3 percent in 1913.[12] This pattern of secular decline followed by secular rise is roughly the same as that of the price level, which implies that real interest rates on forward-looking contracts such as bonds showed great swings. Ex post, creditors gained at the expense of debtors in the fourth quarter of the nineteenth century (the rise of populism and strong antibank feeling during that period shows that the debtors were very much aware of it) and lost in the first quarter of the twentieth century. Real ex post rates of return on twenty-year bonds purchased in 1872 (a price peak) and held until maturity were 10.4 percent, compared with a nominal yield of 7.5 percent; similar bonds purchased in 1896 (a secular price trough) and held until maturity yielded only 1.2 percent in real terms, compared with a nominal yield of 4.3 percent (figure 2.2).

Yields on British consols followed roughly the same pattern as prices; they declined gradually from a postresumption high of 4.42 percent in 1820 to a low of 3.02 percent in 1852, rose to a local high of 3.41 percent in 1866, declined gradually and slowly to a low of 2.45 percent in 1897, then rose to 3.39 percent in 1913 (and up to 4.43 percent in 1925, when the gold standard was resumed in Britain).[13] Calculations of real rates of return are more arbitrary for perpetuals, but for holding periods of twenty to twenty-five years, as in the United States, real rates of return varied much more than nominal rates of return. It is thus not true, as is sometimes claimed, that a gold-based unit of account offers a stable basis for long-term contracts and "eliminates entirely windfall losses and windfall gains among debtors and creditors."[14] Variations in real short-term interest rates were even greater over the period 1879–1913, moving from a high of 11.5

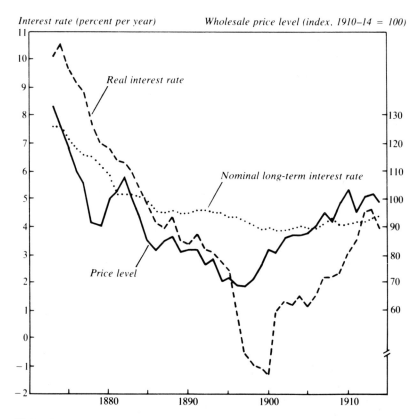

Interest rate (percent per year)   *Wholesale price level (index, 1910–14 = 100)*

Figure 2.2
US Wholesale prices, long-term interest rates, and long-term real interest rates for a
twenty-year holding period, 1873–1914. The nominal interest rate is the yield on American
railroad bonds. Sources: Warren and Pearson, *Gold and Prices*, 13–14; and Frederick
R. Macauley, *The Movement of Interest Rates, Bond Yields and Stock Prices in the United States
since 1856* (National Bureau of Economic Research, 1938), A108–A109.

percent (May 1891 to May 1894) to a low of −2.3 percent (June 1897 to November 1900).[15]

If the relevant public really expected the long-term price level to be stable, long-term interest rates should be *negatively* correlated with the price level, high levels giving rise to expectations of a subsequent fall in prices, which would be reflected in a lowering of nominal long-term interest rates; the reverse effect would take hold when the price level was low relatively to historical levels. Instead, long-term interest rates are positively correlated with the price level, both in Britain and in the United States. The data suggest that the public did not correctly foresee the long-term price changes that were to take place, and they adjusted their expectations (as reflected in interest rates) only slowly to the price movements that had actually taken place.[16] Nominal interest rates, in other words, did not adjust adequately to correct for rates of inflation; on the contrary, on balance they adjusted with such long lags that the correction turned out to be perverse.

In view of another claim that is sometimes made for the gold standard, that it is conducive to long-term contracts (British consols being the extreme manifestation of long maturities), it is worth noting that, while high-quality bonds could typically be floated in the United States for twenty-five or thirty or sometimes even one hundred years, mortgage loans in the nineteenth century were typically very short, averaging about four years for farm mortgages.[17]

Increase in Monetary Gold Supplies

Prices were not stable under the gold standard in part—but only in part—because the stock of gold varied substantially in its rate of growth.

The general level of prices in terms of currency can be written as a product of the currency price of gold and the terms of trade between gold and commodities: $/goods = ($/gold)(gold/goods). Under a gold standard the currency price of gold is fixed (indeed, the currency is defined in terms of gold). The price level will be stable only insofar as the terms of trade between gold and other goods is stable. But stability in the terms of trade is unlikely in the presence of substantial variations in the supply of gold, except insofar as the public's demand for gold is perfectly elastic in terms of other goods—a claim even nonmonetarists would decline to make.

Variations in the growth of monetary gold were due mainly to fluctuations in gold production, but to some extent also to variations in nonmonetary demand for gold. As a consequence of new production from California and Australia, the stock of monetary gold doubled between 1848 and 1859, after having shown negligible growth in the preceding two decades.[18] It took until 1895 to double again—a period of thirty-six years—whereupon it again doubled in the nineteen years to 1914 as a result of sharp increases in gold production in South Africa, Canada, and Alaska during the late 1890s (which was partly the result of new discoveries, partly the result of improved extractive techniques). Table 2.3 shows world gold production (and also in figure 2.3), increases in monetary gold, and estimated monetary gold stocks. Although major developments do not always appear at the beginning of each decade, table 2.3 clearly shows the great variation in additions to monetary gold stocks over the decades, from a low of 11 percent during the 1880s to a high of 88 percent during the 1850s. The clear correlation with price movements during the century led a number of observers—Cassels, Kitchin, Keynes, Warren and Pearson, among others—to generalize the relation. Warren and Pearson, for instance, argue that, on the basis of history during the preceding century, prices rose whenever the rate of growth in monetary gold exceeded the rate of growth of total output (or physical production, as they call it), and fell whenever the growth in gold fell short of the growth in production. The key rate of growth was reckoned by many authors to be between 2.5 and 3 percent. If gold stocks did not increase this rapidly, prices were bound to fall.[19]

The general relation between the quantity of money and the level of prices had been part of background knowledge at least since David Hume's famous parable in 1752 involving a hypothetical destruction of four-fifths of England's money supply, leading to a decline in prices and an improvement in the balance of trade. With this "model" of the economic system in mind, the tenfold increase in annual new gold supplies that took place between the late 1830s and the mid-1850s and the not quite so sharp increase in the decade spanning the turn of the century should have affected prices through expectations, on the currently voguish rational expectations view of the world. Yet the impact on prices of these sharp increases in gold production (which, as noted, also represented a sharp increase in the rate of growth of monetary gold stocks) was more gradual, delayed, and spread over a long period of time. Whereas world monetary gold stocks grew 90 percent between 1849 and 1859, and 45 percent between 1895 and 1905, wholesale prices in the United States rose only 24 percent and 29 percent during the two periods, respectively, and prices in Britain rose 28 percent and 16 percent in the same two periods.[20] Warren

Table 2.3
World Gold Output and Monetary Stocks[a] (Millions of fine ounces).

| Period | Production | Monetary gold stock | | |
		Additions to monetary gold stock	Percent increase	End-of-period stock
1493–1600	23.6	n.a.	...	...
1601–1700	29.3	n.a.	...	...
1701–1800	61.1	n.a.	n.a.	39
1801–39	19.8	7	18	46
1840–49	14.7	6	13	52
1850–59	60.4	46	88	98
1860–69	61.0	30	30	128
1870–79	54.6	22	17	150
1880–89	51.4	17	11	167
1890–99	95.1	59	35	226
1900–09	173.2	104	46	330
1910–19	213.8	122	37	452
1920–29	180.5	98	22	550
1930–39	256.5[b]	205	37	755
1940–49	260.1[b]	228	30	983
1950–59	268.3[b]	166	17	1149
1960–69	388.2[b]	30	3	1179
1970–79	339.2[b]	−49	−4	1130
1980	29.2[b]	4	...	1134

Sources: Data for 1493–1929 were computed from Warren and Pearson, *Gold and Prices*, pp. 92–93, 121, 125. Gold production data for 1930–66 are from Fred Hirsch, "Influences on Gold Production," *International Monetary Fund Staff Papers*, vol. 15 (November 1968), p. 486; since 1967 from Bank for International Settlements, *Annual Report*, various issues. Data on monetary gold after 1930 are from estimates by the International Monetary Fund and from IMF, *International Financial Statistics*, various issues.
n.a. Not available.
a. The dollar value before 1933 can be calculated by multiplying by $20.67; 1934–68, by $35. For metric tons, divide by 32,151.
b. Excluding the Soviet Union.

Millions of fine ounces

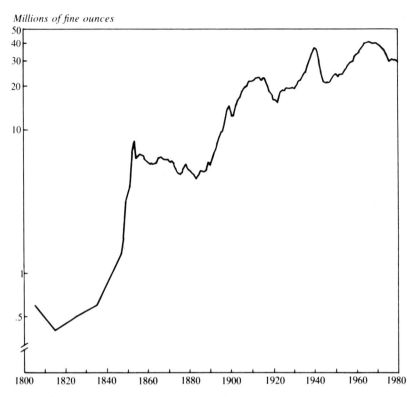

Figure 2.3
World gold production, 1805–1980. Sources: Same as table 2.3.

and Pearson reckon a delay of about thirteen years before the full impact of increased gold supplies is felt on prices.[21] Why the prolonged period of adjustment? Several explanations are possible. First, the public may not have known the full magnitude of the increases. That is almost certainly true, since statistical information was much scarcer then than it is today. But the public might just as well have overestimated the true extent of the increase, given the enormous publicity and excitement that attended the gold discoveries in each period.

Second, based on quantity theory reasoning it is the total money supply that counts, not a single component of it. Allowance for monetary silver and bank notes reduces the rate of increase in money brought about by the new gold supplies, but not by enough to bring the figures into correspondence.[22] This is especially true for Britain, where silver coins were of relatively minor importance; but they were also temporarily of less importance in the United States during the 1840s, full-weight coins having been largely exported as a result of the Currency Act of 1834. The allowance for bank deposits takes us further from the explanation in the later period; as shown below, they grew more rapidly than gold. But such deposits should perhaps not be counted because, like credit cards today, they were not yet recognized as money.

Third, the public may have believed, contrary to the Hume hypothesis, that new money "stimulates trade," that as a consequence of the new gold production, output of other goods would be increased as well, and therefore that prices would not rise proportionately with the increase in the money stock. This third interpretation is consistent with Fetter's puzzled observation that there was very little contemporary comment on the likely impact of new gold on prices until the 1860s, that is, until after the increase in prices had been observed (recall that the work of Jevons and Laspeyres took place in the 1860s).[23] And certainly the debates of the 1880s and early 1890s over the monetary standard suggest the widespread belief that increased money would stimulate trade; it was not argued that more money would merely increase prices. This interpretation might also help to explain the failure of long-term interest rates to rise (at all in the first period, commensurately in the second) following large increases in gold production.

As noted above, gold was not the only source of money. During 1879–1913 monetary gold in the United States grew by a factor of 3.5, whereas the money supply (as it is now calculated, including time deposits) grew by a factor of about 8.4; bank deposits accounted for the difference, growing by a factor of 9.8 during this period.[24]

Table 2.4 shows the growth in various forms of money in eleven industrial countries between 1885 and 1928. Monetary gold grew 120 percent during 1885–1913, while monetary silver grew only 25 percent in these countries. The major change, however, was in demand deposits, which increased by 400 percent, rising from 39 to 63 percent of the money supply as it is now defined. The financial system apparently responded, with a lag, to the perceived shortage of money during the 1880s and early 1890s with institutional innovation. This factor, to the extent that it influences prices, compounds the puzzle raised above about the impact of sharp increases in gold production on the price level: the impact on prices should have been even greater than the increase in gold stocks alone would suggest.[25]

The central lesson to derive from this brief review is that the supply of monetary gold was highly erratic even during the heyday of the gold

Table 2.4
Comparative Evolution of Money and Reserve Structure, Selected Countries and Years, 1885–1928 (Billions of US dollars).

Money supply and reserves	Three countries[a]		Eleven countries[b]		
	1885	1913	1885	1913	1928
Money supply	6.3	19.8	8.4	26.3	50.4
Gold	1.4	2.0	1.8	2.7	0.1
Silver	0.7	0.6	1.0	1.2	0.3[d]
Credit money	4.1	17.2	5.6	22.4	50.0
Currency[c]	1.6	3.8	2.3	5.9	13.0
Demand deposits	2.6	13.3	3.3	16.5	37.0
Monetary reserves	1.0	2.8	1.6	4.5	10.6
Gold	0.6	2.1	0.9	3.2	7.9
Silver	0.4	0.6	0.6	0.8	0.4[d]
Foreign exchange	...	0.1	0.1	0.5	2.3
Total gold and silver	3.1	5.4	4.3	7.9	8.7
Gold	2.0	4.1	2.7	5.9	8.0
Silver	1.1	1.2	1.6	2.0	0.7[d]

Sources: Robert Triffin, "The Evolution of the International Monetary System: Historical Reappraisal and Future Perspectives," Princeton Studies in International Finance 12 (Princeton University, 1964), pp. 56, 62, for all series with the exception of foreign exchange held as monetary reserves in 1913, which was taken from Peter H. Lindert, "Key Currencies and Gold, 1900–1913," Princeton Studies in International Finance 24 (Princeton University, 1969), pp. 10–11, 23, and the holdings of silver by the United States in 1928, which was taken from US Bureau of the Census, *Historical Statistics of the United States, Colonial Times to 1970* (Government Printing Office, 1975), pt. 2, p. 994.
a. United States, United Kingdom, and France.
b. United States, United Kingdom, France, Germany, Italy, Netherlands, Belgium, Sweden, Switzerland, Canada, and Japan.
c. Including subsidiary (nonsilver) coinage.
d. United States only.

standard. The one feature the gold standard did secure was stability of exchange rates among major currencies, except for those that remained on silver. Under the gold standard, price stability and other domestic objectives were, when necessary, relinquished to preserve stability in exchange rates.

The Interwar Period

There is no need to examine closely the brief restoration of the gold standard during the late 1920s. The experience was so brief and unsatisfactory that it provides no basis for an assessment of the gold standard in more normal times. Most European countries called in the gold still held by their publics before the First World War and concentrated it in the hands of the central banks. The restored gold standard was a gold *bullion* standard, such as had been recommended by Ricardo over one hundred years earlier, whereby the monetary authorities bought and sold gold at a fixed price only in large quantities, and did not coin the gold. Moreover, to conserve gold further (for it was recognized that at the much higher postwar price and activity levels the prewar gold standard regime could not be restored), there was strong encouragement toward a gold *exchange* standard, whereby the monetary authorities of countries would hold, instead of gold, currencies that were convertible into gold, notably sterling. With considerable deflation, Britain returned to gold convertibility in 1925 at the prewar gold parity (85 shillings per ounce). France returned to convertibility in 1926 at a parity one-fifth of the prewar parity. It is widely considered that these parities overvalued the pound and undervalued the French franc, in each case putting considerable strain on the pattern of international payments and, through them, on domestic economies. Britain remained depressed throughout the 1920s, with unemployment never dropping below 10 percent after 1920. The system was supported for a while by international lending, but it collapsed in 1931–33 under the impact of the world depression, to which the fragile restoration of the gold standard contributed. There is probably not that much to be learned from this period about a gold standard, except that "incorrect" exchange rates can put great strains on national economies and, if they are important, on the system as a whole.[26]

It is perhaps worth observing, in the light of subsequent events, two prophesies in this period that concerned the role of gold. Joseph Kitchin, on the basis of his extensive study of the supply of gold during the nineteenth century and its relation to the price level, testified before the Royal Commission in 1926 with respect to prices in England (on a base of 1913 = 100) that "it would seem evident from a study of the chart that they may go a considerable way toward 90 in the next few years."[27] Prices were then at 143; by 1932 they were at 93.

The second is an observation by Keynes in January 1929, that new gold production could add only about 2 percent a year to monetary gold stocks, against a normal requirement of about 3 percent, thus necessitating economy of gold to the extent of 1 percent a year. But in recent years one legislature after another had stipulated a minimum gold backing for the currency outstanding, a provision that made no sense to Keynes in a regime (such as prevailed everywhere outside the United States) in which currency was not readily convertible to gold. These requirements, Keynes reckoned, denied the use of two-thirds to three-quarters of monetary gold for meeting external drains, and thus introduced a great source of fragility into the system: "It is not much with which to meet all the chances and fluctuations of economic life. It follows that a very little upsets them [the central banks] and compels them to look for protection by restricting the supply of credit ... raising of rates all round helps no one until, after an interregnum during which the economic activity of the whole world has been retarded, prices and wages have been forced to a lower level."[28] This is exactly what happened.

The Supply of Gold in the Late Twentieth Century

As table 2.3 makes clear, gold production in the non-Communist world rose during the 1930s (stimulated in part by higher gold prices), receded in the 1940s, and rose gradually to an all-time high in the 1960s. New gold production is supplemented from time to time by sales from the Soviet Union, which is assumed to be the second largest gold producer, after the Republic of South Africa. Sales by the USSR are largely keyed to its own requirements for foreign exchange, which in turn are influenced mainly by harvest conditions. But the Soviet Union also pays attention to market considerations. It withdrew from sales altogether in the late 1960s, when it became clear that something dramatic would probably happen to gold. After attempting for several years to prevent market prices from rising above the official price of $35 an ounce, the United States also ceased selling into the London market through the "gold pool" in 1968 and the market price started its long rise. The Soviet Union again in 1981 reduced its sales of gold (despite large needs for foreign exchange) and allegedly tried to borrow against gold collateral to avoid further depressing the market price.

The principal source of monetary gold to most countries of the world since the Second World War was neither new production nor Soviet gold sales, however, but a redistribution of gold held by the United States. Total monetary gold stocks grew about 200 million ounces ($7 billion at the official US price of $35 an ounce) between 1945 and 1969, whereas the United States sold over 250 million ounces during the same period. Thus the "world" demand for gold was satisfied to a large degree from the United States, which in 1945 held 59 percent of the world's monetary gold. Even so, the holdings of dollars by foreign monetary authorities rose during this period by $13 billion, dollars being fully convertible to gold by monetary authorities at the US Treasury, so the demand for international reserves outside the United States was satisfied nearly as much in that way as with augmented gold holdings. Robert Triffin early pointed out the nonsustainability of a system in which dollars provided major additions to international reserves, gold reserves grew only slowly (and US gold reserves declined), and the dollar remained convertible to gold.[29] Official gold convertibility of the dollar was in fact suspended in August 1971.

World gold production declined steadily during the 1970s, despite a sharp rise in both the nominal and the real price of gold (see figure 2.4). Gold prices have been so erratic that it is difficult to know what price has been used for planning decisions on production, reopening old mines, and developing new mines. The market price of gold briefly reached $800 an ounce in early 1980, but declined rapidly again from that peak. For the sake of round numbers, and without too much injustice to the truth, one can assume that the "planning" price of gold has risen tenfold in the 1971–81 decade, from $35 an ounce (official price) to $350 an ounce. In real terms, using the US GNP deflator as a rough and ready indicator of world inflation rates, this represented a rise by a factor of five.[30] This increase was not smooth, but tended to come in bursts; in late 1978, for instance, the market price of gold was about $225, a fourfold increase in real prices during the 1970s up to that point.

Despite this sharp increase in real prices, gold production has declined. South African production, in particular, declined by one-third between 1970 and 1980 (see table 2.5). This performance marks a sharp contrast with the last major increase in the real price of gold—during the 1930s, when world gold production rose substantially. Either production lead times must be substantially longer today (gold having experienced a steady but gradual decline in real prices since the Second World War), or South Africa is supressing production that would be profitable at today's prices. It is said that marginal mines have been brought into production during the 1970s and production has been cut in the more profitable mines.[31] If so, considerable central direction of South African gold mining is implied, or at a minimum a strongly oligopolistic structure combined with expectations that real gold prices will decline in the future.

South Africa estimated its gold reserves in 1979 at 530 million ounces, 51 percent of the world total and 64 percent of the total in the non-Communist world (implying world reserves of about 1,040 million ounces).[32] This would imply non-Communist world production at current rates for another twenty-seven years. Numerous allowances must be made with respect to this sort of calculation. "Reserve" figures are conceptually tricky—they imply a known geology, price, technology of extraction, and costs. But

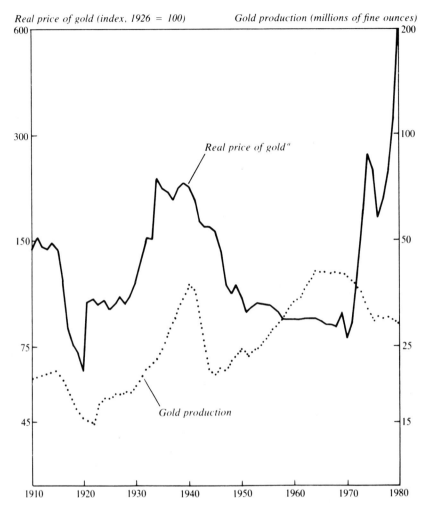

Figure 2.4

World gold production and the "real" dollar price of gold, 1910–1980. (a) Average of daily
London fixing prices deflated by the US producer price index for finished goods. Sources:
Based on the figure presented in Fred Hirsch, "Influences on Gold Production," *International
Monetary Fund Staff Papers*, vol. 15 (November 1968), 416. Data before 1966 are from the
same source, 486–488. Data from 1967 to 1980 are as follows: gold production—Bank
for International Settlements, *Annual Report*, various issues; gold prices—International
Monetary Fund, *International Financial Statistics*, various issues; US producer price index—
Council of Economic Advisers, *Economic Report of the President*, February 1982.

Table 2.5
New Gold Supplies, Selected Years, 1965–80 (Millions of fine ounces[a]).

Country or region	1965	1970	1975	1980
South Africa	30.5	31.1	22.2	21.0
Canada	3.6	2.3	1.6	1.5
United States	1.7	1.7	1.0	0.9
Other	5.2	4.4	5.0	5.8
Total non-Communist world	41.0	39.5	29.8	29.2
Addenda				
Gold sales by the Soviet Union	15.7	1.6	4.7	2.8
Gold sales by the International Monetary Fund[b]	...	...	...	2.1

Source: Bank for International Settlements, *Annual Report*, various issues.
a. Gold is measured in troy ounces, equal to 31.104 grams, or about 10 percent heavier than an avoirdupois ounce.
b. Gold sales by the International Monetary Fund began in 1976.

they give a rough idea of informed judgment on the remaining gold to be extracted.

An approximate estimate of nonmonetary gold in the world would be about 1,500 million ounces, derived by subtracting monetary gold holdings from known and estimated gold production over the centuries. This is about one-third higher than monetary gold holdings (excluding those in the Soviet Union). Current new production, virtually none of which has gone into monetary gold holdings for over a decade, amounts to 2.7 percent of monetary gold holdings and about 1 percent of the total outstanding gold. It is unclear how sensitive the huge nonmonetary holdings are to gold prices and to price expectations.

Contemporary Proposals for Restoring Gold to a Monetary Role

Proposals for reinstituting a monetary role for gold cover a wide range, from reestablishing gold backing for the currency at an official price to full-fledged restoration of a gold currency. I will discuss these proposals under two broad headings: gold backing of all kinds without convertibility; and proposals calling for some form of gold convertibility, ranging from foreign monetary authorities' holdings to all holdings of dollars. I address only proposals for the United States, although as noted above, a desire to restore fixed exchange rates represents part of the interest in gold, and that requires other countries to reintroduce gold as well. But so far there has been little interest from other countries in moving toward gold convertibility.

It is worth recalling at the outset that the United States had full gold convertibility for the dollar from 1879 to 1933 (with export restrictions imposed briefly during World War I); gold convertibility for foreign monetary authorities from 1934 to 1971; and gold backing for the currency from 1879 to 1968.[33] The only country that maintains any formal monetary role for gold (apart from holding gold among central bank assets) is Switzerland, about which more will be said below.

Gold Reserve Requirements

The idea behind gold backing without convertibility is to limit the growth in the supply of money and presumably also to bolster psychological support for the currency by those who still attach a monetary significance to gold and do not fully comprehend that, ultimately, money is a social convention.

The most limited proposal for gold backing calls for stipulating that the currency in circulation must be backed by the existing official gold stock of the United States at its current official price of $42.22 an ounce, and that the allowable growth in outstanding currency should be limited to 3 percent a year after a transition period, assured by revaluing the existing gold stock by 3 percent a year.[34] For the indefinite future, this proposal amounts only to a monetary rule in thin disguise; gold plays no essential role. One might just as well back the currency with the Washington Monument or the Statue of Liberty, endowing each with an initial value and stipulating that the value should increase at the fixed rate of 3 percent a year. Such a proposal will not be considered further here.

Gold backing for all or some portion of the money supply could also be required at a fixed price of gold, or at the market price of gold, which fluctuates substantially. If the gold backing requirement does not bind—that is, if the value of the monetary gold exceeds the requirement for gold reserves—we would be in the realm of discretionary monetary policy, as at present. When the reserve requirement does bind, the monetary authorities would have to buy gold in order to increase the money supply. Unlike under a regime of convertibility, the purchase would be at the discretion of the monetary authorities.

This kind of arrangement poses difficult but not insuperable technical problems over the valuation of monetary gold, because in general the market price must deviate from the official price if orderly monetary growth is to be maintained (otherwise the permissible monetary base would fluctuate—wildly, in recent experience—with the market price of gold). For example, the Treasury could buy gold necessary for increasing the money supply at market prices, and resell it to the Federal Reserve banks at the fixed official price, absorbing the difference as an expenditure (or, if the official price were above the market price, as a receipt).

But the key point is that this would be a discretionary regime, not an automatic one, unless in addition a rule governing monetary growth were also imposed. It would involve extra discipline only insofar as directors at the Office of Management and Budget and their superiors balk at budgeting for gold when market prices are considerably higher than the official price, or the Secretary of the Treasury balks at the balance-of-payments implications of gold purchases. A rough idea of the magnitudes is suggested by the fact that a 4 percent growth in the official US gold stock—implying a 4 percent growth in that component of the money supply covered by gold reserves, if the reserves are binding—would involve a gross expenditure of $4.2 billion if the market price were $400 an ounce, and a net expenditure on the budget of $3.75 billion if the gold were resold to the Federal Reserve at the present official price. If the official price were increased, say, to $200 an ounce (with a corresponding increase in the required gold reserve, to keep it binding), the gross expenditure by the Treasury for 4 percent growth would be the same, and the net expenditure would be reduced to $2.1 billion. Obviously official US purchases of the 10.6 million ounces a year required for 4 percent annual growth, amounting to 35 percent of current world gold production, would very likely drive up the market price of gold considerably.

In short, gold backing by itself does not provide monetary discipline. The United States had backing for many years, and during most of that period the gold reserve requirements were not binding. The gold reserves would have permitted much more rapid growth than what actually took place. On the occasions when the reserve requirement became binding, it was lowered, and eventually removed. The national debt ceiling provides an analogous restraint on US government borrowing; it is there in principle, but in practice it is regularly overridden by other considerations, even by "conservative" Congresses.

Switzerland is the only country that currently requires gold backing for its bank notes, in a ratio of 40 percent. (Switzerland ceased to provide for convertibility of those notes into gold in 1954, the year the London gold market reopened.) Swiss official gold holdings grew only 7 percent during the inflationary decade of the 1970s, but the Swiss money supply grew by 65 percent. How was this possible? Switzerland entered the period with ample gold holdings relative to the required backing, more than double the legal requirement in 1970. The ratio fell steadily through the decade to 53 percent in 1981, still well above the required 40 percent. The restraint in Swiss monetary expansion has been discretionary, not conditioned by a binding gold reserve requirement.

What will happen when the reserve requirement becomes binding? Switzerland would have two options, apart from relaxing the requirement itself. It could raise its official price of gold (which still stands at 4,596 Swiss francs a kilogram, about $80 an ounce at current exchange rates), which is well below the market price, and which can be changed by simple government decree (after consultation with the Swiss National Bank). Or Switzerland could buy sufficient gold at market prices, something that country could probably do without greatly affecting the market price of gold. Either action would be discretionary in nature.

Gold Convertibility

Gold convertibility exerts its discipline in quite a different way. The proposals involving convertibility vary, some calling in effect for full convertibility of all Federal Reserve notes and 100 percent gold money thereafter. Bank notes could be issued by private banks, but they would in effect be depository receipts for gold.[35] Others are more limited, for example, calling for restoration of the pre-1971 gold convertibility for foreign monetary authorities.[36]

Although the modus operandi would very substantially from one proposal to another, the underlying idea is the same: whenever some substantial group of dollar holders became dissatisfied with monetary developments and unsure about the future value of the dollar, they could and presumably would convert their dollars to gold. These conversions in turn would require the Federal Reserve to defend its gold reserves by tightening credit conditions or otherwise persuading the relevant public that gold conversions were unwarranted. The system in principle would be symmetrical: as gold reserves increased, the money supply would expand; this feature has not been emphasized by most proponents of gold convertibility. Moreover, historically central banks have often offset ("sterilized") the expansionary effects of gold inflows, as the United States did during the late 1930s and again during the late 1940s.[37] Sterilization obviously would not be possible when gold (or gold certificates) is the sole form of money.

Since new gold production is small relative to outstanding gold stocks, the requirement for convertibility, it is argued, will automatically limit the rate of money creation, hence inflation, since there is a natural limit to how rapidly gold reserves can grow. Too rapid monetary growth would lead to conversion, which in turn (to preserve convertibility) would necessitate monetary retrenchment.

Note that most proposals for convertibility—those that fall short of a move to 100 percent gold money—provide for some elasticity to the supply of money, so long as the relevant public is not of a disposition to convert dollars into gold. This feature indeed could conceivably be a source of instability, since in periods of high "animal spirits" in the business and financial community outstanding Federal Reserve credit could rise substantially, only to be sharply reduced as the buoyant spirits give way to pessimism and a period of heavy conversion sets in, leading to a drop in Federal Reserve credit below its historical trend under the regime.

There is no doubt that a regime of gold convertibility could be made to function technically. But could if function politically? That is, could the political authorities resist the pressures they would be under to take countervailing action in periods of distress, either too rapid expansion or too rapid contraction? That would depend in part on how serious the distress was, which in turn would depend in part on the credibility of the monetary regime itself: expectations of long-run price stability will reduce the inertial character of inflationary impulses to the US economy, and hence improve the ability of the economy to absorb both monetary and real shocks with reduced cost in terms of lost output and employment. The argument, in short, is that a constrained monetary standard will dissuade the government and the public alike from believing they can "inflate" out of economic difficulties, and a gold standard would provide a constrained monetary standard.

Or would it? Can convertibility be credibly established? Or would the public believe that a restored gold standard is bound to be a fair weather vessel, likely to capsize and be abandoned in the first serious storm?

One difficulty with the credibility of a requirement for convertibility of US dollars into gold is the already huge volume of liquid dollar assets around the world. Federal Reserve liabilities at the end of 1980 were $158 billion; the US money supply was $415 billion (M1) or $1,656 billion (M2); foreign monetary authorities held an estimated $240 billion in liquid dollar claims ($157 billion directly in the United States and the remainder in various "Eurodollar" centers around the world), and other foreigners held an additional $700 billion, give or take several tens of billions, in dollar deposits (other than European interbank deposits) outside the United States. US gold reserves, by contrast, amounted to only $11.1 billion at the official price of $42.22 an ounce, and $111 billion at $422 an ounce (which has no virtue beyond being ten times the US official price and roughly equal to the market price at the end of 1981; the market price fell substantially below that in early 1982).

Full convertibility would hardly be credible, given the relation of assets to potential claims. Of course, not all outstanding liquid dollar claims would formally be convertible into gold; presumably the convertibility requirement would strictly apply only to Federal Reserve liabilities. But that provides no comfort, since the financial system functions on the supposition that all liquid dollar claims can, on short notice, be converted into claims on the Federal Reserve, either federal funds or currency. To deny or repudiate this more general convertibility is tantamount to a breakdown in the financial system, both domestic and international. Moreover, a major strength of the international financial system at present is that for large holders (that is, leaving aside bank notes) it is a closed system, so funds can be moved around in it but cannot be withdrawn from it, except by the Federal Reserve System. This feature served the international economy well in "recycling" the large OPEC surpluses during the last decade; it would be altered by gold convertibility, which would provide a potential leakage to the system at the initiative of dollar holders, and thus could threaten the system as a whole with a convertibility crisis, as in 1931.

With too little gold relative to the potential for conversion, a gold convertibility system would be seen as a fair weather system; expectations about future economic developments would not be changed radically; and the real costs of monetary adjustment would continue to be high, casting further doubt on the political sustainability of a gold convertibility regime.

A straightforward way to deal with these problems is to set a price of gold sufficiently high that there cannot be any doubt about the ability of the United States to sustain even large-scale conversion, at least for some time. If $422 an ounce will not be persuasive, perhaps $844 an ounce would be, and $1,288 an ounce certainly should be (the last figure would result in a valuation of $333 billion on the existing US gold stock).

But with a much higher price, another, equally acute, problem arises: not only would new gold production increase substantially, but sales from the large existing gold stocks and hoards would take place. The US authorities would find themselves flooded with gold. Consider the privately held stocks first. Much of the estimated 1,500 million ounces of privately held gold no doubt is held for traditional reasons, partly for ornament, partly as precautionary protection against untoward political or economic events. But much of it, especially during the 1970s, was also acquired as an investment.

With a credibly high official price of gold, the prospect for further capital
gains on these investments would vanish, and gold as an investment would
lose its luster, except to a small degree for portfolio diversification against
remote contingencies. Thus there would be large-scale dishoarding. Even
some central banks might sell their gold under these circumstances, and for
similar reasons: prospective earnings on alternative assets would be much
higher.

It is unclear what the supply schedule is for new production, although it
is presumably upward sloping with respect to the price of gold in terms
of other goods and services. In any case, as noted above, production is
not determined simply by marginal costs today, but rather is subject to
oligopolistic manipulation by the two major suppliers, South Africa and the
Soviet Union, which are large enough to face a downward sloping demand
schedule for gold. With a high and credible US official price of gold, in
contrast, the demand schedule becomes perfectly elastic even for large
producers, and there would then be no reason for them not to produce as
much gold as it is economical to produce.

Thus there would be a flood of gold into the United States, on a more
modest scale if convertibility were limited to foreign monetary authorities,
on a vast scale under full convertibility. What should the United States
then do? To monetize the gold would be strongly expansionary.[38] This
expansion would presumably endure until the price level had risen sufficiently to reduce new gold production to the point at which it just satisfies
the secular growth in demand for gold. That prolonged adjustment hardly
satisfies the expectation of price stability sought by advocates of gold
convertibility. The monetary authorities could sterilize the monetary impact
of the additional gold, as they did at various times past. But then that
would mean a return to a world of discretionary monetary policy much as
what prevailed from 1934 to 1971, a period during which reliance was
placed on the monetary authorities, not gold convertibility, for monetary
restraint.

With large holdings of (sterilized) gold in official hands, there would be
ample room for monetary expansion without threatening convertibility.
When that room was exhausted many years later, people would rightly
wonder why suddenly this constraint of gold supply, which had not been
operative for many years, should suddenly provoke a restrictive monetary
policy. They would simply remove it.

Is there a price that just balances between these conflicting considerations—too low a gold stock to make continued convertibility credible,
or such a high gold stock that it would exert no monetary discipline and

de facto would be a regime of discretionary management? Conceivably there could be such a price, one that would persuade hoarders to disgorge enough gold such that a combination of the higher price and the enlarged quantity of monetary gold would make the system credible but not too undisciplined. But my guess is that there is no such price. The relevant public would be skeptical about continued convertibility up to quite a high price, and only then would be won over; but the price that would be persuasive would be too high to provide the discipline.

Whether there is such a price is irrelevant, however, because there is no way of finding it. Any guess, however well informed or rationalized, would obviously be seen to be a conscious policy choice. And therein lies the problem of a restored gold standard as a source of discipline and automaticity: once the price is recognized as a discretionary variable, the discipline that a gold standard could conceivably exert would be lost.

One proposal deals directly with the difficulties of choosing a price by allowing the market to determine the price in the first instance, and then allowing the price to change (again, determined by the market) in periods of great stress. In particular, the starting official price would be the average market price in the five days preceding restoration of convertibility, following six months' notice of the intention to introduce a regime of convertibility. The official price would then be fixed indefinitely at this level, unless gold reserves dropped below 25 percent of the target level of gold reserves (set by the ratio of gold reserves to Federal Reserve liabilities on the day before resumption of gold convertibility) or rose above 175 percent of the target level. In either of these events, a "gold holiday" would be declared for ninety days to allow the private market to set a new price. During gold holidays the government would not engage in either purchases or sales of gold, nor would the Federal Reserve be permitted to alter the monetary base by more than 1 percent.[39] Within 50 and 125 percent of this target, monetary policy would be discretionary, but the degree of discretion would be reduced as the outer limits were approached. For instance, if gold reserves are above 125 percent of target, the monetary base must be increased by 1 percent a month, and this rises to 2 percent a month if reserves are above 150 percent of target. Below 50 percent of target, the monetary base must be reduced by 1 percent a month.

This scheme, like the adjustable peg system of exchange rates, would provide strong incentives to speculate for or against gold as the highly visible reserve level approached the critical boundaries, which, combined with the mandatory adjustments in monetary base, would introduce a strong source of instability into the monetary system. Moreover, while the method for choosing the official price would ensure that the "market" accepted that price at the outset, the same method would lend itself to manipulation by large holders of gold, and in particular to manipulation by South Africa and the Soviet Union, the principal sources of new gold. They would have a strong interest in as high an official US price as possible, and therefore would surely take all possible steps to withhold new gold supplies from the market during the critical six-month period after the announcement. Although the price of gold is primarily an asset price because it is the price that persuades the public to hold existing stocks of gold throughout the world, even relatively small changes in the stock relative to changes in demand can have a substantial impact on price. Thus, at the margin, withholding supplies would raise the price. Expectations by the public concerning future sales by these countries would have no influence on current market prices, since after resumption day the United States would provide a perfectly elastic demand at the indicated price, so such sales would not be expected to depress future market prices.

Finally, shifts in market sentiment about gold or the dollar could under this regime trigger prolonged monetary contractions or expansions. With no distinction among different sources of disturbance, this feature could result in greater monetary instability rather than achieving its stated purpose of greater stability. For instance, another disturbance in the oil market resulting in much higher oil prices would require severe monetary contraction if either the public or the oil-exporting countries decided to acquire gold, but no contraction if they did not decide to acquire gold, and that decision in turn would be heavily influenced by the political circumstances surrounding the disturbance, not merely (or even mainly) by monetary conditions in the United States. This proposal would certainly not offer the prospect for long-run price stability that many proponents of the gold standard desire, and that Laffer ("price stability would return in short order") claims for it.[40]

Another approach may be possible to deal with the excess of outstanding dollar holdings over existing US gold reserves, and the difficulties that poses for determining an appropriate price for gold. Some of the outstanding dollars might be "locked up" in a substitution account under the auspices of the International Monetary Fund to reduce the contingent claims on US gold. If enough dollars were converted to SDR (special drawing rights) claims on the substitution account, usable only to finance payments deficits, perhaps US gold valued at, say, $422 an ounce would represent a credible reserve.

There are two difficulties with this idea. First, most of the outstanding dollars outside the United States are in private rather than official hands and could not be placed into a substitution account without first driving them into official hands, presumably by creating prospects for a weak dollar. Such an exercise would itself be hazardous and would threaten the objective of monetary stability that motivates consideration of a restored gold standard.

Second, at present, for a variety of reasons, many official holders of dollars would be reluctant to exchange them for SDR-denominated claims in a substitution account, even claims that provide considerable liquidity to each holder in case of balance-of-payments need. The terms of the substitution account would have to be very attractive to induce many developing countries to participate in the scheme. The process of negotiation over these terms and even the negotiated outcome would very likely cast doubt on the determination of the community of nations to restore global monetary stability or to help the United States restore the stability of the dollar.

I conclude this discussion of gold convertibility regimes by noting that neither history nor logic offers compelling reason to expect gold convertibility to lead to stable prices. Exchange rates could be stabilized only if other countries also introduced gold convertibility and if maintaining that convertibility became (as it was in the late nineteenth century) the principal objective of policy. But if countries were willing to do that, they could do it without the intermediation of gold.

There is another disadvantage to reinstituting gold in a monetary role that is in any way linked to the market for gold, directly or indirectly. As has already been noted, the principal producers of gold in the world, together accounting for nearly 80 percent of world production, are South Africa and the Soviet Union. Both countries exercise considerable discretion in the amount of gold they actually put onto the market rather than allow competitive market incentives to prevail. Both are, in very different ways, at political odds with other members of the community of nations. Restoring gold convertibility would provide a windfall of considerable magnitude to those two countries. They could sell all they wished without depressing the market, and every $100 per ounce in the price is worth about $1 billion annually to the Soviet Union on its current estimated gold production and $2.2 billion to South Africa. For the reasons given above, a credible regime of gold convertibility would require a substantial increase in price above the current market level. An ill-conceived attempt to avoid this price increase and to rely on new supplies to provide for limited monetary growth would place the monetary system of the United States hostage to political decisions in one or both of these countries.

No Escape from Discretion

The choice of a price for gold plays a central role in the viability of any restoration of gold to a monetary role. Yet the choice of a price, while crucial, is unavoidably arbitrary and is known to be arbitrary. So long as this is so, a rule based on a supposedly fixed price of gold cannot be a credible rule. If gold were to become unduly constraining, its price could be changed, and that would be widely known—indeed, it is intrinsic to the process of setting a price in the first place. In this respect, the situation today is fundamentally different from the situation in the nineteenth and early twentieth centuries. Then the dollar price of gold was historically given and not open to question (except for minor adjustments on several occasions to preserve the relation to silver). The price was not conceived as a policy variable. Now it is, indeed must be. Yet gold ceases to provide monetary discipline if its price can be varied. So long as the price of gold is a policy variable, a gold standard cannot be a credible disciplinarian. It provides no escape from the need for human management, however frail that may seem to be.

Other Commodity Standards

The failure of the gold standard to achieve price stability was well understood by many who lived through it, and provoked thought about what arrangements might produce greater stability. Most of the public debate in the nineteenth century focused around the alternative of silver (which conceptually had the same disadvantages as gold), of bimetallism, and of using paper currency elastically to supplement gold in periods of stringency. In the twentieth century serious proposals have arisen for broadly based commodity money, for a "tabular" standard that alters the definition of money according to the movement of some commodity price index, and for monetary policy to be keyed formally and directly to a price index. Each of these ideas had nineteenth-century antecedents.

Bimetallism and Symmetallism

Bimetallism endows two metals, gold and silver, with full monetary status at a fixed price. Because variations in supply and in nonmonetary demand are unlikely to be perfectly correlated, this system can generally be expected to provide greater price stability in the long run than monometallism, provided the monetary authorities do not run out of either metal—that is, provided they hold reserves large enough to maintain the fixed price between the metals so that both of them stay in circulation. Variations in the relative supply of gold and silver plagued bimetallism over the years. It was Newton's overpricing of gold at the English mint that failed to retain the recently reminted silver coins and inadvertently placed Britain on the gold standard. The gold value of the US dollar was adjusted in 1834 to correct for the previous undervaluation of gold, and overdid it (the silver-gold mint ratio was changed from 15 : 1 to 16 : 1), leading to an overvaluation of gold and the export of silver. Generally speaking, French coinage was sufficiently important during the nineteenth century to keep the price of silver relative to gold around France's official mint ratio of $15\frac{1}{2}$: 1. But after the Nevada silver discoveries of 1859 and the decision of Germany to switch from silver to gold in 1871, followed by Scandinavia, France was unable to hold the ratio and abandoned unlimited coinage of the silver five-franc piece in 1874.

Alfred Marshall pointed out the difficulties in maintaining a fixed price between any two commodities over time, and suggested that "true bimetallism" should define the currency in terms of fixed quantities of the two metals, leaving the relative price free to vary. Marshall favored a symmetallic standard, as Edgeworth called it, over a monometallic one. At first he shied away from actually recommending it on the grounds that a change in the monetary standard would be too disruptive to justify the modest gains from it, but as agitation over the standard mounted, he began to advocate it.[41]

Commodity Reserve Currency

A logical extension of Marshall's proposal would be to enlarge the list of commodities, fixed in quantity, in which the monetary unit is defined and against which it is issued. This was done by Benjamin Graham and his unrelated namesake, Frank Graham, in the 1930s. Benjamin Graham proposed that the dollar be defined in terms of a fixed-weight bundle of twenty-three commodities (reduced to fifteen in his international variant) and that the Federal Reserve issue notes against warehouse receipts for the bundle thus defined.[42] His proposal was to supplement the existing monetary system with commodity money. Frank Graham would have included a much longer (but unspecified) list of commodities in his commodity bundle, and he would have substituted commodity money for all other forms of money, at least in terms of future growth. At the margin, he favored what was called 100 percent money; in effect all new currency and demand deposits would represent warehouse receipts for the commodity bundles. He recognized that this preferred variant was not realistic and he was willing to settle for less.[43]

Benjamin Graham selected his proposed commodities on the basis of their economic importance and their storability. Commodity production was monetized under the scheme, but the relative prices of commodities were left free to vary; only the average price level was held constant in terms of dollars. Graham was motivated in large measure by antidepression considerations; he felt that support for primary commodity prices in times of economic slack would help stabilize overall economic activity. By the same token, release of commodities (demonetization) would help to limit booms, both by supplying commodities out of stocks and by contracting the money supply. His scheme in effect would provide perfectly elastic demand for the commodities (taken as a bundle) included in the monetary unit in times of depressed economic activity, and perfectly elastic supply (so long as physical stocks lasted) in times of boom.

Stabilizing the price level of a limited bundle of storable commodities will stabilize the general price level only if the terms of trade between the commodities in question and manufactured goods (and services, if the "general" price level is taken to be the consumer price index) are unchanging over time.[44] Apart from both the improbability of satisfying this condition and the real costs of storing the monetized commodities (reckoned by proponents to be about 3 to 4 percent annually of the value of the stored commodities)—a factor that also applies to gold, although on a smaller scale—it is unclear why there has not been more enthusiasm for commodity-reserve proposals. Such proposals have found little interest beyond intellectuals. I suspect that conservatives really want gold, for reasons of history and sentiment, whereas nonconservatives prefer managed money.[45] Also, the schemes are basically too complicated to appeal to a wider public.

Benjamin Graham pointed out in 1961 that between the Commodity Credit Corporation and the strategic stockpile, the US government during the 1950s acquired enormous reserves of both agricultural and non-agricultural commodities valued at $16 billion (over 10 percent of the money supply in 1960). Part of these acquisitions were even monetized through the federal budget deficit and the Federal Reserve's acquisition of Treasury bills. So the costs were incurred anyway, but in the name of other objectives and sometimes with a destabilizing rather than a stabilizing influence on price movements.[46]

The idea of a commodity currency was revived in 1964 in an international context by Albert Hart, Nicholas Kaldor, and Jan Tinbergen. They proposed an International Commodity Reserve Currency (ICRC) in lieu of an increase in the price of gold or reliance on a world fiduciary money as a solution to the problem of growing reliance on the US dollar as a reserve currency and increasing dissatisfaction with that arrangement.[47] They were flexible on the composition of the ICRC, suggesting thirty commodities for illustrative purposes only. The commodities should be chosen for their importance in international trade, and with that in mind the composition of the ICRC should be reviewed and if appropriate altered at five-year intervals. (They do not address the question of the *relative* price changes that would occur when individual commodities are greatly increased or reduced in importance following these reviews, and are consequently purchased or sold from stocks.) This scheme is not designed to stabilize national price levels because countries are free to pursue autonomous monetary and exchange rate policies, but rather is intended to stabilize the "real value" of the international unit of account. Curiously, their proposal also includes parallel treatment of gold, which would not be included in the ICRC bundle. The International Monetary Fund was thus to be left the task of stabilizing the price of gold in terms of the ICRC, reminiscent of bimetallism. Given sponsorship of the proposal by the United Nations Conference on Trade and Development, one can assume that it was designed to appeal to developing countries by providing demand for primary products in the bundle; but, as with the Graham proposal, relative prices are left free to vary, so there is no perfectly elastic demand for any particular commodity.

Indexation

The complexities of a multiple-commodity standard can be avoided by the simple expedient of indexing all dollar-denominated contracts by a suitably broad price index, provided the supply of money is limited. The basic idea goes back at least to Joseph Lowe, who suggested in 1822, long before price indexes were constructed, that contracts be adjusted for changes in the general value of commodities. The idea was promoted a decade later by George Poulett Scrope, who is sometimes credited with inventing the "tabular standard," since he mentions the possibility of adjusting the legal tender as well as contracts. Writing in 1875, Jevons proposed that indexation of contracts be adopted on a voluntary basis at first, but that later it might be made compulsory for all contracts in excess of three months, indirect evidence that the real value of deferred payment was not preserved under the gold standard. He argued that indexation would represent an easy change; all that was necessary was a dispassionate government office to collect and collate the price information, publishing its results fully so they would be subject to public review and criticism.[48] Marshall also advocated indexation, and urged the Royal Commission on the Depression of Trade and Industry to attend to developing a purchasing power index, or government unit, as he called it. He believed that once it was understood it would be popular in contracts; unlike his proposal for symmetallism, about which he was somewhat diffident, he considered indexation on the urgent and active agenda for reform.[49] In fact, the British government did not publish a consumer price index until 1914, nearly thirty years later; the US government did so in 1919.

The Tabular Standard

Indexation can be carried a step further, to include money itself, along with some link to the supply of money. This is known as the tabular standard, and is alluded to by Scrope in 1833, described by Jevons in 1875, advocated by Irving Fisher in 1920, and recently revived by Robert Hall.[50] Fisher proposes that the definition of the dollar in terms of gold (he was writing during the gold standard period) should be indexed to the cost of living. Contracts would be written in terms of dollars, without indexation, but indexation would be automatic by adjusting the dollar. If, for example, the relevant price index fell, the number of grains of gold that defined the dollar as a unit of account would be reduced by a corresponding amount. In other words, for purposes of settling debts, the goods value of the dollar would be preserved, since more gold would be required to settle a given debt denominated in dollars. The reverse adjustment would take place if the relevant price index rose.[51]

This scheme amounts to full indexation of all contracts, including gold-convertible paper money, against changes in the real value of gold, with gold remaining the formal basis of the dollar. In addition, Fisher would have adjusted the gold money supply in parallel with adjustments in the gold value of the dollar. If prices fell, for instance, the gold content of the dollar would be reduced, that is, the dollar price of gold would be raised, and gold would flow into the Treasury (against the issuance of gold certificates) from private hoards, from abroad, and eventually from new production. The reverse would occur if prices rose. Fisher would have reinforced this natural influence by issuing new gold certificates against the capital gains on existing Treasury stocks of gold, or retiring gold certificates in the event of rising prices, although this was not an essential part of his proposal.[52]

Robert Hall has recently revived the ideal of a tabular standard (without endorsing it), but he would substitute for the role of gold in Fisher's standard a weighted average of four commodities (ammonium nitrate, copper, aluminum, and plywood, ANCAP for short) whose price index has tracked very closely the US consumer price index over the past thirty years.[53] The dollar would be defined in terms of a specified combination of physical quantities of these commodities, and they would be legal tender in settlement of debts. Fiat money would presumably disappear, and bank notes could be issued freely, fully redeemable in ANCAPs. When the consumer price index rose, the dollar would be redefined to contain more ANCAPs. In this way, contracts with deferred payment written in terms of dollars would involve repayment that was constant in terms of purchasing power, as measured by the consumer price index. Unlike the Grahams, Hart-Kaldor-Tinbergen, and Fisher, Hall would not require or even permit the government to engage in purchases or sales of the commodities comprising ANCAP. The government would simply define the dollar in terms of ANCAPs and would endow them with the attribute of legal tender, so that private and government debts in effect would be settled in ANCAPs or paper claims to them. Private arbitrage, which would involve some physical storage of the commodities in ANCAP, would ensure that a paper dollar or dollar demand account remained equal in value to the current ANCAP definition of the dollar.

Hall suggests that this would be a perfectly workable arrangement, but sees no advantage in it over a well-managed fiat money. He prefers a system whereby monetary policy would be keyed to deviations of the consumer price index from its target values (ultimately, after a transition period, zero change): for each percent the consumer price index is above its target the Federal Reserve would engage in open market sales with a view to raising the Treasury bill rate by 0.1 percent; and it would act similarly each month that the consumer price index exceeded its target, so the effect would be cumulative.[54]

Conclusions

Consideration of the gold standard involves three quantities: gold; paper money (including demand deposits) called dollars; and some composite of goods and services in which members of the public are directly interested, for example those used to construct the consumer price index, a composite that we can call goods. There are three "prices" linking these three quantities: the dollar price of goods, the dollar price of gold, and the gold price of goods, or the commodity terms of trade between gold and other goods. Because any one of these relative prices can be derived from the other two, only two of them are independent: (dollar/goods) = (gold/goods) × (dollar/gold) or ($/G) = (A/G) × ($/A), where G stands for goods and A stands for *aurum* (or ANCAP). Inflation involves the first of these three prices, $/G. In attempting to limit inflation, advocates of the gold standard would fix the third price, the dollar price of gold (or, equivalently, the gold content of the dollar). This can be done if the government has a sufficiently large stock of gold relative to the stock of dollars outstanding and if, when necessary, it devotes control of the supply of dollars to that objective. Alternatively, it can be done by going to a pure metallic currency, in which "dollars" *are* gold. These advocates contend that by fixing the dollar price of gold, $/A, they will stabilize the dollar price of goods, $/G. Both history and logic refute this contention, however, because in general the relative price between gold and other commodities, A/G, is variable over time. To be sure, there is some feedback from A/G to the supply of gold, because this price influences the cost of extracting gold. But this influence occurs only with long lags, and even then it is weak because gold is an exhaustible resource, not in perfectly elastic long-run supply. It would be necessary to argue that in the long run both discovery and technical change adapt so as to assure a fixed terms of trade between gold and goods. Certainly this price, A/G, in fact showed great variation in the nineteenth century, and it also showed a great change during the 1970s when gold prices rose much more than goods prices did (A/G fell by about 80 percent). In short, A/G is too variable to permit $/G to be stabilized by fixing $/A.

The Graham and the Fisher and Hall schemes seek to control the dollar price of goods directly. The Graham plan would do so by buying and selling a bundle of goods against dollars at a fixed price, with a sufficiently broadly defined bundle so that its price is highly correlated with all goods. Even so, it is necessary to be concerned with long-run divergences in the relative price between their suggested composites and goods more generally. Frank Graham would also control tightly the quantity of dollars by making commodity bundles the exclusive source of (additional) money.

The tabular standard of Fisher and Hall would define the dollar as some commodity or composite commodity, then would adjust the definition of the dollar at regular intervals to ensure dollar price stability of a large bundle of goods and services, such as the consumer price index: $/G$ can be stabilized (to be sure, as Hall points out, not always without economic hardship) by adjusting $/A$ to offset exactly changes in the real price A/G, which under a commodity standard is the sole source of instability in the general level of prices.

In summary, if stabilizing the dollar price of commodities is the objective, fixing the dollar price of gold is not the way to achieve it. Direct action on the dollar price of goods is more likely to be successful. But as was noted at the beginning of this paper, an objective—perhaps the dominant one—of the advocates of a restoration of gold is to reduce greatly or even eliminate discretion in the hands of the monetary authorities. It is noteworthy that all of the commodity-based proposals except that of Benjamin Graham sharply reduce or eliminate altogether discretion in monetary management.[55]

Seen this way, these proposals, taken together, raise the interesting philosophical question of why one should think that experts are more clever at devising operational, nondiscretionary monetary regimes than they are at monetary management within a discretionary regime. If the desire for a nondiscretionary regime is really simply another way— misguided, as shown above, in the case of gold—of assigning priority above all others to the objective of price stability in the management of monetary policy, that can be done directly by instructing the Federal Reserve unambiguously to take whatever action is necessary to ensure price stability. If collectively we are ambivalent about that priority, that is the principal source of the problem, not the nature of the regime.

Notes

1. Establishment of the Gold Commission was not at President Reagan's initiative, however. He was responding to a statutory requirement to study US policy on the role of gold in the domestic and international monetary systems. In 1980 President Carter signed an act to increase US quotas at the International Monetary Fund, to which this requirement had been added as a rider by Senator Jesse Helms.

With much disagreement among its members, the Gold Commission recommended against restoration of any formal monetary role for gold. In its one positive recommendation, the majority of the commission favored issuance of gold coins by the US Mint, denominated by weight, sold at market prices, and exempt from capital gains taxation. See *Report to Congress of the Commission on the Role of Gold in the Domestic and International Monetary Systems* (Government Printing Office, 1982).

2. The point was made explicitly twenty years ago by Arthur Kemp, however, who observed that the ability to carry wealth, especially gold coins, has provided individuals with the opportunity to escape from political tyranny throughout history. See Kemp, "The Gold Standard: A Reappraisal," in Leland B. Yeager, ed., *In Search of a Monetary Constitution* (Harvard University Press, 1962), pp. 137–54, especially pp. 152–53. This volume, incidentally, offers an excellent sampling of the debate twenty years ago on sound versus unsound money and the desirable degree of discretion to leave in the hands of the monetary authorities—with a heavy majority of the contributors being against much, if any, discretion.

3. The oldest known gold coins date from the sixth century B.C. See Brian Kettell, *Gold* (Ballinger, 1981), pp. 20–21.

4. Arthur I. Bloomfield, "Gold Standard," in Douglas Greenwald, ed., *Encyclopedia of Economics* (McGraw-Hill, 1981), p. 452.

5. Variations in exchange rates were thus influenced by the gradual decline in shipping costs, by interest rates, and by changes in mint charges. In the 1880s the range for fluctuation in the pound-dollar rate of exchange was about 1.3 percent; that between the British pound and the French franc was about 0.8 percent. See Oskar Morgenstern, *International Financial Transactions and Business Cycles* (Princeton University Press, 1959), p. 177.

6. An excellent discussion of this period, brief but well documented, can be found in Arthur Nussbaum, *A History of the Dollar* (Columbia University Press, 1957).

7. During the 1880s, for instance, no less than 80 percent of the natural increase in British population emigrated, and one-third of the natural increase in Germany. Calculated from B. R. Mitchell, *European Historical Statistics, 1750–1970* (Columbia University Press, 1975), pp. 20, 24, 138, 139.

8. These standard deviations are calculated as the standard error of estimate of the fitted equation, $\ln P_t = a \ln P_{t-1}$, where P_t is the wholesale price index in year t. This statistic for Britain showed a higher standard error for the more recent period than for the gold standard era, 6.2 percent versus 4.6 percent. Moreover, if price changes are measured over five-year intervals, as from $\ln P_t = b \ln P_{t-5}$, the standard error is higher in the more recent period for both the United States and Britain. The standard errors for the United States and Britain, respectively, are 13.7 and 11.3 percent in 1884–1913 and 21.0 and 37.8 percent in 1953–79.

9. The indexes are dominated by tradable goods, so under fixed exchange rates, and except for changes in import tariffs, that would ensure close correspondence in the latter part of the period when transport costs were low.

10. W. Stanley Jevons, *Money and the Mechanism of Exchange* (D. Appleton, 1875), p. 326. His "Serious Fall in the Value of Gold Ascertained, and Its Social Effects Set Forth" appeared in 1863 and his "Variation of Prices" in 1865.

11. *Official Papers by Alfred Marshall* (London: Macmillan, 1926), pp. 10, 15.

12. Frederick R. Macaulay, *The Movement of Interest Rates, Bond Yields and Stock Prices in the United States since 1856* (National Bureau of Economic Research, 1938), pp. A108–A109.

13. See George F. Warren and Frank A. Pearson, *Gold and Prices* (Wiley, 1935), p. 403.

14. Jude Wanniski, *Business Week*, December 7, 1981, p. 27.

15. See Lawrence H. Summers, "The Non-Adjustment of Nominal Interest Rates: A Study of the Fisher Effect," Working Paper 836 (National Bureau of Economic Research, 1982), p. 18. Summers averages real commercial paper rates over the economic cycles as defined by the NBER, using monthly Warren and Pearson wholesale prices to deflate nominal interest rates. In a variety of statistical tests, he finds no statistically significant effect of inflation on interest rates.

16. Keynes called the movement of long-term interest rates in parallel with prices the "Gibson paradox," after a person who made the observation and tried unsuccessfully to explain it in the 1920s. Keynes' own explanation ran in terms of a tendency of the market rate of interest to lag behind changes in the natural rate of interest—that is, the rate required to equate savings with investment, with the consequence that a decline in the natural rate would lead to a depression in economic activity and a decline in prices, whereas a rise in the natural rate (ahead of the market rate) would lead to a long-term investment boom and a secular rise in prices. He attributed more of the great secular swings in prices to this factor than to purely monetary factors, on the grounds that basically, through a variety of channels, the supply of money (or efficiency in its use) responds to the demand for it. See John Maynard Keynes, *A Treatise on Money* (London: Macmillan, 1930), vol. 2, pp. 198–208.

17. Based on specific questions in the 1890 census, reported in Douglass C. North, *Growth and Welfare in the American Past* (Prentice-Hall, 1966), p. 141.

18. MIT President Francis Walker called it "the greatest financial storm of two centuries." See Francis A. Walker, *International Bimetallism* (Henry Holt, 1897), p. 129. Walker's little book gives an excellent history of the monetary use of metals and, in particular, of the interaction between silver and gold.

19. See Warren and Pearson, *Gold and Prices*, pp. 94–97.

20. US prices rose more sharply between 1849 and 1855—by 36 percent—and then fell again.

21. Warren and Pearson, *Gold and Prices*, p. 132.

22. Laughlin reckons gold to be 72 percent of the British money supply (gold, silver, and uncovered notes) in 1895, 37 percent of the US money supply, and 38 percent of the world money supply (most of the silver being in China and India). Gold can be estimated as about one-third of the world money supply in 1848, although the ratio would be much higher in Britain and the United States (before the coinage under the Bland-Allison Act). Monetary silver was also growing during these periods, rapidly from 1895 to 1905, but most was then going to the

Far East. See J. Laurence Laughlin, *The History of Bimetallism in the United States* (Greenwood Press, 1968; originally published in 1896), pp. 205–06.

23. Frank W. Fetter, *Development of British Monetary Orthodoxy, 1797–1875* (Harvard University Press, 1965), pp. 240–46.

24. See Milton Friedman and Anna J. Schwartz, *A Monetary History of the United States, 1867–1960* (Princeton University Press, 1963), table A-1.

25. It is of interest to note, however, that contemporaries did not consider demand deposits to be part of the money supply; their inclusion is long after the fact. Both Jevons and Marshall considered demand deposits to be fundamentally different from money, because, as Marshall put it, in contrast to a bank note, "a cheque requires the receiver to have formed some opinion for himself as to the individual from whom he receives it," *Official Papers*, p. 35; also Jevons, *Money*, pp. 336f. By 1911 Irving Fisher treats demand deposits as money, but with different attributes (including velocity) from other forms of money. Should contemporaries have reasoned otherwise, or is the concept of money so slippery that it can only be determined long after the fact?

26. An exhaustive treatment of this period can be found in William A. Brown, Jr., *The International Gold Standard Reinterpreted, 1914–1934* (National Bureau of Economic Research, 1940). Brown contends that the key to the pre–World War I gold standard was the preeminence of Britain as a market for goods and as a source of saving, and of London as a bank-clearing center and a source and repository of short-term credit. This preeminence was lost in the 1920s. Thus Brown argues that while the form of the gold standard was restored, its substance was not.

27. Warren and Pearson, *Gold and Prices*, p. 95.

28. "Is There Enough Gold?" *The Nation and Athenaeum*, January 19, 1929. Also reproduced in Donald Moggridge, ed., *The Collected Writings of John Maynard Keynes: Activities 1922–1929, The Return to Gold and Industrial Policy*, vol. 19, pt. 2 (Macmillan, 1981), pp. 775–80.

29. See especially Robert Triffin, *Gold and the Dollar Crisis* (Yale University Press, 1960); the argument had been advanced earlier in articles.

30. This price was about 75 percent higher, in real terms, than the maximum real price of gold (measured in British prices) in the century before World War I, which occurred in 1896. The likely instability in the real long-run price of gold is discussed in William Fellner, "Gold and the Uneasy Case for Responsibly Managed Fiat Money" in *Essays in Contemporary Economics Problems* (Washington: American Enterprise Institute, 1981), pp. 97–121. This interesting paper came to my attention after my own essay was written.

31. See Federal Reserve Governor Henry Wallich, "Are There Alternative Ways of Fighting Inflation?" remarks at Cornell University, October 28, 1981, p. 10.

32. Data provided by the Embassy of the Republic of South Africa, Washington, D.C. Recent CIA estimates place Soviet gold stocks at 1,800 metric tons, or about 58 million ounces.

33. In 1933 the gold coins and gold certificates in the hands of the public were all called in. The Banking Act of 1934 established the requirement that the Federal Reserve Banks should hold 35 percent in gold against their deposit liabilities and 40 percent against outstanding notes. In 1945 these requirements were reduced to a uniform 25 percent against both deposits and notes. In 1965 the reserve requirement against deposits was eliminated, and in 1968 the reserve requirement against notes was eliminated.

34. Robert E. Weintraub, "Restoring the Gold Certificate Reserve," appendix to a study prepared by the Subcommittee on Monetary and Fiscal Policy of the Joint Economic Committee, *The Gold Standard: Its History and Record Against Inflation*, 97 Cong. 1 sess. (GPO, 1981), pp. 21–24.

35. See H. Res. 391, a bill submitted to Congress by Representative Ron Paul in January 1981.

36. I leave aside suggestions that gold convertibility be reestablished only for residents of the United States on the grounds that it would always be possible for foreigners to arbitrage around such restrictions in the absence of a comprehensive set of exchange controls.

37. Offsetting actions by central banks, in periods of contraction as well as periods of expansion, even took place often in the heyday of the historical gold standard. See Arthur I. Bloomfield, *Monetary Policy Under the International Gold Standard: 1880–1914* (Federal Reserve Bank of New York, 1959).

38. It is for this reason that Sir Roy Harrod over the years favored an increase in the official price of gold. See, for example, his *Reforming the World's Money* (London: St. Martin's Press, 1965), chap. 3.

39. See S.6, "Gold Reserve Act of 1981," submitted to Congress by Senator Jesse Helms in *Congressional Record*, daily edition (January 5, 1981), pp. S22–26. The basic idea derives from a proposal by Arthur Laffer, "The Reinstatement of the Dollar: The Blueprint," A. B. Laffer Associates, February 29, 1980. Laffer likens his proposal to that made by the United States in 1972 for management of exchange rates around target levels of international reserves.

40. Laffer, "Reinstatement of the Dollar." Laffer makes much of the analogy between his proposal and the official US proposal of 1972, described in the *Economic Report of the President, January 1973*, concerning an exchange rate regime. But the underlying purposes of the two proposals are completely different. The 1972 proposal was designed to introduce greater symmetry of adjustment between countries in deficit and those in surplus into a system that presupposed national autonomy in monetary policy and was designed to accommodate that autonomy as much as possible, while still preserving the alleged advantages of temporarily fixed exchange rates. The Laffer-Helms proposal, in contrast, is designed to impose severe limits on autonomy in national (at least US) monetary policy.

41. Marshall, *Official Papers*, pp. 14–15, 30–31.

42. Graham's short list comprised wheat, corn, cotton, wool, rubber, coffee, tea, sugar, tobacco, petroleum, coal, wood pulp, pig iron, copper, and tin. At 1937 prices, coal and wheat were the most important (over 13 percent each), tea and tin the least (2.1 percent each). See Benjamin Graham, *Storage and Stability* (McGraw-Hill, 1937); and *World Commodities and World Currencies* (McGraw-Hill, 1944), p. 45. The scheme was originally proposed by Graham in 1933. W. Stanley Jevons suggested a "multiple legal tender" that could be interpreted as a commodity standard in the same vein, but he actually proposed indexation of contracts by a commodity price index, without distinguishing between the two. See Jevons, *Money*, p. 327.

43. See Frank D. Graham, *Social Goals and Economic Institutions* (Princeton University Press, 1942).

44. In the United States the price of crude materials—including oil—rose by 201 percent between 1947 and 1980; wholesale prices of finished manufactures, by 265 percent; and prices of services (in the consumer price index), by 429 percent.

45. It is of interest, though, that F. A. Hayek viewed commodity money favorably; see his "A Commodity Reserve Currency," *Economic Journal*, vol. 53 (June–September 1943), pp. 176–84.

Keynes and Friedman both opposed it. Keynes, though highly supportive of stabilization schemes for individual commodities, opposed a commodity reserve currency on the grounds that it would have the same disadvantages as a gold standard in failing to persuade organized labor that they should keep their demands for money wages in line with the increase in efficiency wages (that is, productivity). He considered the risk of excessive money wage demands as one of the major obstacles to maintenance of a full employment economy. See his 1943 letter to Benjamin Graham, reprinted as an appendix to B. Graham in Yeager, ed., *In Search of a Monetary Constitution*, pp. 215–17.

Milton Friedman also opposed a commodity-reserve currency on the grounds that a full commodity-reserve currency, lacking the mystique and historical legitimacy of gold, would in time become financially burdensome because of the real costs associated with it. This in turn would result in dilution of the concept, through various economies, which would lead in effect to discretionary policy, which he also opposed. It is therefore dominated both by a gold standard, with its mystique, and by a properly managed fiat money, which Friedman favors. See his "Commodity-Reserve Currency" in *Essays in Positive Economics* (University of Chicago Press, 1953), pp. 204–50.

46. See Benjamin Graham, "The Commodity-Reserve Currency Proposal Reconsidered," in Yeager, ed., *In Search of a Monetary Constitution*, pp. 185–214.

47. See A. G. Hart, Nicholas Kaldor, and Jan Tinbergen, "The Case for an International Commodity Reserve Currency," in Nicholas Kaldor, *Essays on Economic Policy*, vol. 2 (Norton, 1964), pp. 131–77; also A. G. Hart, "The Case as of 1976 for International Commodity-Reserve Currency," *Weltwirtschaftliches Archiv*, vol. 112, no. 1 (1976), pp. 1–32.

48. Jevons, *Money*, p. 331; characteristically, Jevons also discusses Lowe, Scrope, and other antecedents. See also Frank Fetter, *British Monetary Orthodoxy*, p. 139; and Joseph A. Schumpeter, *History of Economic Analysis* (Oxford University Press, 1954).

49. Marshall, *Official Papers*, p. 12.

50. See Jevons, *Money*; Irving Fisher, *Stabilizing the Dollar* (Macmillan, 1920); and Robert E. Hall, "Explorations in the Gold Standard and Related Policies for Stabilizing the Dollar," in R. E. Hall, ed., *Inflation* (University of Chicago Press, 1982).

51. Irving Fisher, *Stabilizing the Dollar*. Fisher observes in the preface that most of his ideas were conceived before the First World War, in other words during the heyday of the gold standard. Some of Fisher's comments on the disasters of the gold standard can be found on p. 117.

52. Ibid., appendix I. To avoid the problem of constant reminting, Fisher would have retired all gold coins and moved to a convertible gold bullion standard. According to him, "gold" in circulation was overwhelmingly in the form of gold certificates, yellowbacks, with most of the monetary gold already in the hands of the Treasury.

53. Robert Hall, "Explorations in the Gold Standard."

54. Robert E. Hall, "A Free-Market Policy to Stabilize the Purchasing Power of the Dollar" (Hoover Institution and Stanford University, December 1981). To work, this proposal assumes that the response of the price level to changes in the supply of money is reasonably rapid; long response lags could lead to explosive oscillation of both money and prices. Hall's proposal was anticipated in 1832 by Charles Jones, who "advocated a policy of price stabilization by a national bank of issue through open market operations, buying public debt when a twenty-commodity price index fell, and selling public debt when the price index rose." See Fetter, *Development of British Monetary Orthodoxy*, p. 139.

55. In this respect, the proposal of Helms and Laffer is a compromise: it retains discretion in monetary management within a range, but increasingly limits that discretion as the official supply of gold continues to shrink or to rise. In doing so, it gives gold a major signaling or thermostatic function, but thereby ignores the function of gold as a commodity and the false signals that it might send.

3   Flexing the International Monetary System: The Case for Gliding Parities

Dissatisfaction with the present international monetary system mounted steadily from the mid to the late sixties. In the two years preceding October 1969 it permitted five major currency crises, involving gold and most of the major trading currencies. Calls for reform became legion. Defenders of the present monetary system have pointed out that the world economy has performed spectacularly well during the past two decades, probably better than during any corresponding period of history, and that while the crises were unsettling, they were largely superficial and were prevented from penetrating into domestic economies, as financial crises usually did in the past. A system that has done so well, they argue, should not be scrapped, but rather should be operated as it was intended to be when drawn up at Bretton Woods a quarter of a century ago.

I will argue that the success of the world economy during the past two decades occurred to some extent in spite of the Bretton Woods system rather than because of it, but that the system may be made to work without drastically overhauling it.

The Bretton Woods System on Paper

Let me first recall very briefly the main features of our international payments system. On the financial side, these are embodied principally in Articles of Agreement of the International Monetary Fund, laid down at Bretton Woods in 1944. On the side of merchandise trade, ground rules are embodied in the General Agreement on Tariffs and Trade (GATT), dating from 1947. In essence, these two documents call for freedom of international payments for goods and services exchanged among countries, for

The International Adjustment Mechanism, Conference Series 2 (Federal Reserve Bank of Boston, 1970), 141–156. Reprinted by permission.

low tariffs, for fixed and stable exchange rates, for non-discrimination among countries, and for the avoidance of direct control over foreign trade. Drawn up against the background of the 1930s, they are designed to avoid beggar-thy-neighbor trade and exchange policies and at the same time to allow countries that degree of national autonomy in monetary and fiscal policies necessary to maintain full employment.

The rules did not extend to international capital movements. Against the background of the extremely disruptive movements of capital during the interwar period, British officials who co-authored the Bretton Woods Agreement were extremely doubtful about permitting private capital to move freely among countries. The IMF Articles of Agreement not only permit controls over capital movements, but actually require all participating countries to help enforce whatever capital controls other participating countries have imposed. At the same time, however, the dominant country of the postwar period, the United States, has always attached considerable importance to freedom of private capital movements, and other countries have increasingly accepted this objective as well. Moreover, it has become increasingly clear that in times of financial unrest no sharp distinction between trade and capital transactions is possible.

It was recognized that imbalances in international payments would develop under the Bretton Woods system. Temporary imbalances were to be financed, partly out of national reserves, partly by borrowing at a new institution, the International Monetary Fund. "Fundamental" imbalances— surpluses as well as deficits—were to be corrected through discrete adjustments in exchange rates, from one fixed level to another.

The difficulty in this distinction between temporary and fundamental imbalances is that by the time the need for a change in the exchange rate becomes known to those officials who must make the decision, it is also known to everyone else. Discrete changes in exchange rates offer windfall gains to those who can shift their assets from one currency to another in correct anticipation of a change. Currency speculation has grown markedly in total volume, to the point at which in May 1969 nearly four billion dollars flowed into Germany in the course of a week in anticipation of a revaluation of the German mark, and over one billion dollars on a single day. (Four billion dollars amounted to nearly one-quarter of the total German money supply.) Here the logic of proscription on capital movements comes clear. To the extent that capital movements may be *effectively* restrained, both the possibility for large private gain and the disruption of market tranquility generated by large speculative flows are greatly reduced.

Actual Performance of the Bretton Woods System

This, in brief, is the international payments system. If it is defective, why has the world economy fared so well? I believe there are two reasons. The first is that the Bretton Woods system did not come fully into force until around 1960. We did not *start* with this system right after the Second World War. It represented the objective, not the reality. International commerce was severely restricted in the late 1940s, and the Bretton Woods Agreement allowed for a five-year transition period. The transition lasted nearly three times that long, and during the transition a process of *differential* trade liberalization provided a de facto balance of payments adjustment mechanism that was absent in theory. Early in the period, European and other countries discriminated heavily against American and Canadian goods, and to a lesser extent against goods from one another. As the payments positions of various European countries improved, they accelerated their trade liberalization. Those in payments difficulty slowed down the rate of liberalization and occasionally even reversed it. So long as restrictions on trade and other transactions could be relaxed differentially in accordance with balance-of-payments requirements, sources of imbalance could be corrected without frequent adjustments in exchange rates.

This process of differential trade and payments liberalization had largely run its course by the early sixties, but here a second unanticipated development obscured the underlying weaknesses of the adjustment process in the Bretton Woods system. I refer to the large US payments deficits after 1958, which (when put on a consistent accounting basis) had their counterpart in the balance-of-payments surpluses elsewhere in the world. The reasons for the large US deficits are controversial and need not detain us here. But their presence made the need for adjustment by other countries rather less pressing. In the absence of US deficits, tensions between the French franc and the German mark, for example, would have occurred long before 1968. It is noteworthy that in 1968 the United States ran a balance-of-payments surplus, in a sense relevant for this discussion, for the first time since 1957, and an even larger surplus was run in 1969. These surpluses throw into relief tensions among other currencies that were earlier obscured by US payments deficits. With the help of differential trade liberalization in the fifties and large US payments deficits in the sixties, the Bretton Woods adjustment process was spared frequent or severe testing.

Somewhat paradoxically, the possibility of relying on US payments deficits has also run its course, for other countries have become apprehensive about permitting the United States to spend abroad unchecked, whether it be for military adventures or for private foreign investment. Under the influence of European pressure and (unnecessarily) alarmist pronouncements by the US financial community, American officials themselves became committed to elimination of the payments deficit.

So these two mitigating circumstances cannot be expected to persist into the future. In addition, however, there is a third complicating development. That is the sharp increase in the international mobility of capital. Under the influence of the revolution in communications and the vastly increased flow of information about the rest of the world, banks, firms, and individuals distinguish far less between domestic and foreign assets than they once did, and the erosion of this distinction is continuing. With increased awareness of investment opportunities abroad comes also increased awareness of the possibility for speculative gains on currency changes. The potential movements of funds in response to anticipated changes in exchange rates has become quite phenomenal. Potential movements are increased further, and the possibility for distinguishing in practice between transactions on current and capital account is further diminished, by the substantial growth of the multinational firm. Such firms can readily shift not only working balances but also commercial credits among their operations in different countries in such a way as to speculate in favor or against particular currencies. They may even adjust the commodity prices at which intrafirm transactions take place for the purpose of developing a long or short position in a particular currency.

Under these circumstances, reliance on discrete changes in exchange rates as the principal weapon for adjustment to fundamental payments imbalances becomes impracticable, for anticipated currency revaluation results in a transfer of public and national wealth (in the form of foreign exchange reserves) into private and usually foreign hands, while currency devaluation results in an arbitrary redistribution of wealth among private individuals and to a lesser (but increasing) extent will also transfer national wealth to foreigners. An additional deterrent is the fact that currency devaluation usually involves questions of national prestige and even the political fate of those with immediate responsibility.[1] Governments are reluctant to admit the failure implicit in a devaluation of the currency, and therefore procrastinate to the point at which devaluation cannot be avoided and currency speculation is correspondingly aggravated.

Not surprisingly, under these circumstances, countries have adopted a series of substitute measures, often violating the letter or the spirit of the postwar agreements, to keep their payments position under control but at the same time to avoid changes in currency parities. Most of the reversals in liberalization have involved capital movements, on which as noted above controls are technically permissible under the Bretton Woods Agreement. But countries have also engaged in extensive interference in foreign trade and services, resorting to a miscellany of ad hoc devices such as tying foreign aid, redirecting government procurement, selling arms, cutting embassy staffs, limiting foreign travel, et cetera. Canada (in 1962), Britian (in 1964), and France (in 1968) all imposed temporary measures directly interfering with private merchandise imports, in direct violation of their international commitments. Other countries have adjusted their tax systems in such a way as to encourage exports or to discourage imports. The Bretton Woods system also gives rise to considerable debate where the responsibility for certain imbalances lies, who should do what, who is not doing enough, and so on; it invites pretentious moralizing and contentious politicking, damaging to the international cooperation the system is supposed to foster.

The Bretton Woods payments system has become unworkable. We still do have exchange adjustments, such as the devaluation of sterling and other currencies in November 1967, but they almost always take place under *force majeure* rather than as an integral feature of a smoothly working adjustment mechanism.[2] To protect existing exchange parities, countries increasingly violate basic principles and purposes of the payments system. The absence of an international adjustment mechanism will plague us increasingly in the seventies unless something is done about it. I see no escape from the choice between somewhat greater flexibility of exchange rates, on the one hand, or, on the other, more frequent resort to restrictions and other interferences with international transactions. Homilies about the need for countries to maintain tighter control over internal demand, even when they are to the point, are not likely to be received with grace or to be translated into action with the regularity and persistence required to avoid one or the other.

Compromise Solution: A "Gliding Parity" System

A possible compromise between the need for a long-term adjustment mechanism and a desire to preserve both a moderate degree of external "discipline" on domestic policies and pressures for international cooperation in framing economic policies resides in a scheme whereby exchange parities change slowly over time, but more or less automatically and in the direction required for payments adjustment. A system of "gliding parities" would provide a reasonable degree of certainty and stability in the short run, but would at the same time permit the gradual economic adjustments so necessary in the long run. In the remainder of this paper, I will argue for a particular version of the gliding parity proposal,[3] will indicate its merits and its limitations, and will compare it with alternative proposals for introducing greater exchange flexibility into the payments system.

Under this proposal, a country would be expected to change its exchange parity weekly whenever its payments position warranted a change. The weekly change in parity would be fixed at .05 percent, cumulating to about 2.6 percent a year if changes were made in the same direction every week. A change in parity would be triggered by a movement in the country's international reserve position. If reserves rose more than a stipulated amount during a given week, the country would announce at the end of the week an up-valuation in its parity for the following week, and vice versa for a decline in reserves. The movement in reserves would determine whether the parity changed or not, but not the amount of the change in parity, which would be fixed at .05 percent. Market exchange rates need not change by the full amount of the parity, however, for the country's central bank might adopt a stragtegy of supporting the market rates temporarily even after a change in parity.

Changes in parity would be presumptive rather than mandatory. Where special circumstances influenced reserve movements, a country might ignore the presumption that the parity should be changed. But a country that failed to alter its parity when an alteration was indicated would be required to explain and justify its decisions before other trading nations, which would meet on a regular basis several times each year to review international monetary developments. Any country that systematically ignored the presumptive rules and offered an unacceptable justification would be open to sanctions: for a country in deficit, no credit from the IMF and other international sources of balance-of-payments support; for a country in surplus, discriminatory "exchange equalization" duties against its products.

An arrangement such as this would provide relatively smooth accommodation to certain kinds of disturbance to balance-of-payments equilibrium. In particular, it would prevent or inhibit payments disequilibrium arising from:

1. gradual shifts in the patterns of demand, as incomes grow and tastes change, toward or away from the products of individual countries;

2. gradual changes in international competitiveness or other supply conditions, such as might arise from exhaustion of natural resources or from small differential rates of change in labor costs due in turn to different national choices regarding tolerable increases in money wages;

3. modest influences on trade positions due to alterations in national policies, such as changes in indirect tax rates and corresponding border tax adjustments.

This arrangement would not be well suited for coping with large disturbances to international payments, such as very large wage settlements or engagement in major overseas military adventures. For this reason large discrete changes in exchange parities, as called for under the Bretton Woods system, could not be ruled out. (The cumulative effects of small changes in parity might of course obviate some large parity changes that would otherwise be necessary.) The arrangement would offer somewhat greater scope, as compared with the present, for independent national monetary policies, but monetary conditions would still be subject to strong international influences, as they are today.

Effect on Trade and Capital Movements

Gliding parities would affect both trade and capital movements. The effect on trade would arise from the gradual change—upward or downward—in exchange rates, making goods and services in a country whose currency was appreciating less competitive than they otherwise would be, and the reverse for a country in deficit. In some cases these changes in exchange rates would merely neutralize opposite changes in other elements affecting competitiveness, for example small changes in wage costs or in border taxes, and thus would be preventive of changes in price competitiveness rather than corrective. In other cases they would produce compensatory changes in trade flows to offset disturbing changes in trade or other international transactions. In the latter cases, trade flows would have to be sufficiently sensitive to relative price movements for the system to work well. Empirical evidence suggests that the required degree of price sensitivity exists for most countries.

Influence on International Investment

Gradual changes in exchange parities would also influence long-term international investment, but the influence would be limited and, on balance, would mark an improvement as compared with the Bretton Woods system. Under fixed parities, portfolio capital may inappropriately flow to countries with high nominal interest rates resulting from inflationary pressures—at least until a change in parity is regarded as imminent. Under gliding parities, exchange depreciation and/or appreciation will offset such yield differences, without, however, inhibiting long-term capital movements inspired by real, as opposed to nominal, differences in interest rates. Similarly, gliding parities would help to neutralize inappropriate incentives or disincentives to foreign direct investment based on divergent trends in money wage costs or certain national tax changes under (temporarily) fixed exchange rates while leaving uninhibited capital flows based on differences in real rates of return.

The impact of a gliding parity on short-term capital movements, hence its implications for monetary policy, is somewhat more complicated. The case in which gradual parity changes are widely expected must be distinguished from that in which the financial public is unsure whether parities will glide and, if so, in which direction. In the first case, monetary policy will have to be governed by balance-of-payments considerations if large outflows of interest-sensitive funds are to be avoided. In the second case, monetary policy will have somewhat greater scope than under the Bretton Woods system for devotion to domestic stabilization.

Strong and one-sided expectations about the direction in which the parity and actual exchange rates will move will be reflected in forward exchange rates. For example, a currency at its floor and expected to depreciate at the maximum rate would trade at a discount of at least $2\frac{1}{2}$ percent (annual rate) in the forward market vis-á-vis the intervention currency. Under these circumstances, strong interest arbitrage incentives would develop; and unless the country in question permitted its relevant interest rates to rise above those prevailing elsewhere by a corresponding amount, interest-sensitive capital outflows would ensue. In this respect, however, the gliding parity arrangement would not restrict the flexibility of monetary action any more than it is at present under similar circumstances.

Greater Scope for National Monetary Autonomy

On the other hand, if expectations about future exchange rate movements are diverse, a system of gliding parities would offer somewhat greater scope for national monetary autonomy than present arrangements. At present, a country whose exchange parity is not expected to change in the near future finds its flexibility to use monetary policy for domestic purposes increasingly circumscribed by a large and growing volume of interest-sensitive international capital.[4] While forward exchange rates are not technically pegged by official action, their movement is limited under these circumstances to a band hardly wider than the band officially allowable for spot exchange rates, for movements outside the spot floor and ceiling rates evoke speculative forward purchases or sales of the currency. The practical limits on forward exchange rate movements similarly limit deviations in domestic interest rates from those prevailing in major foreign financial markets, because deviations in excess of those permitted by the range of forward exchange rates would evoke large-scale inward or outward movements of covered, interest-sensitive funds, thus weakening or even vitiating the intended effects of tight or easy monetary policy on the domestic economy.

Because under a gliding parity arrangement exchange rates could move in the course of a year by as much as 2.6 percent in either direction outside the band around parity, forward exchange rates could also range outside the initial band without evoking large, one-sided speculative forward purchases. To the extent that uncertainty prevailed about the direction and extent that the parity would glide, therefore, monetary policy would be given somewhat greater scope for pursuit of domestic objectives without being undercut by international capital movements.

A Case for Presumptive Rules for Parity Changes

It is tempting to make the rules governing changes in parity automatic and mandatory. Too often domestic politics and national prestige become involved in government decisions regarding exchange parities, and a fully discretionary system would very likely result in less frequent changes in parity than would be desirable. Even apart from the difficulty of devising automatic rules appropriate to all circumstances, however, governments as a practical matter are not likely to bind themselves to courses of action that they may not always conceive to be in their best interests. This difficulty can be resolved by laying down *presumptive rules*, of the type indicated in this proposal, which no country is obliged to follow, but which each country would be expected to follow in the absence of sound and persuasive reasons for not doing so. A procedure could be established in the International Monetary Fund or elsewhere for close and continuing examination by other member countries of those cases in which the presumptive rules were not followed.

Presumptive rules of parity changes must be based on some measure of balance-of-payments performance. Movements in reserves, spot exchange rates, and forward exchange rates all convey some information about a country's payments position. No single indicator will always be appropriate. However, simplicity is a virtue, and presumptive rules will be less seriously deficient if they are based on reserve movements tempered where necessary by other indicators on a discretionary basis, than if they are based on observed spot or forward rates. Forward rates may be held at a premium or discount by differences in national interest rates even when there is no net movement of funds, and such a premium or discount signifies nothing about a country's balance-of-payments position. A currency trading at a forward discount is not necessarily or even normally an over-valued currency.

An alternative version of gliding parities, the one most frequently discussed, would make the parity at each moment in time depend on some average of the spot exchange rates prevailing in the recent past. If the spot rate were below the parity, this would generally induce a fall in the parity; spot rates above parity would raise the parity. Under this scheme, the spot exchange rate is used as the key indicator of a country's payments position.

Two Difficulties

There are two difficulties with this proposal, apart from its automaticity, which has been discussed above. First, it neglects entirely the great importance of non-market transactions, such as the purchase of German marks for US forces under NATO. Even when by agreement these transactions take place at market rates, they exert no direct pressure on the spot market since they occur outside the market. Thus a country's currency may be technically weak even when the country has a strong payments position, and vice versa. While conceivably this problem could be solved by requiring all foreign exchange transactions to go through the market, the parties involved would frequently object to such a stipulation, not only because of the transactions costs involved but also because of the influence that large purchasers could exert on the market. (US official purchases of marks for use in Germany amount to nearly one billion dollars a year, for instance.)

Second, the authorities of a country might influence the movement of its parity by intervening in the exchange market, for example, by selling home currency to prevent appreciation, thereby thwarting the purposes of the scheme. To prevent this, it has been suggested that official market intervention within the exchange rate band must be prohibited. Apart from the fact that few governments are likely to agree to such a proscription, it will not solve the problem, for countries can influence market rates by other means, such as monetary policy.

Under the arrangement proposed here, in contrast, monetary authorities would be free, as now, to intervene in the exchange markets at times of their choosing. But they would have an incentive not to intervene within the band, since intervention (implying reserve movements) would presumptively require a change in parity in the direction which the authorities were resisting. Reserve sales to inhibit a fall in the market rate would call for a reduction of the parity, while purchases of foreign exchange to inhibit a rise in the rate would call for an increase in the parity. Any country that desires to maintain a constant exchange rate between its currency and some other currency can of course do so by following a monetary policy appropriate to that objective; its monetary policy then becomes fully dependent on conditions abroad, and monetary policy is truly (if one-sidedly) "coordinated," a necessary condition for a durable regime of fixed exchange rate without controls on international transactions

There is, finally, some positive advantage in keying parity changes to reserve movements, since this would relate balance-of-payments adjustment explicitly to demands for reserves and would thereby highlight any national inconsistencies in the global demand for reserves. Under the Bretton Woods system, countries declare exchange parities but do not declare their demands for reserves, with the result that global demand may exceed global supply (or vice versa) and balance-of-payments adjustment policies may work at cross purposes as many countries attempt, unsuccessfully in the aggregate, to increase their reserves.[5] Under the presumptive rules proposed here, changes in parity would be keyed to national reserve changes relative to some normal, desired reserve increase. The declaration of desired reserve increases would, in turn, assure that the total demand for reserves matched the total supply—if necessary by adjusting the total supply (e.g., creation of SDRs).[6]

Transitional Problems

A difficulty with any new proposal is the transition during which it is put into effect, especially when the initial situation may be characterized, in this case, by large actual or suppressed imbalances in payments.

It would be highly desirable with any innovation in the rules governing exchange rates to begin from a position of approximate payments equilibrium, at least among the major trading countries. As a practical matter, this may not be possible, even with some initial realignment of rates, since such changes may not be exactly right. Fortunately, however, transitional problems for a system of gliding parities are markedly less than for many other proposals regarding changes in the exchange rate regime. In particular, initial equilibrium, while desirable, is by no means a necessary precondition for the introduction of gliding parities.

Inaugurating the system from a position of disequilibrium would, for a time, assure the direction in which certain exchange parities would move; and this assurance, in turn, would provide incentive for speculating on currencies expected to rise in value and against those expected to fall. But this incentive would not necessarily be greater than that before the introduction of gliding parities in what is, by assumption, a position of widely recognized disequilibrium. The only new element is the certainty of parity change, but with that certainty also comes the certainty of small changes spread over a period of time (provided the new regime itself is credible) and the assurance of eventual correction (provided new sources of disequilibrium do not equal the corrective capacity of the parity changes). Moreover, the financial incentives of small changes in exchange rates can be compensated by corresponding differences in interest rates—lower on assets in an appreciating currency, higher on assets in a depreciating one. Thus, starting the arrangement in the presence of payments imbalances might require, at the outset, an adjustment in certain national interest rates to compensate for expected changes in parities. Since relative rather than absolute interest rates matter here, such an adjustment should be the subject of international discussion and agreement. Furthermore, where financial institutions maintain a rigid separation between capital and income on their accounts either by law or by accounting convention, some provision should be made for offsetting one against the other insofar as changes in capital valuation would result from changes in exchange parities.

Gliding Parities and Widened Band Proposals Compared

Before concluding, let me contrast this proposal for gliding parities with the proposal for introducing greater exchange flexibility by widening the band within which market exchange rates are free to fluctuate without required intervention by the monetary authorities. In my view, these two proposals serve basically different functions, and thus are complementary rather than competitive in their effects. So long as the exchange rate is within the band, wider bands introduce greater uncertainty with respect to the movement of exchange rates in the near future. As a consequence, a wider band permits greater national autonomy in the pursuit of monetary policy, for forward exchange rates are similarly free to move more widely than is true with a narrow band. Gliding parities permit somewhat greater monetary autonomy, but not so much as a much wider band would.

Second, a wider band would reduce the need for reserves to cover seasonal, cyclical, and other reversible balance-of-payments disturbances. These disturbances would be compensated by movements in market exchange rates, aided by stabilizing private speculation. To the extent that the parities remained credible, the need for international liquidity would be reduced.

A wider band would not permit adjustment to secular, or cumulative, disturbances to international payments, such as might arise from persistent divergences in national price or demand-for-import trends. These are the kinds of disturbance that a system of gliding parities is designed to accommodate. Once the floor or ceiling of a widened band is reached, a country would find itself in just the same condition as it does today under similar circumstances. Since I believe that such long-run divergences in balance-of-payments trends are inevitable, I cannot regard a widening of the bands as a permanent solution to the adjustment problem. It leaves us with all of the same problems outlined earlier in the paper. I find unpersuasive the claim that wider bands would make discrete parity changes easier. A market rate at the floor or ceiling of the widened band would certainly make the need for parity changes more obvious than it sometimes is today, but that need would be as obvious to private parties as to government officials, and would stimulate massive speculative flows of funds.

A widening of the bands is often linked with a proposal to permit parities to glide. However, it is not true, as has sometimes been claimed, that there is an organic connection between the width of the band and the permissible rate at which parities may glide. Under the proposal described earlier whereby the parity is linked automatically to an average of historical market rates, the band width, hence the possible deviation of actual market rates from the parity, obviously influences the rate at which the parity would glide. But when parity changes are keyed to reserve changes, a gliding parity is consistent with a variety of band widths; the two proposals are separable, and each can be considered on its merits.

Finally, I should add one tentative reservation about widening the bands or indeed any other proposal that might lead to substantial fluctuations in actual market exchange rates. Our understanding of the considerations which lead people to hold money is still highly imperfect. Ronald McKinnon has suggested that stability in purchasing power is an important consideration in the willingness to hold money and that, where the exchange rate of a currency fluctuates substantially against other currencies, residents may be tempted to move their holdings of cash balances from the fluctuating currency into a more stable one—a tendency that would increase in proportion to the importance of foreign goods in their expenditures.[7] Thus, stable currencies might "drive out" unstable ones, and evoke in turn national attempts to preserve national currencies through the use of controls to prevent flight into other currencies. Of course, as is frequently pointed out by the advocates of greater exchange flexibility, flexibility need not lead to instability. It need not, but it might; and therein lies the risk. This objection is not a serious one, however, for relations among major currencies.

While a system of gliding parities would be highly novel insitutionally and, in that sense, would represent a sharp departure from present arrangements, its impact on trade and payments and on the need for close cooperation among major countries would be limited and, in that (more relevant) sense, it would represent a modest but possibly significant step in the evolution of the present international monetary system. Relations among currencies would be relatively stable, movements in exchange rates would be severely limited, pressures for coordination of national monetary and other policies would remain high, and movements in foreign exchange reserves—augmented when necessary by official borrowing from the IMF and elsewhere—would continue to absorb the bulk of swings in payments positions.

Within limits, however, a system of gliding parities would prevent the cumulative imbalances that arise from disparate national rates of growth or disparate national rates of wage inflation, and by so doing it would reduce the need to resort to the import surcharges, tax devices to improve foreign receipts, and direct controls over international transactions that have once again become a common feature of the international economic landscape.

Notes

1. In a sample of two dozen devaluing countries, mostly less developed countries, the probability that a Minister of Finance would lose his job within a year

following a devaluation was increased three-fold over the corresponding experience of a control group. This illustrates the conflict between personal and national interest that may arise for the individuals responsible for framing national policy. See my "Currency Devaluation in Developing Countries: A Cross-Sectional Analysis," Gustav Ranis (ed.), *Government and Economic Development*, Yale University Press, 1971.

2. The French devaluation of August 1969 was an apparent exception, for the timing of the devaluation caught financial markets off guard; but most international firms and many individuals had already taken a short position in francs.

3. This proposal is taken from my "Gliding Parities: A Proposal for Presumptive Rules," prepared for the Conference on Exchange Rates at Burgenstock, Switzerland, in June 1969, and to be published in *Approaches to Greater Flexibility in Exchange Rates: The Burgenstock Papers*, Princeton University Press, 1970.

4. Countries whose parities are expected to change also experience difficulty in preserving monetary autonomy, but for different reasons.

5. Thanks to the reserve-currency role of the dollar and the relative indifference of the United States to its payments position, this problem was not acute during the fifties, since dollar outflows satisfied any residual demand for reserves in the rest of the world.

6. Each country would thus have two reserve indicators under the scheme: (1) the target increase to allow for secular growth in reserves and (2) the amount by which reserve changes would have to exceed or fall short of this target increase before a change in parity was indicated.

7. R. I. McKinnon, "Optimal Currency Areas," *American Economic Review*, 53 (September 1963), pp. 717–24.

4　　　　　　　　　　Flexible Exchange Rates,
　　　　　　　　　　　　1973–1980: How Bad
　　　　　　　　　　　　Have They Really Been?

Grand claims were once made for a system of flexible exchange rates. The classic statement was by Milton Friedman (1953), and the most complete development was Egon Sohmen's *Flexible Exchange Rates: Theory and Controversy* (1961).

Robert Triffin, while never discussing flexible exchange rates in analytical detail, has over the years entertained some skepticism about their merits. His grounds for doing so revolved around the loss of discipline on fiscal and monetary authorities that flexible exchange rates permit with respect to anti-inflation policies. Triffin has also been concerned with the possibility that flexible exchange rates might lead to such turbulence in cost-price relationships that they would engender protectionist actions. He has feared the disintegrative impact that flexible exchange rates might have upon economic and, hence, upon political relations between nations, an impact that would run strongly counter to his lifelong objective of promoting economic integration among nations, and especially among European nations.[1]

By March 1981 we had eight years' experience with major currencies floating against one another in exchange markets. What can we say about this experience—and pariculary against the grand claims that have been made for flexible exchange rates and Triffin's concerns about them?[2]

First, it is necessary to admit that on any comparative measure, the world's macroeconomic performance during the late 1970s, when generalized floating prevailed, was worse than its performance during the final years of the adjustable peg system. For example, real economic growth was only 60 percent as rapid during 1973–1979 as it was in the preceding

The International Monetary System under Flexible Exchange Rates: Global, Regional, and National (essays in honor of Robert Triffin), ed. R. N. Cooper, J. de Macedo, P. Kenen, and J. Van Ypersele (Cambridge, Mass.: Ballinger, 1982), 3–16. Copyright 1982, Ballinger Publishing Company. Reprinted with permission.

seven-year period; unemployment rates in industrialized countries were 50 percent higher, and inflation rates were more than double.

These lamentable developments, however, cannot be attributed to the introduction of flexible exchange rates. Post hoc does not imply propter hoc. To appreciate this, we need only recall two other factors that greatly affected economic performance during this period—the quadrupling of world oil prices in 1973–1974 and the further doubling of those prices in 1979; and the tremendous expansion of international liquidity in the period 1970–1973, the last years of the fixed exchange rate system. These factors together forced national economic policymakers to deal simultaneously with high unemployment and high inflation, a task to which our standard tools of economic management are not well suited.

If we make allowance for the severe disturbances to which the world economy was subjected during this period, I conclude that the experience under floating exchange rates has been a reasonably good one. It is worth keeping in mind that the smoothness of a ride depends on the size of the bumps on the road as well as on the quality of the shock absorbers. If we abstract from sharp day-to-day movements, floating exchange rates performed about as well as one would have expected, given the disturbances. Protectionist actions were largely avoided (indeed, major trade liberalization was agreed), and world trade continued to grow.

In what follows, I first want to make some analytical distinctions that pertain to movements in exchange rates. Then I will discuss the actual movements in exchange rates during 1973 to 1980. Following that, I consider the possibility that flexible exchange rates may have been a substantial cause of some of the disturbances experienced by the world economy during this period. I conclude with some observations about where we go from here.

Real versus Nominal Movements in Exchange Rates

One attribute of flexible exchange rates is that they can correct for differential national rates of inflation at the border, leaving all real variables unchanged. Fixed exchange rates, in contrast, lead to an alteration of relative prices among countries—or between tradable goods and nontradable goods within countries—when there are divergences in relevant national rates of inflation.

Divergences in national rates of inflation, however, are not the only source of possible disturbance to international transactions. Real disturbances—changes in the underlying demand for or supply of particular goods and services—call for correction through the price mechanism. Flexible exchange rates in some circumstances can help to bring about this adjustment. Indeed, when factor prices in nominal terms resist decline, and where some "money illusion"[3] exists, movements in exchange rates may be the most efficient way to bring about the required decline in real factor prices.

This distinction between correction for divergence in inflation rates and adjustment to changes in real variables is crucial, for it indicates that changes in nominal exchange rates under a flexible rate system can plausibly lead to a wide range of changes in "real" exchange rates (changes in exchange rates corrected for inflation differentials), from none at all to a change fully equivalent to the change in nominal rates. In contrast to the impression sometimes conveyed in a literature preoccupied with purchasing power parity, we should not be surprised, either in theory or in reality, to find a variety of changes in real rates corresponding to any given change in nominal rates. The outcome will depend inter alia on the initiating combination of disturbances.

An exchange rate is the rate at which one money exchanges for another. It therefore reflects the whole range of factors that influence the demand for money, not merely the demand for foreign goods and services. Domestic demand for foreign securities and foreign demand for domestic securities are also important factors in the foreign exchange market. Indeed, the current fashion is to treat the exchange rate as that "price" that clears the market with respect to the holding of foreign assets in national portfolios. It is admitted that over time exchange rates can have an important effect on investment at home and abroad, hence on net foreign investment, hence on foreign trade. But since the time it takes for investment flows to respond to differences in relative yield is very much longer than the time it takes for market prices to adjust to changes in asset preferences, portfolio balance considerations are thought to exercise the dominant short-run influence on exchange rates. It is only over time that changes in the current account balance, which is equal to net foreign investment, can correct portfolio imbalances with respect to the holding of foreign assets.[4]

As will become clear below, I believe it is an oversimplification to concede even dominant short-run influence of portfolio considerations on exchange rates, except tautologically. Imbalances in current payments may so influence expectations about future exchange rates (hence today's desire to hold securities) that a major role in exchange rate determination must be given to imbalances in goods and services that are perceived to be non-sustainable. These perceptions, it is true, are reflected in portfolio decisions.

Thus seemingly alternative explanations for exchange rate determination, properly considered, are not alternatives at all, but different aspects of the same underlying process whereby perceptions are translated into expectations and expectations in turn are translated into market prices.[5]

Exchange Rate Developments, 1973–1980

Let us turn from these analytical considerations to the events of 1973–1980. If we abstract from week-to-week movements, exchange rate movements are not that difficult to explain. Newspapers quote bilateral exchange rates, such as that between the German mark and the US dollar. What is important for a country's economy, however, is not one single exchange rate, but some average of all relevant exchange rates. This average can be called the "effective" exchange rate. It is usually a weighted average of bilateral exchange rates, where the weights correspond to the trading pattern of the country in which we are interested, or sometimes to the trade of a group of countries. (This kind of weighting obviously focuses on trade. A different set of weights would be appropriate if we were to focus exclusively or predominantly on financial transactions.) Second, as already noted, differences in national inflation rates may alter exchange rates simply to avoid affecting relative prices between or within countries. A change in an exchange rate corrected for differential inflation rates is called the change in the "real" exchange rate.

With these distinctions in mind, consider the exchange rate of the US dollar during the period of floating rates. Contemporary newspaper accounts conveyed the impression that the dollar took quite a beating in exchange markets during this period. It therefore will come as a great surprise to many that the effective exchange rate of the dollar relative to currencies of other industrialized countries showed no change in December 1980 from its position in March 1973, when generalized floating began following the February 1973 devaluation of the dollar. Inclusion of the currencies of developing countries in the "effective" rate would show an appreciation of the dollar over this period.

There were some ups and downs in the value of the dollar during this period, but they were not large and they followed almost a textbook pattern in their movements. The effective rate appreciated modestly in 1973 and again in 1975–1976; it depreciated in 1977–1978 and appreciated slightly in 1979–1980 (see table 4.1). The real effective exchange rate of the dollar (wholesale prices of manufactured goods are used to measure the relevant inflation rates) followed a similar pattern, except for

Table 4.1
United States, Exchange Rate, 1973–1980 (March 1973 = 100).

	Effective Exchange Rate[a]	Real Effective[b] Exchange Rate	Current Account[c] Balance ($ billion)
	December		
1973	101.6	95.1	7.1
1974	101.0	97.7	4.1[d]
1975	105.0	102.5	18.3
1976	106.4	101.1	4.5
1977	102.9	98.2	− 14.1
1978	97.5	94.9	− 14.3
1979	98.7	96.5	− 0.6
1980	99.9	99.7	+ 0.1

a. Index of fifteen currencies of industrialized countries, weighted by the US 1976 trade in manufactures with those countries.
b. Effective rate corrected for differentials in wholesale prices of nonfood manufactured goods.
c. Including government transfers.
d. Excludes a $2 billion write-off of Indian rupee holdings.
Sources: Morgan Guaranty Trust Co.; IMF, International Financial Statistics.

an initial depreciation of the dollar in 1973, when inflation rates in other industrial countries sharply exceeded those in the United States.

The principal observation to make on these movements is that contrary to widespread impression, movements in the exchange rate of the dollar did not correct for differential rates of inflation—indeed, the United States had a better than average record in this regard—but rather were real, alternately improving, worsening, improving, and then again worsening the competitiveness of US goods and services in international trade. Moreover, the real effective exchange rate followed a classic pattern: It declined in response to a deterioration in the current account position of the United States, and it appreciated in response to an improvement in the current account. Whatever the exact channel of causation, the relationship was a close one.

A similar pattern can be observed for the Japanese yen. Movements in the real effective exchange rate of the yen correlate well with Japan's position on current account, with the yen generally depreciating in response to a worsening of the current account and appreciating in response to an improvement (see table 4.2; the Japanese current account improved greatly during 1980 and was in surplus by the end of the year).

Similar effects can be discerned in movements of the German mark, although the more striking pattern there is the relative stability of the real

Table 4.2
Japan, Exchange Rate, 1973–1980 (March 1973 = 100).

	$/Yen	Effective Exchange Rate[a]	Real Effective[b] Exchange Rate	Current Account[c] Balance ($ billion)
	December			
1973	96.5	93.1	106.6	−0.1
1974	89.8	85.7	90.2	−4.7
1975	88.3	86.4	84.8	−0.7
1976	88.3	91.0	88.4	3.7
1977	97.6	109.1	99.0	10.9
1978	124.4	129.6	108.0	17.6
1979	119.5	103.5	86.9	−8.7
1980	124.8	122.0	100.8	−10.8

a. Index of fifteen currencies of industrialized countries, weighted by Japan's 1976 trade in manufactures with those countries.
b. Effective rate corrected for differentials in wholesale prices of nonfood manufactured goods.
c. Including government transfers.
Sources: Morgan Guaranty Trust Co.; IMF, International Financial Statistics.

exchange rate (except for the depreciation in 1975 and again in 1980). The mark appreciated substantially over this period, which served to offset inflation that was higher for Germany's trading partners than for Germany. Thus, in this case, in contrast to the US dollar and to an extent considerably greater than for the yen, the movements in real exchange rates were far smaller than the movements in nominal exchange rates (see table 4.3).

Establishing a visible correlation between two variables, of course, does not define the causal connection between them. By affecting the demand for foreign currency, current account imbalances could influence exchange rates directly, or as noted above, they could affect expectations about future exchange rates and hence, through attempted adjustments in portfolios, could affect today's exchange rates. Or there could be some common factor that influences both the exchange rate and the current balance. Moreover, the causation acts in both directions, with exchange rates influencing the current balance as well as the other way around. It is widely accepted, however, that a considerable period of time—perhaps as long as two years—is required before a change in the real exchange rate will have substantial effect on the volume of trade, especially trade in manufactured goods. In the short run, a depreciation of the currency, by raising domestic currency prices of imports, will worsen the balance on goods and services (measured in domestic currency). If this condition were dominant and were to persist, the exchange market would be unstable. But if it is temporary,

Table 4.3
West Germany, Exchange Rate, 1973−1980 (March 1973 = 100).

	$/DM	Effective Exchange Rate[a]	Real Effective[b] Exchange Rate	Current Account[c] Balance ($ billion)
	December			
1973	105.2	107.2	105.6	4.6
1974	109.3	111.4	104.7	10.1
1975	114.9	108.2	97.4	3.9
1976	112.2	122.4	103.8	3.6
1977	121.8	130.1	104.8	4.0
1978	140.6	135.0	105.2	8.7
1979	154.3	140.2	105.9	−6.3
1980	143.3	133.9	98.7	−15.0

a. Index of fifteen currencies of industrialized countries, weighted by Germany's 1976 trade in manufactures with those countries.
b. Effective rate corrected for differentials in wholesale prices of nonfood manufactured goods.
c. Including government transfers.
Sources: Morgan Guaranty Trust Co.; IMF, International Financial Statistics.

we have the so-called J-curve effect, whereby a movement in an exchange rate first moves the current account balance in one direction, before the volumes of imports and exports have had an opportunity to adjust fully, but over time moves the current balance in the opposite direction, after traders have had a chance to adjust to the new prices. This J-curve effect seems to have played an important role in the sharp growth of Japan's surplus during 1977 and 1978. Appreciation of the yen, induced by the growing surplus, also aggravated the surplus by raising the dollar value of exports. Moreover, an anticipated change in a currency's value may induce traders to accelerate or defer their purchases of foreign goods, so that in addition to the J-curve effect, there is actually some disequilibrating movement of goods in a period of expected exchange rate change. Again, during late 1977 and early 1978, Japanese exports may have been stimulated for a time rather than retarded by the great appreciation of the yen.[6]

The experience during these years of floating exchange rates illustrates that both real and monetary elements influenced exchange rates. Indeed, it is possible to classify countries according to the dominance of monetary or real factors. In the case of Italy, the substantial depreciation of the lira was due almost wholly to higher rates of inflation in Italy than in its major trading partners. By mid-1980 the lira had depreciated almost 50 percent since March 1973, but the real effective exchange rate was not quite 5 percent below that of the earlier period. Most of the appreciation of the German mark (DM) was also to offset differential inflation rates, although some movement in the real DM rate also occurred. At the other end of the spectrum, movements in the effective exchange rate of the dollar and the French franc (except for the very late 1970s) were largely real, with only a small part representing corrections for divergence in national inflation rates.

Japan and Switzerland fall between these extremes: A substantial part of the movement of effective exchange rates is explained by better than average performance of those two countries with respect to inflation, but substantial real movements in their exchange rates also took place. For example, between March 1973 and September 1978 (the peak), the effective exchange rate of Switzerland appreciated 84 percent. During the same period, the real exchange rate of the Swiss franc appreciated 34 percent, declining sharply thereafter. This large real appreciation occurred during a period in which the Swiss current account surplus was an extraordinary 5 to 6 percent of Switzerland's GNP.

The only really aberrant case among major countries—aberrant in the sense of not falling within the patterns just described—was the United Kingdom. The British pound depreciated heavily during the first several years after floating, stabilized, and then appreciated strongly, despite rates of inflation substantially in excess of those of most of its major trading partners. Indeed, in real terms the British pound appreciated 50 percent between late 1976 (a low point) and mid-1980. This appreciation was accompanied by modest but steady improvements in the current account balance. Much more important, however, was the increased production of North Sea oil, combined with a sharp rise in oil prices and Mrs. Thatcher's policy of economic retrenchment in late 1979 and 1980. This case represents a dramatic illustration of the influence of real (as opposed to monetary) economic developments on a country's exchange rate.

Flexible Exchange Rates as Insulators

An alleged advantage of flexible exchange rates is that they insulate national economies from disturbances coming from abroad. By the same token, they "bottle up" domestic disturbances in the originating country. On this argument, a country could neither import world inflation nor export its home-grown domestic inflation under a regime of flexible exchange rates, for movements in the exchange rates would compensate at the border for disturbances originating on the other side.

This traditional view of flexible exchange rates is a considerable over-simplification. Their powers of insulation depend very much on the nature of the disturbance, and in some instances flexible exchange rates may actually transmit disturbances across national boundaries more strongly than a system of fixed exchange rates. Flexible exchange rates are likely to be most successful at neutralizing disturbances when the disturbance is a general rise in the price level. For a small country under fixed exchange rates, a rise in the world price level would stimulate demand for national products and would lead to a rise in the domestic price level. An appreciation of the currency to offset the rise in world prices would compensate at the border, preventing either relative price or wealth effects inside the country.

A world increase in demand for the country's particular export products, in contrast, will raise incomes and stimulate domestic demand. With flexible exchange rates, its currency would appreciate and partially damp the sale of exports, as well as discouraging imports—on both counts relieving pressure on the domestic economy. But relative prices will have changed, total wealth will have been increased, and resources will have been reallocated, so the insulation provided by flexible rates is incomplete.

An increase in foreign demand for a country's securities will also lead to appreciation of its currency. That, in turn, will both diminish aggregate demand and lead to a reallocation of resources away from tradable to nontradable goods, possibly with transitional unemployment. In this instance, therefore, far from insulating the domestic economy from foreign disturbances, a flexible rate will have transmitted the disturbance more forcefully than would have been the case under a fixed exchange rate. Under a fixed rate, an increase in demand for the country's securities will be offset by the monetary authorities, who in preventing an appreciation of the currency will add to its foreign exchange reserves—that is, will export capital—in a manner that partially or even fully limits the impact of the shift in portfolio demand on the markets for goods and services and labor at home.

During the 1970s, flexible exchange rates undoubtedly insulated West Germany from imported inflation, a point much emphasized by German authorities in support of flexible rates. But changes in real economic variables are real, not monetary, and their impact can only be mitigated, not offset, by changes in exchange rates. For example, the sharp rise in the Swiss franc weakened but did not altogether stop the influence on its trading partners of Switzerland's deflationary policy during this period, a policy that was motivated by the desire to reduce the large number of foreign workers in Switzerland at the beginning of the period. By the same token, depreciation of the dollar in 1977–1978 reduced but did not eliminate the expansionary impact on the rest of the world of expansionary US domestic policies.

To sum up, exchange rates during this period of floating have not been "unstable" over time, and indeed, the movements have been fully explicable in terms of correction for inflation differentials combined with a corrective response to current account imbalances.

It remains to be seen how powerful changes in real exchange rates are as an adjustment mechanism leading to the correction of imbalances. Preliminary indications are favorable. Goods and services do seem to follow a J-curve: First the imbalance worsens in response to a currency depreciation, but thereafter, with a lag, both the volume of exports and the volume of imports respond in a corrective fashion. In this respect, the experience under floating exchange rates must be considered a qualified success. Floating exchange rates do not, however, fully insulate national economies from external disturbances, nor do they fully bottle up domestic disturbances.

Flexible Exchange Rates as Sources of Disturbance

An assessment of flexible exchange rates would not be complete without addressing the question of whether the presence of flexible rates actually created the disturbances that plagued the world economy during this period. This is a subject for endless debate, but I believe the answer is negative. There are occasions, as noted in the previous section, when flexible exchange rates can aggravate the transmission of disturbances, especially when there are sharp portfolio shifts between foreign and domestic securities. There were episodes during the period 1973–1980 in which porfolio movements undoubtedly did disturb national economies. But it would be an error to attribute the general turmoil of the period to flexible exchange rates.

The most notable feature of the 1970s, as compared with the 1950s and 1960s, is the sharp increase in rates of inflation. But this sharp increase antedated the switch to flexible exchange rates, as did the large growth in world liquidity that supported the inflation. As Triffin has pointed out on numerous occasions, international liquidity grew enormously—doubling on most measures—between 1969 and 1972.[7] But that growth took place in a period of fixed, not flexible, exchange rates. Indeed, the introduction of flexible rates—which was resisted for years by monetary officials—was an unavoidable response to the difficulties already being experienced.

Then there was the sharp increase in oil prices in 1973–1974, following the introduction of floating exchange rates. But the price increase cannot plausibly be attributed to floating. Some observers argue that it was an autonomous action, representing a coalescence of OPEC market power in the wake of the huge increase in demand for OPEC oil during the preceding five years and the Saudi Arabian embargo associated with the Yom Kippur War. Other observers contend that the oil price increase was an endogenous reponse to world inflation, a reaction to the alleged decline in the real oil price in the early 1970s.[8] Whatever one's views on the hypotheses, and they are not mutually exclusive, flexible exchange rates played no role in either of them. In principle, currency instability could have been a precipitating event. But in fact the US dollar (the currency in which oil prices are denominated) was relatively stable between March 1973—after the February devaluation, a feature of the earlier adjustable peg exchange rate system—and December 1973. Its value in SDR (Special Drawing Rights) was unchanged, and it experienced only minor movements up or down against other leading currencies.

National divergences in inflation rates existed before the oil shock of 1973–1974, but that shock aggravated them. Different economies responded to that price increase in different ways. Price and wage inflation accelerated in all countries, but to differing degrees. At one extreme was the United States, where price increases accelerated more than wages; real wages actually fell in the United States, alone among industrial countries. Some countries—most notably Japan—experienced a wage explosion in the immediate aftermath of the OPEC price increase but brought wage settlements down to pre-1973 norms within two years. Still other countries—notably Britain and Italy, among others—experienced an enduring wage and price inflation. But since all of these countries had floating currencies, that fact can hardly account for the divergence in national experience. Because of the divergence in national experience, floating currencies served as a necessary shock absorber for the world economy. Without them, payments imbalances would have been far worse, and protectionist reactions—which in fact were largely avoided—would have been irresistible. Thus, flexible exchange rates can surely be credited with preserving an open world economy during this period.

It is possible that flexible exchange rates made it more difficult to control inflation in countries such as Britain and Italy, although avoidance of tariff protection or new exchange controls is no small contribution toward that end. But by the same token, flexible exchange rates contributed to the success of anti-inflation policies in other countries. This is simply a manifestation of the "bottling up" effect whereby, under flexible exchange rates, each country has to live with more of the consequences of its own behavior and actions; it cannot so easily export the consequences of its policies as it can under fixed rates.

Another source of divergence among countries was their response to the 1974–1975 world recession. The recession was led by the major countries—the United States, Japan, Germany, and Britain. Many developing countries and some smaller industrial countries cushioned the impact of the recession on their own economies (and thereby the depth of the recession itself) by continuing their policies of growth and by borrowing heavily abroad to finance it. Still other countries pursued an economic policy between these extremes.

The United States recovered from the recession with some vigor. Recovery in Japan, Germany, and Britain was more sluggish. The recovery faltered everywhere in 1976. German industrial production, for example, did not return to its 1973 peak until 1977, and in Britain and Japan 1973 levels were not restored until 1978. The United States pressed ahead with new expansionary policies in 1977 and tried, at first unsuccessfully, to persuade other major countries to do the same. This involved the much touted locomotive theory, under which the largest and financially strongest national economies—the United States, Japan, and Germany—would lead the rest of the world out of the recession and by so doing would relieve the severe financial pressures that by late 1976 were besetting many countries. A resumption of the growth of these major economies was necessary to avoid politically dangerous economic stagnation elsewhere, a revival of protectionism, and the prospect of large-scale default on outstanding debts that would have had major repercussions on the international banking system.

US expansion in 1977 relieved the condition of many other countries. But failure to persuade Germany and Japan to join it in expansionist policies led to further divergence among national economic developments, which in turn was largely responsible for the large payments imbalances of 1977–1978. The United States developed exceptionally large current account deficits, while Germany and especially Japan developed large surpluses. These developments in turn played a major role in the exchange rate movements in that period. A closer coordination of economic policies would have avoided some of the exchange market turbulence in 1977–1978. Such coordination was finally achieved at the Bonn Summit meeting of July 1978, and that agreement contributed importantly to the corrective adjustment in subsequent years.[9]

There were occasions in 1977–1978 when exchange rates moved sharply and by substantial amounts in short periods of time. Exchange markets were extremely nervous, and both news and rumors moved exchange rates around erratically. Expectations were fragile rather than solidly based on economic fundamentals. In addition, there was much talk about virtuous and vicious circles, carrying the suggestion not that flexible rates had some partial feedbacks onto domestic prices, which had long been known, but that they were unstable, with depreciation leading to inflation leading to depreciation, in an endless, nonconverging spiral.

We have known for a long time that foreign trade takes one to two years to respond in volume to relative price changes. Are we collectively too impatient to wait for such adjustment processes to work? Do we need instant results? If so, there may be strong psychological, not economic, reasons for eschewing movements in exchange rates. But what are the practical alternatives?

There is no feasible alternative so long as the world economy is subject to major turbulence. The European Monetary System (EMS) is a regional arrangement designed to provide a "zone of stability" in a world that by implication is full of instability. However, even the EMS sensibly contains much more flexibility than earlier proposals for European monetary integration, especially the proposals put forward in 1969–1970 and given a strong political endorsement then by leaders in the European Community. Despite this greater flexibility, Britain declined to join the EMS, and Italy received a special dispensation under the EMS, with a much wider exchange rate band than that of other members.

Exchange rate flexibility must be managed to help stabilize expectations and to break psychological bandwagon movements. A target zone for exchange rates, such as the EMS has adopted, could help to stabilize expectations if it is credible. But it cannot be credible over a period of time so long as the relevant inflation rates diverge. Thus, we are perforce left with a somewhat ad hoc, judgmental system of managed floating. The monetary authorities should strive to limit radical and unjustified movements in exchange rates, which means that they will sometimes have to take large, open positions in foreign currencies. Their interventions can and should be reversed later, so as to allow exchange rates to move over time in response to market pressures. On the whole, this has been the strategy that the leading monetary authorities have followed, in collaboration with one another, and on the whole, it has worked reasonably well.

Notes

1. See Triffin (1978: 12, 14). In the late 1940s, however, Triffin advocated a foreign exchange auction system for nonessential transactions as a technique for eliminating the exchange controls then so prevalent (see Triffin 1966: 166–68).

2. A useful review of the recent literature on flexible exchange rates can be found in Goldstein (1980).

3. "Money illusion" may in fact not involve an illusion at all. Wage earners may be willing to suffer a decline in real wages brought about through a rise in the local currency prices of imported goods even when they are not willing to accept a decline in nominal wages. For a discussion of the phenomenon, see Cooper (1977: 160ff.).

4. See Branson (1980) for a formal exposition of this adjustment mechanism.

5. These interrelations have begun to be recognized. See for example, Dornbusch (1980) and Branson's (1980) comments on it.

6. This possibility has been emphasized by Wilson and Takacs (1980).

7. International monetary reserves grew from $79 billion to $159 billion during this period, and foreign liabilities of commercial banks grew from $121 billion to $217 billion (Triffin 1978: 4).

8. In fact, the real price of Saudi marker crude rose about 30 percent between 1970 and mid–1973, on the basis of the US GNP deflator.

9. These issues are discussed more extensively in Cooper (1982).

References

Branson, William H. 1980. *Asset Markets and Relative Prices in Exchange Rate Determination.* Princeton Reprints in International Finance No. 20, Princeton, New Jersey: International Finance Section, Princeton University.

Cooper, Richard N. 1977. "Monetary Theory and Policy in an Open Economy." In A. Lindbeck and J. Myhrman, eds., *Flexible Exchange Rates and Stabilization Policy.* London: Macmillan.

———. 1982. "Global Economic Policy in a World of Energy Shortage." In J. A. Pechman and N. J. Simler, eds., *Economics in the Public Service.* New York: Norton.

Dornbusch, Rudiger. 1980. "Exchange Rate Economics: Where Do We Stand?" *Brookings Papers on Economic Activity* 1.

Friedman, Milton. 1953. "The Case for Flexible Exchange Rates." In *Essays in Positive Economics.* Chicago: University of Chicago Press.

Goldstein, Morris. 1980. *Have Flexible Exchange Rates Handicapped Macroeconomic Policy?* Special Papers in International Economics No. 14, Princeton, New Jersey: International Finance Section, Princeton University.

Sohmen, Egon. 1961. *Flexible Exchange Rates: Theory and Controversy.* Chicago: University of Chicago Press.

Triffin, Robert. 1966. *The World Money Maze.* New Haven: Yale University Press.

——. 1978. *Gold and the Dollar Crisis: Yesterday and Tomorrow.* Essays in International Finance No. 132, Princeton, New Jersey: International Finance Section, Princeton University.

Wilson, John, and Wendy Takacs. 1980. "Expectations and the Adjustment of Trade Flows Under Floating Exchange Rates: Leads, Lags and the J-Curve." Federal Reserve, International Finance Discussion Paper # 160, April.

5   The Balance-of-Payments Adjustment Process

Outside of a controlled economy, economic decisions concerning what to produce and what to buy are made by millions of decision-making units—families, firms, governments of many levels. It would be surprising indeed if these economic decisions, independently arrived at, resulted in continuous balance in the international payments between the numerous countries of the world economy in which these decisions are taken. Some factors must be brought into play to influence these decisions in such a way as to preserve balance in international payments or to restore it when it is disturbed. These factors are called the balance-of-payments adjustment process.

In a tradition that is now increasingly remote in time, the adjustment process was regarded as automatic—it was called the adjustment "mechanism"—but in today's world of managed mixed economies the adjustment process is also managed. It must therefore be described in terms of the instruments of policy under the influence or control of governments bent on determining the course of national economies. Three broad types of adjustment process can be distinguished according to the instruments that are used to bring payments into balance: management of aggregate money income, management of exchange rates between national currencies, and management of policies designed to influence specific international transactions—the last being designated "controls," although that term is used here to include taxes on particular classes of international transactions, such as imports or capital flows, as well as quantitative restrictions and licensing of foreign exchange.

Most of this paper is concerned with the second of these categories, exchange rates. But since there are still widespread reservations about

Committee for Economic Development, 1973.

frequent changes in exchange rates, it is worth considering first the alternatives: aggregate demand management and use of controls. Then I turn to the question of exchange rates in the context of the current debate over improvements in the adjustment process.

Adjustment with Fixed Exchange Rates

Changes in Aggregate Demand

With exchange rates irretrievably fixed among different national currencies, recourse to some combination of changes in aggregate demand and imposition (or removal) of controls is necessary to preserve balance in international payments. Controls for balance-of-payments reasons have a relatively short history. Changes in aggregate money demand represented the mechanism—largely automatic—that prevailed before World War I. The classical adjustment mechanism worked something like this: Whenever the total foreign payments by the residents of one country exceeded their total receipts, the national money supply (gold under the gold standard) would decline. This in turn would lead to a rise in interest rates, a drop in domestic demand, and—perhaps after a lag—a fall in domestic prices. All these developments would help correct the imbalance—the first by retarding capital outflows or attracting capital inflow, the last two factors by leading to a reduction in imports and an increase in exports. The mechanism, moreover, was symmetric: A country with a payments surplus would experience a rise in its money supply, with corrective effects opposite of those just described.

As a description of relations among national economies, this classical mechanism is badly dated. But it is nonetheless of contemporary interest, for it is the mechanism that in essence operates *within* countries even today. An advantage of the general way in which the adjustment problem was posed in the opening paragraph is that it draws attention to the fact that the adjustment problem is not peculiarly an *international* problem; it arises also among regions within a country and even in individual towns or counties. When trade and payments take place freely among regions within a country in the absence of controls, then the only adjustment mechanism available is that which relies on movements in money income. These in turn influence regional levels of demand and movements of capital and labor between regions. We are not accustomed to identifying regional balance-of-payments problems, for among other things we do not keep regional balance-of-payments accounts or regional figures on "reserves."

But it might be said that New England had an acute balance-of-payments problem in the 1950s, when national demand shifted strongly away from New England's traditional "export" product, cotton textiles, as a result of the introduction of synthetics and the rapid growth of competitive capacity in the American South. For many years New England was a "depressed" area, as money incomes fell sufficiently to keep New England's payments position with the rest of the country in balance.

This analogy is relevant to the present discussions within Europe, looking to eventual monetary unification. With controls on payments generally barred, payments imbalances among European countries will then look much like regional imbalances within the United States, and they will require for correction a similar combination of alternations in money income (leading to regional booms and depressions) and inter-regional factor movements.

One strongly equilibrating factor within the United States, and indeed within all modern economies, is the presence of a national fiscal system, which automatically transfers funds from boom regions to depressed regions through the passive mechanism of differential changes in tax collections (as money incomes fall in a region, national tax collections also fall) and through the active mechanisms of social insurance, unemployment compensation, and "regional" policies. These national fiscal effects greatly mitigate the impact on money incomes of potential payments imbalances among regions.

The reason for mentioning these factors here is to draw attention to the kinds of changes that will be required if European countries are to unify their currencies and if the leading industrial countries were to commit themselves to a world economic order that forbids both changes in exchange rates and the use of controls on international transactions. The international mobility of capital and labor is not such that adjustment to payments imbalances would take place smoothly with relatively little economic pain in the next decade or two—even within Europe. Indeed, capital movements might well be perverse, with capital leaving depressed regions (nations) for better local markets. Thus extensive "regional" policies would be required, possibly supplemented by outright fiscal transfers among regions, as suggested. In brief, an adjustment mechanism that relies exclusively or even extensively on alterations in money incomes flies in the face of the strong national commitment in all modern economies to maintain full employment with some measure of price stability; both commitments would have to be abandoned at the *national* level with a world economy based on fixed exchange rates without controls. We are not likely for some time to have either the international factor mobility or the international political cohesion to make such a system work.

One hope remains. It rests on the factual assumption that payments imbalances in today's world arise largely, if not wholly, from misconceived divergences in national monetary policies. Under a global regime of fixed exchange rates without controls there would necessarily be one monetary policy for the "world" of nations that adhered to this regime, and under those circumstances payments imbalances might not arise, even in incipient form. This is ultimately an empirical question and one that is extraordinarily difficult to resolve decisively from historical information (because all payments imbalances are fundamentally monetary in character, if not in origin). But I believe this is grasping at straws. The hope is misplaced. There are too many real disturbances in the world—arising from technological change, from differential growth in per capita national incomes (starting from very different levels), from divergent demographic trends, from the exhaustion and discovery of natural resources, and from a host of other factors—to be confident that, if we simply harmonized national monetary policies, the adjustment problem under the constraint of full employment would go away.

Controls on International Transactions

Controls on international transactions have historically been used to reduce payments deficits in wartime. Since the 1930s, controls have frequently been used in peacetime as well, and indeed they were the main instrument of payments adjustment in the early 1950s, during the dollar shortage. When they are imposed with care, controls can succeed in their objective of reducing international payments. Import tariffs have persisted for years and have not been undercut in their trade effects by smuggling. Import quotas, such as the US oil import quotas, can also be effective in damping down particular imports. Nonetheless, an adjustment process that relies on controls is subject to some severe disadvantages. First of all, because controls typically fall on particular classes of transactions, they lead to inefficiency in the allocation of resources, resulting in a loss of economic welfare. Second, by creating economic rewards for evasion of the controls, controls lead to illegal activity with a pervasive corrupting effect on business and government and on an honest citizenry. Third, partly because of this, controls in the absence of strong enforcement are eroded in the long run. In many cases it will also be necessary to extend the controls to transactions that are not at first covered but that represent close substitutes for the controlled transactions—as when in the United States the Interest Equalization Act of 1963 was gradually extended to the Mandatory Control Program of 1968. Fourth, when the course of a national economy under fixed exchange rates results in an ever greater deterioration or improvement in trade competitiveness, the tensions created by growing imbalances will eventually become too great to be covered even by severe controls and must in the end be rectified by a change in the exchange rate anyway. Many less developed countries have attempted to preserve payments balance in the face of growing underlying disequilibrium by a continuous extension and tightening of controls, finding only that the above weaknesses became so blatant that the controls were finally shed in favor of an adjustment in the exchange rate.

Use of Exchange Rates for Adjustment

Floating Exchange Rates

If neither money demand adjustment nor adjustment through controls is desirable in today's world, that leaves only the third possible adjustment process, reliance on changes in exchange rates. One might therefore go the whole way and introduce a regime of flexible exchange rates, which might be called a no—par value system to distinguish it from the various par value systems of exchange rates to be discussed. Under a no—par value system, exchange rates would, in principle, be allowed to float freely, determined by "market" forces. Prospective imbalances in payments would exercise upward or downward pressures on a given country's exchange rate in the market, and any excess demand for foreign exchange would automatically be eliminated by a movement in the exchange rate, much as is the case with equity prices or prices on the commodity exchanges today. Balance-of-payments deficits or surpluses would never be observed.

The difficulty with this kind of system is that governments are not likely to allow the exchange rate to be completely determined by market forces. In many areas they simply cannot do so because by the nature of their own activities they are themselves important transactors in foreign exchange, and like any transactor, they would from time to time "speculate" by running up or down their foreign exchange balances. But of course for a large transactor to do this influences the exchange rate. Moreover, the exchange rate for many countries is, like market interest rates, a highly important economic variable, one that simply cannot be left completely free to move by a government whose citizenry holds it responsible for proper management of the economy. For this reason as well, governments will want to retain the freedom to intervene in exchange markets for the purpose of influencing the exchange rate. As long as this is so, a no–par value regime requires rules of intervention if countries are not to intervene at cross purposes, one country trying to push up a given exchange rate between two currencies while the other country is trying to push it down, each for its own domestic economic reasons. Seen in this way, as a regime that requires rules of currency intervention, a no–par value regime differs little operationally from a par value regime with limited flexibility. I therefore turn to such regimes, which provide the substance of current international discussion.

Par Value Systems

It has become conventional to consider three different types of par value exchange rate regimes with limited flexibility: (1) wide bands of flexibility around parity, (2) a period of floating rates between two periods of fixed parity, and (3) gliding parities, that is, an arrangement whereby the parity moves relatively frequently and by relatively small amounts over time, although in any short period of time there is a fixed parity. A regime of gliding parities in turn can be governed either by automatic criteria for changes in parity, or the changes can be left to the discretion of some authority, national or international.

Before discussing the merits of these alternative techniques for introducing flexibility into a par value regime, it is appropriate to ask what is wrong with a continuation of the present regime, laid down in 1944 in the Bretton Woods Agreement. The Bretton Woods regime calls for a relatively narrow band of flexibility around parity, relatively infrequent changes in the parity, and changes that, when they come, are relatively large in size—large enough to correct a "fundamental disequilibrium" and in practice generally more than 10 percent. This adjustable peg system, as it has been called, is subject to increasing strain and even unworkability in today's world for three related reasons.

First, a payments imbalance that is clear and measurably large invites large-scale speculation on a change in exchange rates that is disruptive both to money markets and to exchange markets. Second, the fixed parity becomes a symbol of financial rectitude, so governments are reluctant to change it, even when the need is indicated. Indeed, the experience of a number of governments bears out the political costs associated with altering the parity. Third, large changes, rarely under 10 percent, of a major economic variable administer a substantial jolt to the economy in question, as literally overnight thousands of calculations of profitability are thrown out of kilter, often by an economically decisive amount.

For all these reasons, governments have been loathe to change exchange parities, procrastinating even in the face of large and sustained payments imbalance. In the end, of course, most countries in deficit must devalue their currencies, for they will otherwise exhaust their reserves or distort their economies intolerably. Even those sanctions, however, do not apply to a country in surplus or to a reserve currency country, both of which can finance deficits for long periods of time but only by imposing cumulative strains on the rest of the world. These asymmetries aggravate but are not the fundamental source of the weaknesses of the adjustable peg system.

There is widespread and increasing recognition of these weaknesses, as evidenced by the 1970 IMF report on the adjustment process, by the decisions of Canada, Germany, and Britain to "float" their exchange rates in 1970, 1971, and 1972, respectively, and by the Smithsonian Agreement of December 1971 to permit a substantially wider band within which exchange rates can move freely and by its call for prompt discussions to improve the adjustment process further. But, although the recognition of need for improvement is widespread, there is to date no consensus on the nature of the improvement. It is in this context that the par value regimes with limited flexibility call for careful consideration.

Before I turn to alternative techniques for introducing greater flexibility, it seems useful first to consider the broad principles that should govern a system of limited flexibility. I take for granted the primacy of domestic economic objectives concerning the maintenance of full employment and a reasonable degree of price stability. As we have already seen, without these concerns the adjustment process could operate through changes in aggregate money demand.

An important principle to be established concerns whether, in a world of uncertainty about the presence and extent of balance-of-payments disequilibrium, there should be a presumption for or against changes in exchange rates. The Bretton Woods system errs on the side of exchange rate stability; that is, parities are not altered until it is clearly necessary, which usually means later than they should have been changed. Much greater flexibility, however, would introduce an error of the opposite sort—exchange rates would change even on some occasions in which they might not be warranted. The difficulties that the Bretton Woods system has encountered suggests that we should be willing to accept some error in this direction in order to avoid the past errors of large uncorrected disequilibria.

A second principle of concern is whether the same exchange rate regime needs to be applicable to all countries. The different economic circumstances of different countries suggest a priori that the same regime should not be imposed uniformly. Many countries may prefer to establish relatively fixed exchange rates between their currencies and those of their leading trade partner while remaining relatively indifferent to fluctuations vis-à-vis countries with whom they have less economic contact. But if countries are allowed some scope for selection of the exchange rate regime, what are the limitations that must be placed on the choice of individual countries to ensure that the system as a whole is workable? In fixing its exchange rate vis-à-vis some particular currency, a country in effect accepts the implication that the adjustment process will operate through changes in money demand, or else it must be prepared to impose controls from time to time. A regime of greater flexibility among leading currencies, each with a number of satellite currencies attached to it, has unpleasant overtones of economic blocs and currency imperialism. This suggests the desirability of some international surveillance of the choices made by individual countries, with a view to allowing them to alter their choice at periodic intervals if the initial choice no longer seems to be in the best interests of the countries in question.

A third principle that must be addressed concerns the sanctions to be applied to countries that violate the established rules. This question in today's context applies especially to countries in payments surplus and to the United States as the reserve currency country. Most countries in payments deficit are under the natural sanction of running out of reserves. But even these countries may apply trade or payments controls in violation of international undertakings, and it would be desirable to consider sanctions in these cases as well. For countries in continuous surplus, the sanction of nonconvertibility of the foreign exchange they acquire in the course of running their surplus has been suggested. It has also been suggested that other countries might impose discriminatory taxes on the exports of such countries. Presumably any sanctions of this nature would be applied only under international supervision. The point of an effective system of international sanctions, of course, is that they will never have to be used. A process of international consultation and review, most plausibly centered in the IMF but substantially different from the present annual reviews, should be established to provide a forum for periodic high-level discussions of the problems created for the system as a whole by large imbalances, both deficit and surplus.

Techniques for Achieving Limited Flexibility

Wider Bands
As noted above, a number of different techniques have been suggested for introducing greater flexibility into a par value system of exchange rates. Following the Smithsonian Agreement of December 1971, many countries widened the band of permissible fluctuation of their exchange rates around parity from the customary ± 1 percent or less to $\pm 2\frac{1}{4}$ percent. This widening represents a useful contribution to the adjustment process, but it is not by itself sufficient. The useful contribution is in permitting a greater separation between changes in exchange parities and changes in the actual rates prevailing in the foreign exchange market. With wider bands, parities may in principle be changed by consequential amounts without any change in actual exchange rates, and this possibility should inhibit undesirable speculation on changes in parities. For this to happen, however, the parities must be required to change well before market exchange rates reach the limits of the band, which in turn requires either a wide band of permissible flunctuation or frequent and relatively small parity changes.

Once the market rate reaches the floor or ceiling of the enlarged band, as it will inevitably do if parities remain unchanged in the face of large disturbances or of divergent trends in different national economies, then the many defects of the adjustable peg system will reappear. Some improvement in the method for changing parities must still be undertaken, even with the wider band.

Wider bands serve another, quite different function. By allowing market exchange rates to swing by a greater amount than before, they help to preserve some autonomy for the national use of monetary policy in pursuit of domestic economic objectives. With absolutely fixed exchange rates, divergent national monetary policies would be difficult if not impossible, for any country trying to maintain tight money would find itself swamped by funds flowing in from abroad, for instance. Allowing the exchange rate to appreciate under pressure of such an inflow will inhibit further inflows in search of the higher yields. But this again, while useful, is not a substitute for improvement in the adjustment process itself.

Temporary Floats
A second technique that has been suggested for introducing greater flexibility is to allow countries to permit currencies to "float" freely in the marketplace for a temporary period once it becomes clear that the old parity no longer represents an equilibrium exchange rate. This technique

was used by Germany in 1969, when the mark was permitted to float for about six weeks before a new par value was established. And in a sense it was also used between August and December 1971, when many countries ceased to provide clear market support for their currencies until the Smithsonian Agreement reestablished an agreed set of "central" rates. Finally, Canada embarked on this course in 1950, when there was considerable doubt about just what the right exchange rate for the Canadian dollar should be; but in that case the "temporary" float lasted eleven years.

A period of temporary floating has some clear advantages over a large and direct change from one par value to another. But it also has some disadvantages as an adjustment process. By the time the currency is allowed to float, a substantial disequilibrium has become established, so that, first, it is quite clear in which direction the currency will float, speculation is encouraged, and financial and exchange rate markets are disrupted, as under the adjustable peg system. Second, once a substantial disequilibrium has arisen, the jolt to the national economy from the required change in exchange rate will be substantial—unless the float is spread over a rather long period. A temporary float has the advantage that counterspeculation may set in soon after the float is inaugurated, so the speculative gains (and hence national losses) will not be so great as under a discrete change in exchange rates; the impact of the change on the economy will also be somewhat cushioned. On the other hand, this same phenomenon means that the market-determined rates reached under the float will not, in the short run, represent a useful guide to what the exchange rate should be in the absence of speculative movements and countermovements. It is far preferable, when possible, to *anticipate* the need for adjustment and to prevent a large disequilibrium from arising. Temporary floats are suitable when that is not possible but offer an inferior solution when it is possible.

Gliding Parities
If parities are to be altered before it is entirely clear that a country's payments position is in lasting disequilibrium yet are not to be changed unnecessarily, a number of questions arise concerning how these two objectives, not fully compatible in a world of uncertainty, are to be attained. What criteria are to be used to indicate whether a given parity should be changed? Should certain quantitative indicators be used to indicate change, and if so, what should they be? If the quantitative indicators are to be qualified by the exercise of judgment, whose judgment is to be used? If parities are to be altered "flexibly," what size should the parity changes be,

and how frequently should they be made? And how much scope is there for differences among countries in these regards?

These apparently technical questions are at the heart of present disagreement between the United States and the European (and most other?) countries on the question of the adjustment process. Past experience suggests that a purely permissive environment on changes in exchange rates will result in changes that are too infrequent, too late, and—ultimately when they come—too large. Moreover, as noted, there is little need for countries in surplus to revalue their currencies. The United States therefore has proposed that certain indicators be used to suggest the need for adjustment. While various indicators are possible—recent movements in spot and forward exchange rates have been suggested—the US proposal focuses on reserve levels as the best indicator of a country's payments position and hence its need to adjust. If used, they should be supplemented by consideration of any rapid *changes* in reserves to avoid destabilizing overshooting in the adjustment of rates. Other countries apparently object to anything so mechanical, and they particularly object to using reserve movements as an indicator on the grounds that these can reflect factors—notably short-term capital movements—that should not in their views trigger an adjustment process.

The mechanical reliance on indicators can be mitigated by making them "presumptive" indicators of the need for adjustment rather than automatic. In other words, the indicators could be tempered by judgment, and if there seem to be special reasons for the change in reserves, the indicators could be ignored. But whose judgment is to be used? That depends partly on the nature of the sanctions. But it would be desirable to have procedures for international consultation on this question. The country that chooses to ignore any indicated need to adjust might be called on to explain its reasons to an international forum, logically lodged in the IMF. Alternatively, the judgment on the need to adjust could be applied in the first instance by an international group, which would be charged with reaching an overall judgment on the desirability of applying adjustment measures. In addition to indicators, it might also use more formal econometric techniques, such as those that apparently lay behind the IMF's recommended parity changes in late 1971, which take into account the state of the domestic economy of each country and of its leading trade partners. These could be supplemented by qualitative assessments by the IMF staff, reached in consultation with the country concerned *and* with its major trade partners. The country in question need not take this international judgment as final, but a strong presumption would be created for it to act on the recommendations. Failure to do so would risk invocation of the sanctions.

Which of these two approaches is used depends in part on the nature of the parity changes agreed on. If parity changes are to be small (the advantages of which are that they can be made without changing market rates by enough to encourage speculation and that they can be readily reversed with minimal cost), they must also be quite frequent (e.g., weekly or monthly) in order to achieve the degree of adjustment that might be required. And if they are to be frequent, they cannot be keyed to an elaborate international consultative procedure *before* the changes. Rather, there would have to be an international review process to assess the extent to which a country's changes (or nonchanges) were consistent with international objectives. The existence of this ex post review process would presumably influence the actions of national decision makers. Prior consultation and international assessment would inevitably dictate less frequent and hence, if necessary, larger alteration in parities—and thus would be attended by some of the disadvantages of the present adjustable peg system, although they could be attenuated.

A further question arises in connection with any kind of gliding parity: Are the rules to apply to all countries, including the United States? The applicability to all countries other than the United States would not be strictly necessary. As noted in the section on management of money demand for adjustment, some countries might willingly accept a high degree of exchange stability with respect to their leading trade partner, including the consequences. Others may be more willing and able to rely on controls on international transactions for adjustment in the short run and thus may prefer something similar to the present adjustable peg system, with controls used for payments adjustment over a number of years, ultimately replaced by changes in exchange rates. Such a regime is more manageable for a country that does not have well-developed capital markets and can maintain rather tight exchange controls, so that movements of capital into and out of the country are not easy. Even then, as a number of countries have learned, much capital movement can take place through "leads and lags" in the trade accounts.

When it comes to the United States, the problem arises because of the present use of the US dollar as an intervention currency, which places the initiative for changes in the parity between the dollar and any other currency in the hands of the authorities governing the other currency. Thus, if the dollar-mark parity is altered, it is the Bundesbank, not the Federal Reserve, that must change the intervention points for the mark against the dollar. A certain technical convenience thus arises if the dollar remains passive. But that has the twofold disadvantage: (1) The dollar enjoys only half the flexibility of other currencies *within* the band of fluctuation around parity; and (2) the exchange rate of the dollar may not be changed as much as is desirable if the United States is in overall deficit. The first disadvantage—which other countries may consider an advantage, given the preponderance of the United States in the world economy and the evident desire for as much exchange rate stability as possible—can be eliminated only if the present system of market intervention is changed to eliminate the asymmetric position of the dollar, for example, by shifting to a multiple-currency intervention system, such as that now being attempted within the European Community. The second disadvantage can be eliminated by formal agreements among all central banks on how to handle a change in the par value of the dollar, agreements that would themselves pose no technical difficulty.

If the dollar were not retained in its intervention role, it would be necessary to devise general rules of intervention for all countries; otherwise two countries might find themselves intervening in the same market at cross-purposes, or one country might find that the market intervention by another country conflicts with its economic objectives. One attack on this problem would be to prohibit *all* intervention except at the floor and ceiling of the permissible band of fluctuation; and at the floor and ceiling both countries concerned could intervene cooperatively. But this restriction fails to allow for the point made earlier: The exchange rate is too important an economic variable for most countries to willingly leave entirely free, except perhaps in a regime with a narrow band of fluctuation. Thus more complicated rules are needed. One that has been suggested is that only countries whose currencies are below their parities with other currencies may intervene; but this too might occasionally conflict with the legitimate aims of the countries with the more appreciated currencies.

On the whole, it would be desirable for the dollar to be subject to the same rules for "gliding" as other currencies; it is less clear that the advantages of symmetry within the margins of fluctuation around parity outweigh the advantages of simplicity provided under a single intervention currency.

Criteria for Assessing the Merits of Alternative Adjustment Regimes

Will Limited Flexibility Work?
Heavy emphasis on exchange rate adjustment presupposes that payments positions can in fact be adjusted through changes in exchange rates. Yet

this point has been doubted by some observers, who contend that, for a variety of reasons (e.g., heavy dependence on foreign sources of foodstuffs and raw materials or the oligopolistic structure of most industries), neither demand nor supply is highly responsive to relative price movements in today's world.

This important question can be addressed under two different headings. The first deals with those cases in which imbalance in international payments has arisen, or will arise, because of divergent movements in prices and costs among countries. In these cases changes in exchange rates simply reverse the factors that gave rise to the problem in the first place. If price responsiveness is low, differential rates of inflation will take longer than otherwise to produce payments imbalances; but if they do, changes in exchange rates should be able to correct the imbalances. Indeed, the original proposals for gliding parities were designed precisely to deal with the case in which modern economies experienced modestly divergent price movements under fixed exchange rates. (Exchange rate changes cannot, of course, ordinarily correct the underlying causes of divergent movements in national price and cost levels; they can correct only their balance-of-payments consequences. In particular, if inflation in some countries arises from fundamentally incompatible claims on national output, there is nothing exchange rate changes can do to correct the underlying problem, and in this case currency depreciation runs some risk of accelerating the rate of inflation that inevitably will occur if the authorities attempt to maintain full employment.)

The second heading concerns those cases in which payments imbalances arise for reasons other than divergent price movements—e.g., because of technological change, exhaustion or discovery of natural resources, demographic trends, acts of national policy leading to greater or less spending abroad, and a host of other factors. Here, changes in exchange rates are relied on to alter the balance in goods and services by enough to compensate for the disequilibrating factors, and of course that does presuppose an adequate degree of price sensitivity. Although the evidence is not conclusive on the point, therefore leaving some room for debate, experience does suggest that changes in exchange rates are able to influence the trade balance. The French devaluations of 1958 and 1969 were followed by substantial improvements in France's trade position, and the British devaluation of 1967 and the Canadian devaluation of 1962 had similar consequences, although after a lag of a year or more. German revaluation of the mark in 1969 seems to have reduced Germany's trade surplus, after allowance is made for the enormous deterioration in the US trade balance during the subsequent two years. Moreover, a study of two dozen currency devaluations in less developed countries, whose economies are generally less flexible than those of developed countries, also suggests that currency depreciation improves the trade balance most of the time, although a few exceptions were noted. The accumulation of evidence thus suggests that changes in exchange rates will work but perhaps only after a substantial lag. This is another reason for suggesting that changes in rates should not be delayed as long as they have been in the past, allowing substantial imbalances to develop. Furthermore, one must again consider the alternatives. If changes in exchange rates will not work, neither will other devices (e.g., import surcharges) that rely on the price mechanism. Thus we would be thrown back onto adjustment of aggregate money demand or quantitative restrictions on trade and other international transactions. The costs of both of these alternatives are sufficiently great to warrant giving exchange rates a fair test.

Does It Facilitate or Impede Domestic Economic Stabilization?
In an integrated world economy of the kind that is fostered by a system of fixed exchange rates without controls, economic disturbances are transmitted rapidly and strongly from one country to another. Flexible exchange rates tend to insulate countries from one another to a greater extent, although not wholly. A regime of limited flexibility involving rather wide exchange rate margins and a gliding parity would provide greater insulation than a system of fixed rates but less than a system of freely floating rates.

The implications of these generalizations for domestic economic stabilization vary with the source of the disturbance. It follows that, if an economic disturbance arises outside a country, it is much more likely to disturb economic equilibrium within a country under a regime of fixed exchange rates than under a regime with some flexibility. This fact induced both Canada (in 1970) and Germany (in 1971) to allow their currencies to float; both wanted to resist the importation of inflationary pressures from the United States. The task of domestic economic stabilization is made easier if disturbances from outside are reduced or eliminated. On the other hand, when disturbances arise principally within the country, a certain "automatic" stabilization is achieved under a regime of fixed exchange rates without controls, for the disturbance is quickly transmitted abroad and is thus spread over a larger territory, reducing its impact on the originating country. For example, inflationary pressures in the United States were reduced by the large growth of inflation-induced imports into the United

States in the late 1960s and early 1970s; imports helped first to satisfy burgeoning demand and then to inhibit price increases, as the United States drew in resources from the rest of the world. The same factors that transmitted US inflationary pressures abroad mitigated the impact of inflation in the United States. Similarly, when Germany experienced a mild recession in 1967, much of the slump in demand was "exported" through a decline in import orders and a sharp rise in exports. A system with greater exchange rate flexibility, in contrast, tends to "bottle up" the economic disturbance in the country of origin, causing greater difficulty there.

One of the sources of disagreement over exchange rate flexibility concerns the desirability of spreading as opposed to bottling up economic disturbances. A case can be made for each side in the debate. In a world in which all leading governments are expected to maintain domestic economies on an even keel, however, the weight of the argument perhaps tips, morally, to the regime that places the burden of policy response at the sources of the disturbance, i.e., to an exchange rate regime with some flexibility. This will put greater pressure on national governments to take prompt *domestic* measures to maintain economic stability at home, and that in turn will generally reduce the degree of economic instability in the world economy as a whole.

Currency Speculation
It must be asked of any exchange rate regime whether it encourages or discourages disruptive currency speculation. Speculation often provides advance notice to authorities that there is a serious payments disequilibrium which they have failed to correct promptly. But heavy speculation can be disruptive to money and foreign exchange markets even under these circumstances, and there is also a risk that speculative movements of funds may take place when alteration in exchange rates is not the appropriate policy response to the underlying economic situation (e.g., when a country is running a large payments surplus because of a slump in domestic economic activity). An exchange rate regime that relies extensively on changes in exchange rates of a magnitude that permits substantial profit from anticipating changes accurately will of course evoke much speculation. Speculation can be reduced (1) by having exchange rate changes come so infrequently or irregularly (sometimes up, sometimes down) that their occurrence is always a "surprise" or (2) by having the changes of such small magnitude that there is little to be gained by successful speculation (after allowance for transactions costs). The last objective, in turn, can be

achieved by having small changes in parities or by divorcing changes in parities from changes in actual market rates, for example, with a wide band and small parity changes made well before the floor or ceiling of the band is reached. Small but steady changes in rates over time encourage the holding of currencies whose rate is expected to appreciate, but this type of speculation can be offset by correspondingly modest changes in interest rate differentials between assets denominated in the currency expected to appreciate and comparable assets denominated in other currencies. To this extent, of course, the monetary policy of each country must be influenced by monetary conditions in the rest of the world. But that is inevitable under any system that attempts to maintain some degree of stability in exchange rates in the absence of really effective controls on capital movements.

The US Proposals for Adjustment

In November 1972 the United States submitted a paper to the Committee of Twenty outlining its general views on the adjustment process. It is therefore of interest to see how the US government proposes to deal with the issues raised in this paper.

The US proposals are general, so a summary of them must necessarily also be general. The proposals focus on the *results* of an adequate adjustment process—i.e., on the maintenance of reasonable balance in international payments—rather than on the exact measures for achieving those results. It suggests the establishment of a set of indicators based on a target level of reserves for each country. If actual reserves deviate too radically from this target in either direction, the country would be expected to take corrective steps. Use of exchange rates is encouraged, but not compelled:

The purpose of a reserve-indicator system is to provide strong incentives for countries to act in limited steps, using a variety of tools suited to their circumstances before their situation becomes so urgent as to involve international concern and action. Moreover, while countries would at given points be brought under overt international pressure for adjustment, they would still have a range of policy options at their disposal. The range of "acceptable adjustment measures" for the system would, however, be limited to those consistent with market mechanisms and a liberal world trade and payments order. Exchange rate changes are not seen as the only, or necessarily the most desirable, means of adjustment in all cases. (para. 26)

The proposals encourage decontrol of trade and capital movements by countries in payments surplus, but they abjure the imposition of controls by countries in deficit. Interestingly, there is no mention of the use of aggregate money demand for adjustment, although it may be taken as implicit in the paper that, when a country finds itself with excessive domestic demand and a payments deficit, it should take contractionary monetary or fiscal measures, and that a country in a slump with a payments surplus should first take expansionary actions before altering the exchange rate.

The proposals presuppose a system of par values for exchange rates but also encourage much greater exchange rate flexibility than exists under the Bretton Woods Agreement. They condone wider bands of fluctuation around parity, transitional floating from one parity to another, and more frequent changes in parities. Revaluations would be permitted at any time, and devaluations would be permitted at any time reserves were below their target ("base") level. Such changes would remain fully at the discretion of the country in question, but if reserves deviated too far above target (no precise distance is specified), the IMF by way of sanction "might authorize other countries to impose general import taxes or surcharges against the country concerned, there might be a loss of scheduled SDR allocations, or there might be a tax on the country's excess reserve holdings with proceeds to go to development assistance" (para. 24(c)). The sanctions could be avoided if the IMF made a positive finding that the country was pursuing an agreed program of adjustment, which might involve liberalization of import restrictions or capital outflows and increases in untied foreign assistance as well as or instead of currency revaluation.

Thus the proposals are keyed to results, as measured mainly by reserve levels, and they leave a good deal of room for action by individual countries under surveillance and guidance by the international community as embodied in the IMF. Moreover, they are "designed to encourage equilibrium by promoting needed adjustments actively, rather than simply prohibiting unwarranted moves; and ... apply equivalent incentives for adjustment even-handedly to all nations" (para. 8). But the proposals leave most of the details to be worked out either in negotiation or in the actual operation of the system.

Conclusions

The nub of the difficulty is that there is no effective alternative to extensive reliance on changes in exchange rates for the foreseeable future, that the exchange rate is too important an economic variable to be left to "market" forces or to automatic criteria for change or even to be turned over to the discretion of an international organization, but that national governments have in the past allowed large disequilibria to develop before altering exchange rates. The result has been substantial disruption both before and after inevitable adjustment. All of this suggests the need to establish a *presumption* for change by individual countries, with flexible interpretation, room for international consultation and mutual agreement to ignore the presumption, and, ultimately, internationally condoned and supervised sanctions against a country that persists in ignoring the presumption in the face of strong disagreement by other affected nations. The system must apply to all important trading nations, for the immutable fact is that they are, in their economic relationships, highly interdependent. No large country can do just as it wishes, for its actions impinge sharply on the economies of other countries. Some form of international coordination is inevitable.

The US proposals leave the door open to a variety of adjustment measures, but on close inspection these turn out to be few in number and limited in application; in the end, extensive reliance must be placed on changes in exchange rates, and it is well to face that implication squarely. Moreover, the concentration of the US proposals on reserve *levels* as the indicator of disequilibrium contains the possible danger, given the long lags between adjustment measures and response to them, of leading to instability in the movement of reserves and exchange rates. This instability can be avoided by giving some weight to *changes* in reserves as well as to reserve levels. Thus, as recently as 1969, Japan could be said to have had a deficient level of reserves by many reasonable standards, especially relative to its level of trade. The rapid growth of Japanese reserves would not therefore have led to adjustment measures if desired reserve levels had provided the sole criterion for need for adjustment; yet we know now that Japan wildly overshot the mark, something that might have been avoided if the large surpluses had triggered adjustment measures early, even when reserves were below target.

Finally, because of the large amounts of funds that today are ready and able to speculate on changes in exchange rates, any adjustment process that relies on changes in exchange rates must involve considerable flexibility (wide bands with moderately frequent and reasonably small parity changes, frequent and small parity changes, or "temporary" floating prevailing much of the time), or else they will cause periodic currency "crises" that will inevitably tempt governments to impose extensive controls on international transactions from time to time. There is no fully satisfactory way out of this dilemma until the distant day in which the world arrives at one world money and has made the necessary changes to function efficiently under that condition. Greater flexibility seems the lesser of evils in the near future.

References

Bergsten, C. Fred. *Reforming the Dollar: An International Monetary Policy for the United States.* Council on Foreign Relations, 1972, chap. 4.

Cooper, Richard N. *Currency Devaluation in Developing Countries.* Princeton International Finance Section, 1971.

Fellner, William. "The Dollar's Place in the International System: Suggested Criteria for the Appraisal of Emerging Views." *Journal of Economic Literature,* September 1972.

Fleming, J. Marcus. "Towards a New Regime for International Payments." *Journal of International Economics,* September 1972.

Halm, G., ed. *Approaches to Greater Flexibility of Exchange Rates* (The "Bürgenstock Papers"). Princeton, 1970. See especially papers by Cooper, Halm, and Willett.

Hirsch, Fred. "The Exchange Rate Regime: An Analysis and a Possible Scheme." *IMF Staff Papers,* July 1972.

McKinnon, Ronald. *Monetary Theory and Controlled Flexibility of Exchange Rates.* Princeton International Finance Section, 1971.

US Government. "The U.S. Proposals for Using Reserves as an Indicator of the Need for Balance-of-Payments Adjustment," *Economic Report of the President,* January 1973.

Williamson, John: *The Crawling Peg.* Princeton International Finance Section, 1965.

6

IMF Surveillance over
Floating Exchange Rates

UNDER THE amended IMF Articles of Agreement, to take formal effect sometime in 1977, countries are free to adopt any of a variety of arrangements for the exchange rates of their currencies; but whatever arrangements they adopt, they undertake to "avoid manipulating exchange rates or the international monetay system in order to prevent effective balance of payments adjustments or to gain an unfair competitive advantage over other members" (Article IV as revised). The IMF is charged with exercising surveillance with respect to these (as well as other) commitments by member countries. This paper is addressed to the stance that the IMF might take with respect to this new, or rather revised, assignment.

The injunctions themselves raise certain questions. First, is a member country enjoined from exchange-rate action that gives it an unfair competitive advantage against each and every other country? "Unfair" is a weasel-word that permits an affirmative answer to the question, but if that is left aside, the answer must surely be negative; an equilibrium exchange rate may well leave a country with an overwhelming competitive advantage over *some* other countries, which advantage is offset by the position of this rate with respect to other countries. Thus the prohibition must refer to some *average* exchange rate with respect to all other countries. But which average? Different methods of calculation may give quite different results, and no one method seems obviously superior to others.[1] Thus any calculation must of necessity be only rough.

Second, what is the "effective balance-of-payments adjustment" that is not to be prevented? The difficulties with various concepts of the balance of payment are well known, especially for countries with extensive capital and banking transactions with the rest of the world.[2] The most straight-

The New International Monetary System, ed. R. A. Mundell and J. J. Polak (New York: Columbia University Press, 1977), 68–83. Reprinted with permission.

forward interpretation of the injunction is that it requires no change in a country's international reserves, net of changes in the valuation of reserves, or net of official compensatory financing (e.g., activation of swap arrangements or transactions with the IMF) in a stationary world, or no deviation from some targeted growth in reserves in a growing world. This formulation, if it is to allow official intervention in exchange markets, obviously involves some time dimension. For example, there should be no deviation from some targeted growth in reserves over a twelve- to eighteen-month period, or over a three- to five-year period. It also obviously (in a growing world) presupposes that there be some targeted growth in reserves, and that in turn suggests (for global consistency of targets and of exchange-market intervention) that the target be an internationally accepted one and that the total supply of new international reserves be adequate to meet the targeted demand for them, either through a decision to create reserves or through a reserve-creating mechanism that is sufficiently elastic to satisfy the aggregate total of nationally determined demands for reserves. Other chapters in this volume address that ticklish problem.[3] Finally, this formulation of adjustment in payments leaves open a number of questions about the countries whose currencies are held as international reserves by other countries. One feasible approach to this last problem is to treat reserve-currency countries like other countries as far as criteria for payments adjustment are concerned, and to make allowance in their targeted growth in reserves, or in other credit facilities, for the fact that they have highly liquid liabilities to other countries.

A third question about the injunctions concerning exchange-rate manipulation is whether the second one includes the first. Can a country have effective balance-of-payments adjustment and still have an unfair competitive advantage? Are these meant to be two separate injunctions, or only one? Is it permissible for a country to intervene in exchange markets (by selling its own currency) so as to achieve a large trade surplus, for instance, and then restore overall payments balance through official credits to foreigners? In short, does the new IMF Article IV stipulate implicit trade-balance targets as well as the requirement for overall balance in international payments? Is this provision, to push the point further, designed to block the use of expansionary monetary policy under a regime of floating exchange rates, where the channel by which monetary policy influences the demand for domestic output is via a depreciated exchange rate, and if so, why? Other countries not wishing the deflation in demand for their products arising from an appreciating exchange rate can also engage in monetary expansion, restoring the previous rate. Or is the term "manipulation" meant to apply exclusively to intervention in foreign-exchange markets, and not to other actions that may influence exchange rates? The context suggests a broader interpretation.

The guiding principle, it seems to me, should be that in their actions countries should not impose costs on other nations except when that is unavoidable from the nature of the problem being addressed. Dampening of a domestic boom, for example, will lead to a fall in imports from other nations, a fall that may be unwelcome. But if the boom had produced a payments deficit, the fall would be unavoidable. Any remaining corrective action, for example, with respect to their own domestic demand, is up to other nations.

Reasons for Intervention in Exchange Markets

Each individual country would like its exchange rate to move in such a way as to maximize its national welfare, somehow defined. To a first approximation, we can take this to mean some combination of net national output and price stability, where the "netting" of national output is taken to mean not merely net of investment for replacement but also net of all frictional costs associated with the reallocation of resources. On this standard, the welfare-maximizing exchange rate will not in general be the momentary equilibrium rate, that is, the rate that would clear the exchange market at each moment of time, exclusive of speculative positions in the currency. The welfare-maximizing rate will generally show less variability than the momentary equilibrium rate. Perfectly foresighted speculation will bring the two rates together, provided that (a) all frictional social costs are reflected in the price signals to those who decide on the allocation of production and consumption and (b) capital markets are perfect in the sense that risk–adjusted borrowing rates are equated at the margin for all potential speculators as well as investors. Condition (a) will not be met to the extent that labor can be dismissed and will remain unemployed because of downward stickiness in wages or because rational individual search behavior in a world of imperfect information leads to a period of frictional unemployment.

That these two conditions are not in fact met will produce a case in principle for official intervention in exchange markets, even if speculators were accurate in their foresight, exclusive of the official intervention. The monetary authorities should intervene to keep the exchange rate at its welfare-maximizing rate.

It is impossible to make this injunction operational, even if the set of welfare-maximizing rates for all countries taken together were consistent (which is unlikely). Our ignorance of economic structure (including its dynamic properties), of market imperfections, and of disturbances to national economies is simply too vast. As Murray Kemp has pointed out in connection with optimal reserve holdings, they depend on all other aspects of the world economic system, including the economic policies and the reserve holdings of other countries.[4] The same is true of the closely related question of optimal exchange-rate policy. Therefore, any guidelines to exchange-rate policy are necessarily in the realm of second-best, or, as Kemp observes, qth best, where q is a number much larger than two. Many other actions should be involved in framing an optimal economic policy. Exchange-rate guidelines can at best be designed to avoid the obviously undesirable or troublesome outcomes, necessarily admitting many possible deviations as compared with the optimal policy sketched above.

For most countries, the exchange rate represents the single most important price after the wage rate, and "the" wage rate is even more elusive than "the" exchange rate. Modern governments are held responsible for management of their national economies, and it is thus neither possible nor desirable that governments be indifferent to movements in the exchange rate. They can influence it indirectly through their other economic policies, but for reasons given above they will also find it appropriate from time to time to intervene directly in the foreign-exchange market.

Governments may intervene in exchange markets with a variety of objectives:

1. to smooth out short-term fluctuations in the exchange rate, which may be disturbing both to businesses and to consumers (the possibility of transacting in the forward market does not solve the problem in itself, since the forward rate may also fluctuate disturbingly);

2. to avoid mistaken signals to reallocate resources, for example, over a cycle in economic activity, and thus to avoid costly but unnecessary resource reallocations;

3. to avoid external impetus to domestic-factor price increases, and especially wage increases, through one-way escalation in the cost of living or some other price index;

4. to alter the level of international reserves held by the country;

5. to generate domestic employment by increasing exports and reducing imports;

6. to dampen domestic inflation by making foreign goods cheaper in the home market;

7. to keep profits from falling in the export- or import-competing sectors of the economy, and no doubt for other reasons as well.

It is the task of any guidance laid down by the IMF to discourage or prohibit exchange-market intervention for reasons that are inimical to the interests of other countries and to the continued smooth functioning of the world economy, while permitting or encouraging intervention for other reasons. Speaking generally, the first three reasons for intervention given on the foregoing list can be viewed as "legitimate" by the international community, the fourth may be legitimate under certain circumstances but will otherwise be suspect, and the remaining three can be viewed as illegitimate reasons for intervening in exchange markets. But even this is too simplistic, for occasions will arise in which an apparently illegitimate action also serves the interests of other countries. So any guidelines can be presumptive only, and must be applied with judgment.

Strategies for Exchange-market Intervention

With managed flexibility, countries need a principle concerning when to intervene. The 1974 IMF Guidelines for the Management of Floating Exchange Rates evisages as possible two quite different strategies, which could be called the "tracking strategy" and the "smoothing and braking strategy." The tracking strategy involves taking a view on what the exchange rate should be, while the smoothing and braking strategy involves taking a view on what maximum rates of change in the exchange rate should be. The former is closer to a system of parities, while the latter is closer to full flexibility of exchange rates.

The Tracking Strategy

A clear exposition of the tracking strategy is offered by John Williamson.[5] He calls it the "reference rate" proposal, and attributes its central features to Ethier and Bloomfield. In essence, it involves the establishment for all countries of a system of consistent "reference" exchange rates, which would be subject to periodic review. Countries would then be permitted (but not obliged) to intervene in the exchange market so as to move the market exchange rate toward the reference rate, but would be prohibited from intervention that would push the market rate away from the reference rate. That is, intervention would track the reference rate. (The 1974 guidelines speak of a "medium-term norm" for each exchange rate and a "target zone" around that medium-term norm, outside of which a country would be permitted to intervene "aggressively," i.e., to reinforce market pressures tending to push the market rate toward the target zone.)

Williamson sees two powerful arguments in support of a reference-rate system. First, a rule for compulsory reserve asset settlement could be introduced into a system of floating rates. Without something like a reference rate, it would be difficult to require a country to convert into primary reserve assets its currency that had been acquired through market intervention at the volition of some other country and without any co-ordination with the reserve-currency country. Presumably by agreeing on a pattern of reference rates, the reserve-currency country would also agree that any of its currency acquired in conformity with the rules of interven-tion would be convertible into primary reserve assets. Second, organized muliticurrency intervention would be possible, thus avoiding the asym-metries for the reserve-currency country attendant on the use of a single intervention currency, for example, the US dollar. An inspection of the pattern of deviations of market from reference rates would indicate the choice of currency that any intervening country should buy or sell against its own currency, so that a number of currencies could be potential can-didates for intervention, thus eliminating the asymmetrical position of the United States. Both of these considerations were important in the discussions of the Committee of Twenty on Reform of the Monetary System, and Williamson would like to see any exchange-rate system incorporate them.

A further argument in favor of the reference-rate proposal is that cur-rency speculation would reinforce official action as long as the reference rates are credible, while at the same time there is enough flexibility so that speculators are not presented with the one-way option they frequently encountered under a system of fixed but changeable parities.

A key prerequisite to this tracking strategy is obviously to obtain agree-ment on the system of reference rates and their changes over time. Some of the literature on gliding parities would be helpful in offering guidance to changes in reference rates over time—changes could be linked to movements in market rates, for instance, or to some combination of market rates and movements in reserves[6]—but that would not help in discovering a set of plausible reference rates from which to initiate the process.

The problem of finding and then changing adequately a system of reference rates is especially difficult in a period of rapid economic change, such as has been brought about recently by world inflation, by the sharp increase in oil prices, and by the ensuing world recession. It is also difficult when there are wide variations in the behavior of important national economies, such as can now be observed, for example, between West Germany and the United States on the one hand, and Britain and Italy on the other. Even when the problem involves mainly divergent rates of inflation, purchasing-power-parity comparisons offer only a general guide, not adequately refined for the setting of exchange-rate norms. Absolute purchasing-power-parity comparisons are notoriously unreliable as a guide to appropriate exchange rates, and relative purchasing-power-parity comparisons are only a moderately adequate guide, even when a satisfactory base period can be found.[7] Yet what would be an appropriate base period for the present—late 1971, 1968, or 1965? None of these years would be satisfactory without substantial adjustment. Nor are general equilibrium analytical models nearly adequate in their present state of development to determine reference rates.[8]

A key problem all along has been our ignorance about the equilibrium exchange rates, and this difficulty would also plague the setting of reference rates. One could, of course, begin with a rough-and-ready set of reference rates and allow for a gradual approach to the "true" set of reference rates, which would itself be changing. But that possibility raises a second difficultly with reference rates, which is their too close resemblance to exchange-rate parities. Although the differences between a set of reference rates as outlined by Williamson and a set of exchange-rate parities are in fact substantial, they are also subtle and might well be missed by government officials and the interested publics, especially in those countries (e.g., France or Japan) where a hankering after fixed exchange rates is still strong. Governments are too likely to treat reference rates, like parities, as offering no line of retreat without surrender, and therefore are likely to intervene too strongly to maintain market rates close to the reference rates. We perhaps need to allow exchange rates to float for a considerable period without any clear point of reference.

The Smoothing and Braking Strategy

For the possibly long interval during which governments are becoming accustomed to exchange-rate flexibility, an alternative strategy for intervention is smoothing and braking. This strategy implicitly acknowledges that we do not know what the equilibrium exchange rate over any time period is, but it allows for the likelihood that the "market" does not know either. The monetary authorities, therefore, intervene to prevent rapid movements in exchange rates except when those are clearly justified by the underlying economic conditions. If the market has been wrong in its collective judgment about the movement of an exchange rate, the monetary authority will have made a profit (capital gain) on its smoothing interventions. If, however, the market has been right, the monetary authorities will lose money by braking a cumulative movement in the exchange rate, for instance, by buying a depreciating currency or selling an appreciating one. But central banks are not endowed with their special legal powers for the purpose of making money. If they lose some money in the pursuit of broader social objectives, the loss may be amply repaid through the attainment of those social objectives.

It is possible to be more concrete. These days wages and other factor costs seem to be quite sensitive to movements, especially upward movements, in the cost of living. In some countries formal indexation of wages to the cost of living is widespread. Under these circumstances, a rapid depreciation of the exchange rate at a time when wage adjustments are scheduled to take place may trigger higher wages than would otherwise obtain, and thus over a period of time justify the expected depreciation of the currency. Prevention of self-justifying speculation against a currency might be one of those social purposes for which, if necessary, some loss of reserves is worthwhile.

Intervention at the wrong time can make matters worse, of course. If a country experiences a sharp deterioration in its terms of trade due to shortages abroad and the currency begins to depreciate, then intervention in the exchange market to prevent the depreciation will involve domestic monetary contraction, and if domestic prices do not fall readily this intervention may lead to prolonged unemployment. Here a choice must be made between allowing the price-increasing effect or the demand-contracting effect of the external disturbance to dominate.[9]

In general, it will be desirable to counteract the impact effects of purely financial disturbances through exchange-rate intervention, whereas the appropriate action in response to real disturbances involves more complex choices among competing objectives. Of course, in a world of uncertainty the monetary authorities will not always be correct in their assessment of the nature of the underlying disturbances. But they must continually weigh the costs and benefits between (a) being wrong in braking the movement in an exchange rate when underlying factors call for such a movement and (b) being wrong in not intervening to brake the movement in a rate depreciating under exchange market pressures when underlying factors do not call for a movement in the rate.

A method of correction is possible against excessive intervention. Direct intervention in spot-exchange markets implies a gain or a loss of international reserves, and the cumulative gain or loss in reserves indicates the degree of one-sidedness in intervention over the corresponding period. Each country could be asked to target a gain (or a loss, or possibly no change) in reserves over some stipulated period. If in the course of market intervention it acquires reserves that along with other factors (such as SDR allocations) lead to increases in reserves above the targeted increase, the country would be required under intervention guidelines to sell the excess reserves whenever it could without causing disorder in the exchange market. Thus over a period of time changes in reserves would correspond to targeted changes in reserves, and a monetary authority that had braked a movement in exchange rates during one period would find itself in some subsequent period pushing the exchange rate in the direction that the market had earlier moved it. In this respect exchange-market intervention would be similar to domestic monetary policy in several leading countries today; monetary actions are governed by short-run price targets combined with long-run quantity targets.

As with any international guidelines, one may ask what incentive countries have to adhere to them, especially, in this case, countries that have intervened to hold their exchange rates down and hence have accumulated international reserves. Ultimately, some system of "pressures" such as those discussed by the Committee of Twenty might have to be introduced, including the possibility of internationally sanctioned discrimination against the goods of a country that had persistently undervalued its currency (as evidenced by its excessive accumulation of reserves). But agreement on the injunctions and on the implementing guidelines should be sufficient to assure adherence to them.

Several questions arise in connection with a braking and smoothing strategy. First, why focus on reserve *changes* rather than on reserve *levels?* Especially since the latter target, rather than the former, seems to follow from the application of the theory of portfolio management. The first answer to this question is that it is inappropriate, without substantial adaptation, to transfer to nations a theory designed for household asset management. (With adaptation we might, however, still find that reserve levels are a more appropriate target than changes in reserves.) The second answer to the question is that both theoretical and simulation results suggest that targeting reserve levels, because of the response lags of changes in trade and other international transactions to changes in exchange rates, would lead to substantial overshooting of targets and hence might increase rather than reduce the variability of exchange rates. Targetting changes in reserves is more stable.[10]

A second question concerns which countries should engage in braking and smoothing interventions, since every exchange rate is intrinsicially two-sided; especially when all relevant countries may not take the same view on when smoothing should take place or on how hard the brakes should be applied. One possible answer is that each country would be free to take a view on changes in the value of its currency with respect to some appropriate average of other currencies and could intervene in the one or several currencies that are most relevant to it. Examples can be constructed where such intervention may complicate the position of the country whose currency is used for intervention, but these will be relatively rare when the principal currency is used, and they can, if necessary, be compensated by intervention in exchange markets by the country whose currency is first used, that country in turn using currencies that are most relevant to it. The possibility of inconsistent interventions can be avoided by a requirement that all countries report their interventions immediately to some common information center, such as the IMF, and the center would immediately notify countries that were intervening at cross purposes.

A third question concerns the time period over which smoothing should take place—or, to state the same point another way, the time period over which reserve changes should be on target. Here there are important differences of view. Some emphasize the desirability of limiting smoothing interventions to strictly short periods of time, several weeks at the outside, to prevent disorderly markets. Others envisage smoothing over a longer period, three to four years, covering an economic cycle. The longer the period, the greater the risk of being wrong, of intervening systematically against changes in equilibrium rates. This consideration suggests adopting the shorter period of time. On the other hand, it is easy enough to imagine a period of prolonged speculative pressure against a currency, for example, for six months, which the monetary authorities might well feel justified in resisting.

Moreover, consider a country that wants to ride out a world cycle in demand for its products, confident that it is a cycle, but because of price inelasticity of demand for its products and its concern about domestic inflation it does not want a temporary depreciation in its currency. Suppose further that international borrowing is costly compared to the alternative of running down its own international reserves temporarily, building them up again when export demand strengthens. Should the world financial community object to this strategy? The country's actions in this instance help to stabilize world demand.

It has been proposed that intervention in exchage markets should take place primarily or exclusively in *forward* exchange markets rather than spot markets.[11] This would have several advantages, notably that forward rates would provide a reference point to speculators in the spot market, that it would help develop forward markets, that arbitrage flows of capital would reinforce rather than work against the intentions of the authorities, and that the central bank could intervene in exchange markets without immediately also affecting the nation's money supply, as spot interventions do. That is, forward market intervention would permit short-term separation between monetary policy and exchange-rate policy. A limitation on this practice is that it would fail to deal with the direct influence of exchange rates on domestic prices and hence on wages, except insofar as importers and exporters buy or sell their foreign exchange in the forward rather than the spot market. Nonetheless, the proposal has merit. While the operating decisions would be up to individual countries, the IMF might nudge them in the direction of greater use of forward markets.

General Observations

Exchange-rate policy cannot be logically separated from other aspects of macroeconomic policy. In principle, any view of the exchange rate and of intervention policy to achieve that exchange rate should take all other aspects of policy into account. The distinctive role of the IMF is not to oversee all aspects of macroeconomic policy in all of its member countries, but to serve as the guardian for the interests of other countries, and of the international financial system generally, with respect to the macroeconomic actions of each of its members—to ensure that the total package of policies does not impose avoidable costs on other countries or otherwise impair the smooth functioning of the world economy. The IMF's assessment cannot focus on exchange-rate intervention alone. There will be occasions when the deliberate or inadvertent undervaluation of a currency will impose a burden on other countries. But there will be other occasions when similar actions by a country will be beneficial to the rest of the world—for example, when world demand is exceptionally high and any source of "hoarding" is welcome. No detailed set of guidelines is likely to apply satisfactorily general injunctions to the manifold and diverse circumstances that may be encountered.

It will be difficult to improve on the guidelines adopted in 1974, short of movement to a full-fledged reference-rate system of the type proposed by Williamson. The 1974 guidelines provide a useful framework for the exercise of judgment, both by individual countries and by the IMF in its consultations with individual countries. They also will occasionally provide grounds for dispute about what is allowed and what is not. But since sensible use of guidelines will always depend on the circumstances, and evaluation of the circumstances will not always be fully accepted, this is inevitable. The IMF should enter discussions on exchange-rate practices with its members early, before complete guidelines are fully worked out, because they never will be. Delay will provide precedent for nonconcern and nonintervention by the IMF.

At the operational level, can the IMF maintain the confidentiality necessary for frank discussion of exchange-rate policies? For example, is it possible in 1976 to have a full discussion in the IMF Executive Board regarding Japan's extensive intervention in exchange markets? Was Japan violating the new Article IV or not? The IMF needs some method and procedure for holding forthright discussions on such matters, and for holding them soon, for it is in the early period that the expectations of member countries will be established with regard to IMF surveillance under the new article.

Notes

1. For an illustration of the differences between several different averages, see Rudolf R. Rhomberg, "Indices of Effective Exchange Rates," *IMF Staff Papers 23* (March 1976), 88–112. Rhomberg argues that for focusing on the effects on a country's trade balance the various exchange rates between the country's currency and those of other countries must be weighted by response elasticities, as is done by the IMF's multilateral exchange-rate model (MERM). Although MERM is concerned with *changes* in exchange rates, it could in principle be adapted to generate equilibrium exchange rates. However, its underlying assumptions, especially with respect to the responses of production to price changes, are too crude to provide persuasive estimates; and in any case it focuses exclusively on trade and makes no attempt to incorporate other important components to a country's balance of payments, such as services and movements of capital.

2. A recent summary can be found in the Report of the Advisory Committee on the Presentation of Balance of Payments Statistics for the United States, *Statistical Reporter*, No. 76–12, June 1976, Office of Management and Budget, US Government. Because of the difficulties, this report advocated eliminating publication of any overall balance-of-payments statistic for the United States.

3. R. A. Mundell and J. J. Polak, eds., *The New International Monetary System* (New York: Columbia University Press, 1977).

4. Murray C. Kemp, "World Reserve Supplementation: Long-run Needs for Short-run Purposes," in *International Reserves: Needs and Availability* (Washington, D.C.: International Monetary Fund, 1970), pp. 3–11.

5. John Williamson, "The Future Exchange Rate Regime," *Banca Nazionale del Lavoro Quarterly Review* (June 1975), pp. 3–20.

6. See Peter B. Kenen, "Floats, Glides, and Indicators: A Comparison of Methods for Changing Exchange Rates," *Journal of International Economics* (May 1975), 5: 107–51. Kenen finds, through a series of simulations, that changes in gliding parities based on changes in reserves generally lead to less error in a variety of situations than do other rules, although changes based on movements in market exchange rates do almost as well.

7. For a recent comprehensive review of purchasing-power-parity theories and evidence, with a conclusion that is sympathetic to the theory but skeptical of its practical application without much further testing and refinement, see Lawrence H. Officer, "The Purchasing-Power-Parity Theory of Exchange Rates: A Review Article," *IMF Staff Papers* (March 1976), 23 : 1–60.

8. See note 1.

9. The OPEC price increase of 1974 represented a major supply "shortage," but it was against virtually the entire world economy, and currency depreciations by each individual oil-importing country, even in unison, would not have represented a helpful response, since a rise in the market value of the Saudi Arabian riyal could not have played a key role in mitigating the impact effects. Appropriate exchange-rate policy thus depends on all the surrounding circumstances.

10. Kenen, "Floats, Glides, and Indicators: A Comparison of Methods for Changing Exchange Rates"; see also A. W. Phillips, "Stabilization Policy in a Closed Economy," *The Economic Journal* (June 1954), 64 : 290–323.

11. See Egon Sohmen, *Flexible Exchange Rates* (Chicago: University of Chicago Press, 1961); Stanley Black, *International Money Markets and Flexible Exchange Rates*, Princeton Studies in International Finance No 32, 1973; and William Day, "The Advantages of Exclusive Forward Exchange Rate Support," *IMF Staff Papers* (March 1976), 23 : 137–163.

7　Eurodollars, Reserve Dollars, and Asymmetries in the International Monetary System

During the past decade economists and a growing number of others have become concerned with the possible instability of the gold-exchange standard. An international monetary system that satisfies a growing portion of its requirements for international reserves by relying on some national currency must eventually face the prospect that the national currency will cease to be convertible into other reserve assets, and this prospect will induce destabilizing shifts in the composition of reserves. In 1971 the prospect became a reality, when the United States abandoned its commitment to buy and sell gold freely, a move that was apparently in part prompted by the anxious attempts of several central banks to convert to gold or otherwise protect the value of their reserves in the face of large acquisitions of dollars.

The presence of this problem has led to a number of proposed solutions, most of which require the consolidation of reserve currency holdings, usually in exchange for some international asset (such as SDRs) at a suitably modified International Monetary Fund, thereby removing or greatly reducing the discretion central banks have over the composition of their reserves.

More recently, growing restlessness and even irritation at the special position of the reserve currencies, the US dollar and to a less extent the pound sterling (as evidenced by the persistent presence of this issue in Britain's negotiations for entry into the European Economic Community), and the advantages that allegedly accrue therefrom to the United States and Britain—an "exorbitant privilege," as de Gaulle called it—have been added to concern over the instability of a system relying on national currencies for international reserves. The result has been a growing demand in the European press and public discussion for greater symmetry among

Journal of International Economics, September, 2 (1972): 325–344. Reprinted by permission.

national currencies, for putting on Britain and the United States the same financial burdens and responsibilities that fall on other countries with respect to their foreign payments.

Symmetry is quite a different issue from the problem of potential instability, but several of the proponents for consolidation of reserves have also echoed the sentiment for symmetry in burdens and responsibilities. These observers have been joined by others, mostly Americans, who seek greater symmetry largely to improve the capacity of the United States to adjust its balance-of-payments position, especially through changes in exchange rates—a perspective obviously very different from that of those Europeans who emphasize the privileges involved in having one's currency used widely abroad.

Thus the arguments in favor of consolidation of foreign-exchange reserves are: (1) that it will reduce an important source of instability in the system, (2) that it will eliminate the special privileges arising from the ability of the reserve currency countries, in effect, to print international money, and (3) that it will permit those countries to deal with imbalances in payments more readily through changes in exchange rates, without being concerned, as they now must be, with a whole range of inhibiting factors not present for other countries.

It is usually assumed in discussing the need for symmetry or for reserve consolidation that certain other central features of the present international payments will remain unchanged. In particular, reliance continues to be placed on private exchange markets for multilateral clearing of international payments, and on maintenance of official exchange-rate obligations by intervention in that market by central banks as buyers and sellers of their own currency against a single foreign currency, usually the US dollar. It is also generally assumed that the vast growth in private international transactions and currency dealings has on balance been a healthy one, so that any changes in these private markets, including the Euro-currency market, should be relatively modest ones, in the interests only of ensuring against instability there. Some observers have expressed deeper concerns about the Euro-currency market, but wide differences of opinion, combined with general recognition of the real benefits to be derived from this market, augur against major changes without a major crisis clearly attributable to the market.

I contend that there is a contradiction between the desire for symmetry among currencies and the disposition to continue present clearing arrangements and the private use of national currencies (where by symmetry I mean inability to distinguish legally among any two national currencies in official arrangements); and in addition that the deep asymmetries in the international monetary system will create problems for reserve consolidation that have not yet been adequately explored.

This paper first draws attention to the fundamental asymmetries in the world financial system, to the reasons for them, and to their implications for official monetary arrangements; it then sketches the radical changes that will be necessary in order to achieve symmetry, draws attention to some of the difficulties created for reserve consolidation by the asymmetries, and offers some possible resolutions to these difficulties.

I   Asymmetries in the World Financial System

The basic asymmetry of course is the dominant economic size of the United States, reinforced by the closely related asymmetries in scale and sophistication of financial markets. These are subject to secular change, but only gradually and over rather long periods of time. These asymmetries in turn lead through a complicated process that will not concern us here to two separate but related asymmetries in the operation of international payments: the extensive private use of the US dollar as a medium of exchange, a unit of account, and a temporary store of value, and use of the dollar as an official intervention currency in a payments system that relies on private markets for multilateral clearing, as the Bretton Woods system in practice does.

Reasons for the Asymmetries

The reasons for these asymmetries are deep-seated, residing in the enormous efficiency of money as an intermediary in the process of exchange. Classical monetary theory recognized the social value of money without being clear about its sources and without integrating money into the theory of exchange. Recent work on these aspects of the theory of money has begun to explore more precisely what is the role of money in exchange, and why some medium of exchange will emerge out of a barter economy.[1] Barter trade suffers from the rarity of a "double coincidence" and the difficulty of carrying on multilateral trade. Under barter, a man with commodity A who wants commodity B must find a trading partner who has commodity B and wants commodity A; or he must find someone who has C and wants A and then someone who has B and wants C, etc. Any trade incurs search costs—the variable costs associated with finding the relevant trading partners; transfer costs—the costs (e.g. transportation) associated with making the physical exchange; and storage costs—the interest foregone and actual losses through theft and spoilage involved while the search and transfer process is going on. There are obviously some trade-offs among these costs, but their totality can be reduced greatly by the institution not only of trading posts, which bring would-be traders together at agreed times and places, but also of a common medium of exchange which by facilitating multilateral trade eliminates the need for a double coincidence.

Qualitatively the problems of a barter economy arise in the international markets for national monies, with the monies taking the place of commodities: the problem is how to facilitate multilateral clearing and avoid the need for double coincidences.[2] The costs of search for double coincidences rise sharply with the number and diversity of participants; with over 100 currencies representing an equal number of very diverse economies the economic advantages of multilateral exchange are considerable. Thus it becomes efficient to have an international medium of exchange, reducing the number of currency markets from over 5000 to around 100 (from $n(n-1)/2$ to $n-1$, where n is the number of currencies). It is quite natural, although not necessary, that this common medium should be the currency of the largest trading nation, for that will reduce both search and transfer costs. Moreover, a medium of exchange is likely to seek a temporary store of value of the same denomination, for that will reduce total transactions costs further and will also reduce the uncertainty arising from a fluctuating price between the store of value and the units of account of trading contracts, which are efficiently the same as those of the medium of exchange. And once it becomes a store of value, the importance of large and efficient (low cost) financial markets is reinforced.

All of this amounts to what we already know: that the world's "public" will find it convenient to hold and use some common medium of exchange for international transactions, formerly silver and gold, then sterling and the dollar. The reasons are deep-seated, not superficial, for these arise from the major economies in making international payments. Any tendency to attribute this process to Eurodollars mistakes the symptom for the cause. US liquid liabilities to private foreigners were $15 billion in December 1971 (some to be sure representing inter-bank liabilities to the Eurodollar market), but they were $7 billion even in 1960, when the Eurodollar market was in its infancy and world trade was only about one-third of that reached in 1971. Furthermore, the reasons adduced above for private foreign dollar holding suggest that these dollars are not merely the unwanted residue of past US payments deficits; on the contrary, the foreign demand for dollars in the sixties may have been one of the *causes* of the deficits, defined in the pre-1971 fashion on the liquidity basis, and may thus have helped to frustrate various American attempts to reduce the deficit.

All of this concerns private markets. Under a system of exchange-rate parities, the responsibility falls on central banks to act as residual buyers or sellers of their currency of issue. The home currency must be traded against something, and it is not only entirely natural but generally most efficient to use the medium most readily accepted in the private community. One can easily conceive of the use of other currencies for intervention, with reliance on the efficiency of the private market for arbitrage against all other currencies. The difficulty lies in the possible need for rapid mobilization and use of large amounts of the medium for intervention purposes; unless the economy whose currency is used is a large one, large-scale use of its currency may play havoc with its domestic monetary conditions; and conversion into cash of balances held tempo-rarily in interest-bearing securities can depress security prices, thereby imposing losses on the holder, if large amounts are sold suddenly. Both difficulties could of course be overcome with the proper international institutional arrangements, but until the advent of the EEC's plans for monetary unification there has seemed no compelling reason to find a substitute for the dollar as a currency of intervention.

Results of the Asymmetries

Use of the dollar as an official intervention currency and private interna-tional use of the dollar in turn have several asymmetrical effects on the actual functioning of the international payments system and on balance-of-payments adjustment through changes in exchange rates. Use of the dollar as an intervention currency limits the maximum movement in market exchange rates between the dollar and any other currency to one-half what it is between any other pair of currencies, for the simple reason that direct intervention controls possible movement vis-à-vis the dollar, whereas market arbitrage is relied upon to provide limits between other trades.[3] This in turn limits the relative price adjustment that can take place through exchange-rate changes between the United States and other countries, compared with other pairs of countries, in the absence of changes in parities, and thereby impedes adjustment in some circumstances.

Second, the use of the dollar as an intervention currency in practice entails at least working balances to be held in dollars, and the dollar thus also takes on the status of a reserve currency.

Third, the use of the dollar as an intervention currency greatly complicates taking the *initiative* for changes of the parity of the dollar. Detailed advance consultation is difficult because of the likelihood of "leaks" and the resulting speculation; while without such consultation, officials of other countries must decide, following announcement of a change in dollar parity, without opportunity to analyze the change in question, whether to alter their intervention points or not, knowing that they will be held responsible to their. publics for any "initiative" one way or the other. This uncertainty concerning how others will respond in turn has led American authorities to consider a change in parity less favorably than they otherwise might have. An alteration of the adjustment process in favor of smaller and more frequent changes in exchange rates should mitigate this problem by reducing the amount at stake in any single change in parity.

The extensive private international use of the dollar also has several implications for the international payments system. First, it means that other countries can be running dollar surpluses when the United States is not running a deficit or, to put it more accurately (since that depends on the choice of definition of deficit and surplus), other nations may be calling on the United States to convert large amounts of dollars into other reserve assets even when residents of the United States are not engaging in net spending abroad, or even (conceivably) when they are selling more goods, services, and securities to nonresidents than they are buying from nonresidents.

Second, private international use of the dollar greatly complicates the *capacity* of the United States to achieve a change in parity against other currencies. Extensive valuation of trading contracts and assets abroad in dollars means that a change in its parity would generate bankruptcy or lesser complications for otherwise viable banks and firms. Thus, when the pound sterling was devalued in 1967, Hong Kong and Jamaica both also devalued at once, although the payments position of neither area warranted it. Hong Kong banks with assets in sterling and liabilities in Hong Kong dollars could have been bankrupt by a large change in the rate between the two. Four days later Hong Kong solved this problem by indemnifying the banks out of official reserves, and revalued the Hong Kong dollar part way. Jamaica had outstanding sugar and banana export contracts in sterling, revenues against a wage bill in Jamaican currency. Devaluation of the pound against the Jamaican dollar would have bankrupted the firms, so Jamaica followed sterling down. It is unclear how Japan handled a similar problem with its ship-building and other industries following the December 1971 revaluation of the yen against the US dollar. But Japan's two-week delay in allowing the value of the yen to rise, during which time the Bank of Japan took in several billion dollars from Japanese residents and banks, suggests the operation of a process of prior indemnification out of official reserves.

II   How Can Symmetry Be Achieved?

Following this exploration of the existing asymmetries between the reserve currencies and other currencies, we can return to the question posed at the outset, and ask whether it is possible to achieve legal symmetry among currencies while still retaining existing private markets and market clearing practices. The answer, it will now be clear, is that it is not possible; more far-reaching changes would be required to achieve symmetry, involving a new nonnational private international currency or at least a clearing union. Before turning to those possibilities it will be useful to dwell on some of the difficulties of introducing symmetry, for these difficulties also bear on the more limited objective of consolidating reserve currency assets.

First, as noted above, use of an intervention currency introduces an asymmetry in exchange-rate movements between the intervention limits. The Bretton Woods Agreement is written with symmetrical requirements for all currencies, but these had to be abandoned in view of intervention practices; as a result, many pairs of currencies have traded at rates outside the 2 percent band width around the ratios of their parities, despite the formal requirement to avoid this.[4] The Werner Committee on Monetary Unification in the European Community also had to wrestle with this problem in its attempt to narrow exchange rate movements among European currencies without narrowing them with respect to the dollar—while still retaining the dollar as an intervention currency. They produced a solution that is technically feasible but cumbersome; it involved the close coordination of market intervention by member countries to narrow the band of exchange-rate variation vis-à-vis the dollar on any given day, but to vary the midpoint of that band from week to week, allowing it in principle to vary over the whole range permitted by a given set of parities (dubbed by wags "a snake in a tunnel"). But on any given day the maximum variation of the dollar with respect to any currency is still only half what it is for any other pair of currencies, and in addition some member countries would be denied desirable variation with respect to the dollar by the requirement to coordinate with other members. Why did the Werner Committee not recommend a European intervention currency which would have greatly simplified achievement of their immediate objective? The answer was no doubt partly the inability to agree on one, but more basically it was rooted in the considerations mentioned in the preceding section, namely the technical advantage in dealing in a currency whose market for other currencies was sufficiently broad that active intervention would influence the market without disrupting it, and the parallel advantage of being able to invest temporarily excess holdings of the intervention currency in interest-yielding assets whose price would not be unduly influenced by movements into and out of cash.[5]

Second, suppose the reserve currency role of the dollar is eliminated by requiring (unrealistically, in view of the need for working balances, taken up below) all reserve assets to be held in some common, nationally neutral form, such as SDRs. Dollars taken up through exchange market intervention must be converted into such assets immediately, and dollars needed for intervention would be acquired through instantaneous conversion of SDRs. What shall be the rate of exchange between dollars and SDRs? Between other currencies and SDRs? One's first inclination is to say each currency will trade against SDRs at its par value. But if the market rates among currencies differ from par value relationships, trading SDRs against currencies at par would create the possibility of profitable arbitrage, with the attractions being all the greater now that the permissible band width has been widened from 2 to $4\frac{1}{2}$ percent. To avoid this, the dollar must trade against SDRs at parity, but other currencies must trade against SDRs at rates influenced by the market rate against the dollar.[6] Thus the dollar would be legally distinguishable from other currencies.

Alternative arrangements are possible, avoiding this need for asymmetry, but they involve costs. For instance, a charge could be levied for conversions into and out of SDRs sufficiently large to discourage conversions for arbitrage gains. On its normal operations, in which currencies do exchange at par, the IMF levies a service charge of $\frac{1}{2}$ percent that partially performs this function. But $\frac{1}{2}$ percent would not be large enough to eliminate arbitrage when exchange margins are as large as $2\frac{1}{4}$ percent on each side of parity, and in any case it would represent a compulsory tax on *all* reserve transactions under the circumstances hypothesized above, a charge that would unduly discourage the use of reserves.[7] A second alternative would stipulate that each country deal against SDRs (at par) in only *one* national currency (any one) other than its own, and could not change its choice of currency except under international supervision; but under this requirement most countries would choose the US dollar, again preserving de facto asymmetry.

Third, in practice use of an intervention currency entails the holding of working balances, so that the monetary authorities are able if necessary to intervene quickly to prevent unwanted movements in exchange rates. But once working balances are allowed, the reserve currency role has again made its appearance. Unless they are subjected to some limit, these working balances are likely to give rise to all the problems of a gold-exchange standard, noted briefly at the outset. Under a market clearing system, the *sources* of dollar accruals to a central bank are not immediately known, and in some cases they may never be known accurately.[8] Thus if the inflows are exceptionally large, the initial presumption must be that they are short-term funds, in principle reversible, and to avoid transactions costs on the turnaround the central bank may reasonably decide to accumulate the dollars it purchases. But once dollars have accumulated, and the inflows are discovered to be nonreversible, it may be awkward (e.g., threaten the system) to convert them into other reserve assets. Moreover, genuine ambiguities over the reversible character of the accruals will permit subtle pressure by the United States not to convert, thereby retaining one of the features of the gold/SDR exchange standard that some observers find most objectionable.

Alternatively, fixing some limit to the magnitude of working balances (e.g., to 15 percent of total reserves as in Triffin's proposal[9]) could also create difficulties for the United States because of the large outstanding private dollar balances and the possibility that they may be shifted into other currencies even when on other counts the US payments position is in balance. These private funds, in the form of demand deposits, short-term time deposits, and marketable US government securities, reached astounding proportions by late 1971: $15 billion in liabilities of US banks, another $30 billion in liabilities of their overseas branches, and an estimated $20 billion in the dollar liabilities of non-US banks in the Eurodollar market. More will be said about them below. But the point here is that the United States does not have enough reserves to cover conversions into other currencies of even 20 percent of these balances. Large-scale conversions would therefore lead the United States to break out of any system imposing convertibility, unless special provisions were made for this contingency, for example through large and virtually automatic lines of credit such as expansible "working balances" of reserve dollars automatically provide. But once again an asymmetry is recognized and a "special privilege" established, unless such lines of virtually automatic credit are also made available (in amounts proportional to some measure of economic size and requirements, e.g., to IMF quotas) to all member countries.

A Neutral International Money

Enough has been said above to support the view that use of an intervention currency is not consistent with complete symmetry among currencies, even leaving aside the asymmetry with respect to movements in exchange rates. A move to freely floating exchange rates would of course establish symmetry in official use of currencies; but it might increase rather than diminish private international use of major national currencies, especially the dollar. Within the realm of fixed parities, a radical solution to this problem would abandon the use of a national currency for intervention purposes and, ultimately, for private market purposes. In the past the monetary metals served as neutral international monetary media; Rueff's proposal for a major increase in the price of gold, the US proceeds of which to be used to retire outstanding dollar balances, would have restored this neutrality if at the same time countries also maintained their currencies' parities by buying and selling gold rather than dollars. A forward-looking arrangement would place this role on a new international currency, a revised SDR, which would be used by national monetary authorities to maintain their market exchange rates within stipulated limits as well as held as reserves. Market intervention in SDRs would eliminate the first two asymmetries mentioned above—the narrower range of fluctuation in exchange rates with respect to the dollar, and the need to trade the dollar against SDRs at par, while not being able to do that for other currencies—but would of course require the development of private markets in SDRs, including SDR-denominated demand accounts and interest bearing securities.[10] Gradually the third asymmetry then might also disappear, as international private holdings of dollars diminished to non-threatening proportions through the United States "earning" them back. But in fact it is difficult to contemplate such a substitution in private use of SDRs for dollars without major incentives to use SDRs and disincentives to the use of dollars. Runaway inflation in the United States soon after private SDRs are launched might for example accomplish the substitution. Even then the mantle might more readily pass to another national currency, or to a new European currency, if it then exists. It is difficult, moreover, to contemplate the successful introduction of an acceptable international currency for private use that does not also threaten the existence of national currencies in all but the largest countries, leading ultimately to a world currency.

An International Clearing Union

Another, more limited, solution to the problem of asymmetries intrinsic in the use of a national currency for international purposes, but one still beyond current thinking about monetary reform, lies in abandonment of the foreign-exchange market for multilateral clearing, thus eliminating the need for market intervention, and establishment in its stead of an International Clearing Union. The Clearing Union would declare consistent fixed buying and selling rates for all pairs of currencies, so that when, for example, a German resident wanted to buy Turkish lire, a German commercial bank would provide the lire against German marks at a fixed rate, drawing the lire from the Bundesbank which in turn would draw them for the Clearing Union. At the end of the day all accounts would be cleared, with Germany's account at the Union being debited and Turkey's account being credited as a result of the above transaction. This approximates the way in which the Federal Reserve System works with respect to its twelve regional banks; the European Payments Union also operated roughly on this basis, with the important difference that accounts were settled only every 30 days and beyond that period special credits were advanced. An International Clearing Union need not involve such granting of credit, although it might do so.

Any substantial difference between buying and selling rates would give rise to private foreign-exchange markets with rates fluctuating between the buying and selling rates, but central banks would be proscribed from intervening in those markets, for that would raise once again the need for an intervention currency.

Establishment of a Clearing Union would not displace the use of dollars in private markets, nor would it deal directly with the possibility of large-scale conversions of these dollar balances into other currencies which would threaten the ability of the United States to maintain convertibility of the dollar into the international reserve asset (here, claims on the Clearing Union). But the Clearing Union itself might be empowered to act as a lender of last resort on such occasions and to provide credit in ample quantity and on reasonable terms. As noted above, such an arrangement would either have to recognize the special problem faced by the United States (and to a less extent by the United Kingdom), thereby acknowledging the asymmetry, or it would have to be made available to all, thereby resulting in a general transformation of the present system of conditional credits to one of (virtually) unconditional ones, except for time limits.

Moreover, a Clearing Union on these lines would result in a narrowing of the range within which market exchange rates can fluctuate around parities, in opposition to contemporary sentiment for widening the band, and would thus result in the need for closer harmonization of national monetary policies to avoid large movements of yield-sensitive funds between nations.

III   Consolidation of Reserve Currency Balances

Full consideration of complete symmetry among currencies requires further discussion, but the observations in the preceding section suggest that it will require changes in the international monetary system far more extensive than those so far contemplated. The question remains: to what extent can official dollar balances be consolidated without complication arising from the asymmetries arising from the private and intervention uses of the dollar? The answer, it seems to me, is that this separation is possible insofar as the objective is to reduce considerably a possible source of instability in the gold–exchange standard,[11] but that a "price" must be paid for this gain in formalization of serveral of the asymmetries that in fact exist. Several of these have already been touched on: the differential exchange margin, the differential treatment on conversion into reserve assets, and the need for special credit provisions arising from private use of the dollar.

Acceptance of these asymmetries may be taken as concessions to the efficiency of a market clearing system based on the currency of the preponderant economic and financial area in a world that otherwise maintains, by and large, formal legal equality among nations. But two other, related, costs are associated with consolidation of dollar balances, one concerning official use of efficient markets and the other concerning the elasticity of global reserve growth. Finally, before the United States can accept full convertibility implied by such consolidation, special credit provisions will also have to be made with respect to private dollar holdings.

Denying Access to Financial Markets

To achieve their purposes over time, consolidation proposals cannot be confined to funding existing dollar balances, but must also deny the possibility for central banks to acquire dollar balances in the future (beyond those required for working balances). In other words, they must deny central banks access to highly efficient money and short-term securities markets outside their own countries. Thus consolidation of dollar balances will lead to some loss in efficiency by reducing reliance on market facilities, and these costs may fall disproportionately on smaller nations. It has been noted, in discussions of direct foreign investment, that the output of General Motors exceeds that of the majority of countries. Similarly, the liquid balances of Exxon Corp. exceed the official liquid balances of over two-thirds of the members of the IMF. Should these countries, which from a worldwide financial perspective are in some respects like medium-sized international firms, be denied the access to efficient financial markets that firms enjoy? This denial presumably involves a considerable efficiency loss, although as noted in the first section we do not know yet how to measure it.

The loss as it will appear to central banks, however, has a number of concrete and identifiable aspects. First, use of the market permits quick and anonymous movement of funds at low transactions costs, a feature that could be reproduced by the IMF, but only without a service charge and thus with the built-in asymmetrical treatment of the dollar noted above. Second, the market provides a source of short-term credit that (given the stickiness of quoted interest rates) often involves maintenance of "compensating balances" with the commercial bank from which the loan was obtained, balances that would be ruled out under the obligatory consolidation proposals. This difficulty could be eliminated by putting a nation's reserves on a net rather than a gross basis for the purpose of calculating allowable dollar balances, although such a practice, by making the true condition of the borrowing country more visible, would reduce some of the present advantages of borrowing reserves to dress up the balance sheet. Third, loans are often obtained by pledging owned reserves as collateral, and it is not clear that commercial banks would accept as collateral claims on the IMF (such as SDRs) that they cannot themselves own (just as they do not lend against real estate that cannot legally be transferred to them); but this problem could presumably be resolved too, if the IMF were willing to facilitate the resolution by interpreting the "balance-of-payments" requirement for SDRs to include making good on outstanding loans and then to underwrite the loan at the time it was made.

Elasticity of Supply of International Reserves

A second loss from consolidation of reserve assets arises from the resulting loss in elasticity to reserve creation. The IMF is finding it difficult to develop persuasive criteria for the amounts of SDRs to be created. Suppose that, despite their best efforts, the authorities guess wrong on the amounts required. If they err on the high side, international spending, especially by developing countries, will increase; the result would be a higher money level of international transactions (reflecting some combination of real and nominal increases), on one hand, and augmentation of the reserves of those countries (which can be called reserve sinks) that do not respond to modestly higher reserve levels, for example, because they pursue active and successful policies of domestic economic stabilization, on the other hand. If the IMF authorities err on the low side, international transactions will contract (below what they would otherwise be), probably through the greater use of restrictive controls, or through a larger-than-normal number of currency devaluations which will raise the national currency value of reserves, these two processes mitigated to the extent that reserves of "reserve sinks" can be drawn down and distributed to the rest of the world. (But the role of reserve sink is likely to be asymmetric, with large countries showing more response to reserve reductions than to reserve increases.)

Official use of the dollar as a reserve currency provides a relatively elastic supply of new reserves to compensate for any shortfall in global reserve creation far faster than could be made good through a sequence of currency devaluations, which in any case experience suggests are likely to be preceded and accompanied by controls and other restraints on international transactions.[12] Thus unless the adjustment process is improved very substantially, this elastic source of reserves, supplied through US payments deficits induced by the shortage of reserves, could help avoid damage to the international economy brought about by restrictive national action.[13]

The loss of this elasticity must of course be weighed against the gains from breaking the link between reserve creation and independent developments in the US payments position, a link that has in recent years introduced capricious changes in international reserves.

It might be noted in passing that both of these costs—the efficiency losses arising from proscribing central bank use of much of the market mechanism and the loss in elasticity of reserve supply to satisfy reserve needs—could be avoided if the consolidation of dollar reserve holdings were made once for all, so that the instability threatened by large existing dollar balances would be removed without limiting the accumulation of future balances. Such a "solution" would not of course solve the problem of stability among reserve assets for all time, for uncomfortably large dollar balances would perhaps accumulate in the future and the consolidation would then have to be repeated; and it would not go even part way toward reducing the other asymmetries that some observers find objectionable. The costs of consolidation would be lower, but so would the benefits.

Elasticity of Supply of Official Credit

Finally, we return to the question of the private dollar balances. Presumably in exchange for consolidation of outstanding official dollar balances the United States will be expected to restore full convertibility of future dollar holdings into other reserve assets. But should the United States resume convertibility without some arrangement also covering the contingency of private dollar balances? And can it be reasonably expected to, except possibly on the implicit understanding that if the contingency of large conversions did arise, the United States would cease to honor that obligation? It should be noted that it was speculative movements in the *private* holdings of sterling, not the official holdings, that gave Britain trouble over the years; and that private foreign dollar balances have gyrated substantially in recent years—to be sure, in response to changes in monetary policy in the United States and other countries—increasing by only $1.7 billion in 1968 but by a startling $8.7 billion in 1969, and then dropping by $6.5 billion in 1970 and by a further $7.4 billion in 1971.

It is of course also true that *American*-owned dollar balances can shift massively abroad on a scale never before imagined, and these are much larger than foreign-owned balances. This is one aspect of the growing interdependence among nations, and reinforces the point. But the key difference between these funds and foreign-owned balances is that, if necessary, the former can be more readily restrained by instructions to American banks, as Britain controlled outflows of resident capital years ago. Distinctions between resident and nonresident capital are of long standing. But the Eurodollar market introduces two new elements into the picture: first, the United States could not fully control nonresident capital even if it desired to, for the institutions involved are beyond the jurisdictional reach of the United States; and, second, the presence of nonresident *institutions* dealing in dollars also makes it much more difficult to control the flow of resident capital.

Nonetheless, the problem of massive conversion of Eurodollars into other currencies can also be exaggerated. Precisely because the Eurodollar market to some extent leads a separate existence from the United States, conversions out of Eurodollars introduce a corrective rise in Eurodollar interest rates, thereby increasing foreign private willingness to hold dollar claims; but if this rise in interest rates induces yield-sensitive outflows from the United States, straining whatever controls the United States may have imposed, the conversions may become very much larger.

The problem of large conversions of private dollars into other currencies could be handled, in the context of reserve consolidation, by permiting the IMF to extend credit *automatically* to the United States to cover large hot-money flows (even those that can be attributed to US monetary policy), in effect providing a gold tranche on a much larger scale. If the conversions out of dollars are short-lived, as they should be if the convenience of holding dollars is as great as I have portrayed it above, then this credit will be reversed automatically. This principle underlies the present network of swap arrangements, which serve a similar purpose. If the conversions are not short-lived, the United States would have a repayment obligation spread over a period of years. If that in turn led to a loss of reserves, depreciation of the dollar would be in order, and should be permitted by other countries.

It comes down to this: either the United States is put on a short tether, like other countries, or it is not. If the tether imposed by convertibility of the dollar into other reserve assets is too short, it will be intolerable for the United States. Any major move out of private dollar balances would force a choice between constrictive domestic economic (especially monetary) policy and inconvertibility, and the latter would undoubtedly be chosen. But if the tether is long enough to cover this possibility, it inevitably confers on the United States a special position in the international financial system.

All of these considerations do not strike at the heart of proposals for consolidation of reserve currencies in some central fund to eliminate the possibility of destabilizing shifts among reserve assets. But full consolidation of official dollar balances involves foregoing some advantages accruing especially to small countries from access to private financial markets. And once-for-all consolidation will by itself be insufficient to restore full convertibility of the dollar into reserve assets without assurances of extensive short-term credit to cover possible conversions of private balances and assurance that the dollar exchange rate can be altered to repay any lasting debt that result from these credits. These considerations thus suggest that the deep asymmetries intrinsic in a market-clearing system will have to be recognized explicitly, and accommodated. To eliminate the asymmetries among national currencies altogether would require more sweeping changes in the international monetary system than are now generally considered desirable, and even sweeping changes in the relative sizes of countries.

Notes

1. See especially Jürg Niehans, "Money in a Static Theory of Optimal Payments Arrangements," *Journal of Money, Credit, and Banking*, Vol. 1 (November, 1969), pp. 702–26; *idem*, "Money and Barter in General Equilibrium with Transactions Costs," and Karl Brunner and Allan H. Meltzer, "The Uses of Money: Money in the Theory of an Exchange Economy," both in *American Economic Review*, Vol. 61 (December 1971), pp. 773–783 and 784–805, respectively; and Morris Perlman, "The Roles of Money in an Open Economy and the Optimum Quantity of Money," *Economica*, Vol. 38 (August 1971), pp. 233–252.

2. This point has also been made by Alexander K. Swoboda, *The Eurodollar Market: An Interpretation*, Essays in International Finance, No. 64, Princeton, International Finance Section, February 1968, pp. 5–10; and "Vehicle Currencies and the Foreign Exchange Market: The Case of the Dollar," in Robert Z. Aliber (ed.), *The International Market for Foreign Exchange*, Praeger, 1969, pp. 30–40.

3. The maximum swing can be even wider between a currency whose authorities use the dollar and a currency whose authorities use the pound sterling as an intervention currency.

4. Art. IV, Sec. 2 of the IMF Articles of Agreement stipulates that all spot currency transactions within a member country's territory shall be kept within one percent of parity—a band width of 2 percent. An IMF decision in 1959 doubled this limit to allow for intervention in dollars (or indeed in any other convertible currency). This decision was superseded by the decision of December 1971 to widen the band width to $4\frac{1}{2}$ percent against the intervention currency, hence as much as 9 percent between any other pair of currencies.

5. After the currency disruptions of late 1971, the European Community agreed that each member of the community accomplish this objective, not by coordinating their market intervention in dollars as under the Werner Plan, but by intervening in the currencies of *each* other member country as needed. Intervention in dollars would be confined to the vicinity of the borders of the new $4\frac{1}{2}$ percent band of flexibility, while exchange-rate variations among member currencies are to be held to the same range by direct intervention, rather than to twice that range as would result from exclusive use of the dollar as an intervention currency. This move not only underestimated the need for greater flexibility, as was illustrated by the floating of the British pound barely a month after the plan started, but also underestimated the difficulty of simultaneous intervention in several currencies whenever a central bank wants to intervene *within* the permissible limits.

6. Strictly speaking, what is required is that the *structure* of market rates among currencies be maintained in dealings against SDRs; *any* currency could be chosen to trade against SDRs at par, or indeed at any other fixed value; but unless the

dollar were chosen for this role arbitrary reserve losses or gains would result from turnaround transactions—selling reserves for intervention dollars and then replenishing them when the market rate between the dollar and the designated currency had changed. In any case asymmetry would result—the point the text tries to establish.

7. The IMF service charge was one of the stumbling blocks to making the gold tranche into a fully usable reserve asset, and since the IMF amendments of 1969 the service charge has been dropped on gold tranche drawings, which still take place at par, with no observation of arbitrage to date. In its dealings in SDRs, however, the IMF follows the practice outlined above, fixing the price at parity in terms of the US dollar, with transactions against other currencies taking place at market rates.

8. More rapid and more accurate reporting from the Eurodollar market will help in this identification, but it will not entirely solve the problem because of the possibilities for credit expansion or contraction in the Eurodollar market. Thus a recorded decline in Eurodollar balances, for example, does not necessarily indicate an equivalent shift of funds either to the United States or into other currencies.

9. Robert Triffin, "How to Arrest a Threatening Relapse into the 1930s," *Bulletin of the National Bank of Belgium* (November 1971).

10. The medium of payment and store of value functions must here be distinguished. In particular, SDRs themselves need not bear interest in order to function effectively as an international medium of exchange—indeed, interest yield might even impair this function by encouraging at the margin deficit-reducing actions, which use social resources, rather than deficit-financing, which does not use social resources; but there must be SDR-denominated interest-bearing assets if SDRs are to function fully as a private international currency.

11. It should be observed that introduction of a system of gliding parities—or indeed any form of frequent change in parity—in which the parity of the dollar is also expected to change, as desired both by those interested in better adjustment and by those concerned with the "inequity" of a system in which the United States does not have to bear the alleged "burden" of initiating parity changes, makes more urgent but also more difficult the task of consolidating reserve currency assets. The task is more urgent because regular movements in the parity of the dollar (and sterling) would encourage shifts in the composition of reserves, into or out of dollars (and sterling). The task is more difficult because it raises the question who carries the exchange risk. For example, if the IMF exchanges a special issue of SDRs for official dollar balances, and then the dollar parity changes, would the United States indemnify the IMF for its loss in SDR-value under a depreciating dollar, or would the IMF carry this loss itself, by building a reserve out of interest earnings on the dollar balances? Since market interest rates would reflect expectations regarding prospective depreciation, the IMF should carry the exchange risk if it earned market interest rates. But to some observers this would appear to be a highly inequitable asymmetry favoring the United States.

This problem could of course be avoided if the parity of the dollar did *not* change under a gliding parity system. But such a special status would not only appear highly inequitable to many observers (see, e.g., John Williamson, *The Choice of a Pivot for Parities*, Essays in International Finance, No. 90, Princeton, International Finance Section, November 1971, pp. 13–14), but might also limit somewhat the effective exchange rate adjustment for the United States, because of threshold effects under any operative gliding parity system. On the last point, see E. Howle and C. Moore, "Richard Cooper's Gliding Parity: A Proposed Modification," and my reply in the *Journal of International Economics*, Vol. 1 (November 1971), pp. 429–436 and pp. 437–442, respectively.

12. In the past decade restraints on imports preceded the devaluations by Canada, Britain, France, and the United States, not to mention large numbers of developing countries.

13. Ronald McKinnon has emphasized this role of dollar reserves, and the efficiency of the mechanism whereby they are supplied, in his *Private and Official International Money: The Case for the Dollar*, Essays in International Finance, No. 74, Princeton, International Finance Section, April 1969, pp. 15–16. John Williamson has argued that the desired elasticity could be introduced by supplementary creations of SDRs keyed to the observed frequency and amount of currency devaluations. This scheme presupposes both an efficient adjustment mechanism (so that devaluation is used instead of controls or unwarranted domestic deflation) and that countries are free to devalue when they choose, even when they show a payments surplus, if in their view they are gaining insufficient reserves. See his *The Choice of a Pivot for Parities*, Essays in International Finance, No. 90, Princeton, International Finance Section, November 1971, p. 19.

8   The Future Of The Dollar

The international monetary system has been in almost continuous turmoil for the past four years. The situation is thus superficially in a high state of flux. In the meantime, we hear statements to the effect that the international reputation of the dollar reached its peak in the mid-1950s, or that the international *position* of the dollar peaked in late 1971, when the world formally accepted a de facto dollar standard. As the dollar's position improved, its reputation declined. And it is asked: How long will the decline in stature continue? How far will it go?

Questions like these leave the economist uncomfortable. The questions themselves are not precise. Even if they were, the context in which they are to be answered is not well defined. To discuss the future of the dollar requires specification of some framework. Is the discussion to be positive or normative: What will happen or what should happen? If it is positive, should it be conditional on other events, or unconditional—that is, a straight forecast of the future? Economists are generally much more comfortable with conditional forecasts, "if ... then ..." propositions that must meet certain standards of internal consistency, and occasionally even of plausibility, but not of certainty or even high probability. If the conditions are not fulfilled, they are neither surprised nor troubled that the "forecast" turned out to be wrong.

A straight unconditional forecast gives the economist further difficulty because it involves forecasting political actions as well as economic events; economic forecasting is at least conditional to that extent, and more often it is further conditioned within an economic framework.

These observations are highly relevent to a discussion of the future of the dollar, for that is deeply tied up with the future of the international

Foreign Policy 11 (Summer 1973). Reprinted by permission. Copyright 1973 by the Carnegie Endowment for International Peace.

monetary system, and that in turn is highly dependent on decisions strongly subject to political motivation and political will. There is no generally accepted framework in which the future of the dollar can be discussed unconditionally, in part because economists have generally treated government as exogenous agents, acting on the system from outside it. This perspective marks a sharp difference from analysis of the firm or the household; the distinctive lesson of classical economic analysis is that it shows that an apparently autonomous agent is in fact tightly constrained, at least in the long run, by the economic environment in which it operates. This perspective has only recently been extended to governments, and then only in a limited context and largely to local rather than to national government.

In spite of these difficulties, partly to provoke discussion and partly to provoke the self-denying effect (whereby a prophency sets in motion avoidance mechanisms), I will make an unconditional forecast about the future of the dollar for, say, the next decade.

It is this: At the end of a decade the position of the dollar will not be very different from what it is now. The dollar will continue to be suspect and the struggle to find acceptable ways to rein it in will continue, but generally they will fail and the dollar will still be widely used both as a private international currency and as an official reserve currency. By then Europe will have greatly reduced its dependence on the dollar for intra-European transactions, probably with a clearing arrangement providing for intervention in European currencies, but with final settlement in dollars, and linked to the dollar for non-European transactions. Other national currencies, and especially the German mark, will play a greater relative and absolute role as international money. While the dollar will therefore have rivals, and the rivals will create new problems of financial stability, the dollar will continue to dominate all of them in importance. The private international role of the dollar will continue to grow.

The basic reason for this forecast is simple: There is at present no clear, feasible alternative. The numerous plans for international monetary reform that have been put forward do not deal satisfactorily with the structural problems inherent in the present situation, and (partly for that reason, but only partly) the relevant governments are still very far apart in what they regard as desirable in an international monetary system. Failing to agree on an alternative perpetuates the evolving status quo. In addition, while there will be progress toward European monetary unification, it will be sufficiently slow to prevent the development of a serious rival to the dollar at the global level. Europeans themselves will resist strongly the evolution of one of the existing European currencies, especially the mark, into a position of dominance, but they will find difficulty in constructing and introducing an adequate substitute.

Furthermore, the behavior of the American economy is likely to be very creditable compared to the economies of other industrial countries. The balance-of-payments problem, as it is now perceived, will not be entirely solved, but price developments in the United States compared with those of other countries will give the dollar a favorable image abroad. There will be great pressures on the US trade balance as a result of rising demands for energy and other raw materials, but that will be true of other industrial countries as well; their continued more rapid growth may in this respect compensate for the fact that in the United States imports will be necessary not only for growth but also, in some cases, to substitute for dwindling domestic supplies. Long-term capital outflow from the United States remains a potential problem, since the United States is still a relatively capital-rich country with correspondingly lower returns to capital for any given technology. But the gap has narrowed substantially already, and capital outflows will remain under enough political control (for example, through the passage into law of some of the provisions of the Burke-Hartke bill) that the outflow will not become embarrassingly large, except of course during periods of speculation against the dollar. And foreign investment in US markets will grow rapidly, compensating for some of the outflow.

The forecast of a single individual is not terribly interesting, especially when it is made without high conviction but merely with more conviction than can be applied to major alternative outcomes. But once some assumptions are stated, an unconditional forecast shades over into a conditional forecast, and that can give rise to dispute over the assumptions and over the alleged link between the assumptions and the forecast.

To provide perspective on the assumptions and on the link between assumptions and forecast, this essay will review briefly how the dollar got to its present position, the structural tensions inherent in the present condition, some proposed solutions and possible outcomes arising out of those tensions, and the deficiencies of the proposed solutions.

A Short History of the Dollar

The dollar emerged as a strong currency after World War I. The US economy had been stimulated by the war, while European economies were set back. Also around this time a truly national capital market developed in the United States, a coalescence of earlier regional markets. The capacity of the country to export capital (after having been a net importer in the nineteenth century) became evident, and, by the late 1920s, 55 percent of all foreign bond issues were being made in the United States, denominated in dollars. The political turmoil of the 1930s, especially in Europe, reinforced the attractiveness of the dollar as a currency of refuge. By 1940, $2.5 billion were held by foreigners in American bank deposits and other liquid claims, and even more were held in American securities. Central banks also held over $1 billion. At the end of World War II, in 1945, foreign central banks held $4 billion in liquid dollar claims. This compared with $10 billion equivalent (at the overvalued exchange rate of 1£ = $4.03) held in sterling, although admittedly most of the holdings of sterling were really long-term war debts to India, Egypt, and other members of the British Empire, held in liquid form.

The story thereafter is well known. The world economy grew apace, and the US dollar, "as good as gold" and convertible into gold at a fixed price of $35 an ounce, provided the desired growth in international reserves. World reserves grew by 26 percent between 1945 and 1960, of which 10 percentage points were in the form of new monetary gold and 14 percentage points were in the form of US dollars. Gold reserves held by the world excluding the United States grew faster than total gold reserves, since other countries added to their gold holdings also by buying from the inordinately high US gold stocks; only two-thirds of their additional gold holdings came from new production; one-third came from the United States.

By 1959 the growth in dollar reserves of a few European countries ran ahead of their desire for additional dollars, and the United States became increasingly fearful about sales of gold from its stocks. During the 1960s the growth in foreign official dollar holdings increased, so that by the end of 1970 there were over $30 billion in dollars in official reserves, amounting to around a third of total international reserves (see table 8.1).[1]

Since the mid-1960s, and especially since March 1968, when the price of gold in the London market was allowed to rise substantially above the official price of gold, it has been said that the world has been on a dollar standard, because the dollar was de facto inconvertible. This is not strictly true. There were in fact many conversions of dollars into gold at the United States Treasury during these years, and indeed in 1970 alone more than five dozen countries converted a total of $630 million into gold. To be sure, most of these were associated with the increase in International Monetary Fund (IMF) quotas that year. But forty-six countries had converted dollars into gold in 1969, and a dozen countries converted dollars

Table 8.1
End of Year International Reserves ($ billion equivalent).

Holdings	1945	1960	1970	1972
Gold	33.3	38.0	37.2	38.9
US gold holdings	20.1	17.8	11.1	10.5
Foreign Exchange[a]	14.3	18.6	44.6	100.3
US liabilities	4.2	11.1	23.8	61.3
UK liabilities	10.1	6.3	6.6	8.2[c]
Other[b]	–	3.6	10.8	16.3
Total Reserves	47.6	60.2	92.5	155.5
Addendum: World exports during the year	34.2	113.4	280.3	368.0

a. Reported assets differ from US and UK reported liabilities by minor differences in concept, by measurement error, by official holdings of foreign exchange other than dollars and sterling, and (mainly) by official deposits in the eurocurrency market.
b. Special Drawing Rights (SDRs) and reserve positions in the IMF.
c. September.
Sources: *Federal Reserve Bulletin; International Financial Statistics.*

into gold in 1971, before suspension of convertibility. What was true is that total dollar assets held by central banks exceeded US monetary gold by enough to raise serious questions about the continuation of convertibility.[2] Large holders of dollars knew that they could not convert substantial amounts of dollars into gold without threatening the US capacity to maintain convertibility, hence the system itself. This restraint on conversions was made formal only in the case of Germany, which in 1967 agreed not to convert dollars into gold. Belgium, France, the Netherlands, and Switzerland among Group of Ten countries all converted some dollars into gold in 1971.

The "de facto inconvertibility" of the dollar into gold was made formal in August 1971 when President Nixon announced his New Economic Policy, which among other things involved the imposition of a freeze on wages and prices and a 10 percent surcharge on many imports as well as the declaration of nonconvertibility. This declaration followed large outflows of dollars from the United States, and the magnitudes of world dollar holdings increased radically in 1971 and 1972. Official dollar holdings rose by over $40 billion, more than doubling official foreign exchange holdings. The US payments deficit, which on a liquidity basis had averaged around $3 billion a year for nearly a decade, suddenly rose to $22 billion in 1971 and $14 billion in 1972. The United States had actually run a surplus on

official settlements in 1968 and 1969, but this became a large deficit of
nearly $10 billion in 1970 and nearly $30 billion in 1971, dropping back to
$10 billion in 1972.

Reasons for Change

The reasons for these sharp changes are three. First, the US trade balance
gradually deteriorated following the Vietnam war boom of 1966, but
the extent of the deterioration was masked in 1969–70 by a weakening
economy. Second, monetary policy turned from being contractionary (with
very high interest rates) through the first half of 1970 to being expansionary
(with much lower interest rates, especially on short-term securities) in late
1970 and 1971 (tight money explains the official settlements surpluses of
1968 and 1969), and heavy American borrowings in the Eurodollar market
began to be repaid after the change. These in turn were converted into
other currencies in which higher yields were available. Finally, in late spring
1971 speculative movements of funds began to augment other outflows in
a major way, and the outflows then became mutually reinforcing. Much has
been made of the drawing power of Japan and Germany, and indeed
between them these two countries added over $20 billion to their reserves
in 1971 and 1972. But that still left an additional $40 billion that was well
distributed among other countries. All industrial countries and many less
developed countries experienced substantial increases in their reserves during
this period.

In short, the legacy of the last several years is huge official dollar
holdings widely spread around the world. In addition, there are large and
not wholly explained private dollar holdings outside the United States.
And over $15 billion of the increase in official foreign exchange reserves in
1971 and 1972 cannot be accounted for by the US deficit, indicating
cycling through the Eurodollar market and the growing use of the mark,
the yen, and possibly other currencies as official reserves.

The Smithsonian Agreement of December 1971 devalued the dollar (in
terms of gold) for the first time since 1934 and revalued the mark and
the yen. US officials were not really satisfied with the extent of those
negotiated exchange rates and were reinforced in this view when (not
suprisingly, in view of the long response lags inherent in modern commercial transactions in sophisticated products) the US trade balance did not
improve in 1972. They therefore took the occasion of some currency
disturbances to devalue the dollar again fourteen months later.

Deficiencies in the Present Monetary System

Analyses of the ailments of the present international monetary system have now become conventional: They revolve around the tensions that arise out of international use of a national currency and out of imperfections in the balance-of-payments adjustment process. The former tensions arise because the reserve currency country ceases in practice to be under any balance-of-payments discipline once it becomes clear that its capacity to convert outstanding holdings of its currency into other reserve assets cannot be tested without breaking the entire system. The latter difficulties arise because discrete changes in exchange rates, the principal and ultimate adjustment measure under the Bretton Woods system, invite large-scale disruptive speculation in anticipation of such changes. They also impose major shocks to foreign industries in close competition with industries in a country the currency of which has been devalued. Moreover, the system has the additional weakness that countries in balance-of-payments surplus are under no strong pressure to alter their exchange rates even when such alteration would be desirable.

While there is now official recognition of the weaknesses of the present system, the emphasis of such recognition varies markedly from country to country. In particular, the United States has concentrated its attention on the deficiencies in the adjustment process, and especially on the unwillingness of surplus countries and (as the US government perceived it, at least before February 1973) the inability of the United States to change exchange rates when necessary, while in contrast "Europe" (which, however, doesn't really speak with one official voice on these questions) has emphasized of late the weaknesses of a system that uses the dollar extensively as an international currency. The United States calls for effective control over its exchange rate, while "Europe" calls for a resumption of convertibility of the dollar. This strong difference in emphasis threatens a total impasse in discussions of monetary reform unless a reasonable bargain can be struck that covers both areas. In the meantime, US liquid liabilities to foreign central banks have grown to over four times US reserve assets, which at the end of 1972 stood at $13.1 billion, including gold, Special Drawing Rights (SDRs), reserve position at the IMF, and small holdings of foreign exchange. Under the circumstances the United States simply cannot accept any obligations of convertibility and hence "discipline" on its balance of payments without greater assurances on its capacity for exchange rate adjustment than other countries are apparently willing to give. The position of European countries is complicated in considerable measure at present by their firm commitment and tentatives steps to achieve monetary unification, although ultimately such unification should make payments adjustment vis-à-vis the United States easier.

Quite a number of possible futures arise out of the impasse noted above, but it seems useful to distinguish two broad classes of possibility. The first involves a disappearance of the reserve currency role of the dollar, or at least reduction to *de minimis* and geographically confined proportions. The second involves an entrenchment and reinforcement of the international role of the dollar, perpetuation of a "dollar standard."

The second outcome is said to be totally unacceptable to many European and some other countries, although apparently they were less troubled by the incipient dollar standard embodied in the Smithsonian Agreement of December 1971 than by the immediately available alternatives. Moreover, it has been argued that the world could do a lot worse than the dollar standard so long as the American economy is well managed, even when the criteria of good management are exclusively domestic ones, that is, concentrating on maintenance of full employment and reasonable price stability without explicit regard for the balance of payments.[3] The United States, as the balance wheel of the world economy, should stay on an even economic keel, and then other countries could adjust to the United States. Whatever might be said about this arrangement from the point of view of optimum economic management, it is clear that such an arrangement would continue to rankle and would induce a continual struggle to alter the regime. The regime therefore is allegedly unstable and would sooner or later degenerate into a dollar bloc of those countries that were not offended (or found the benefits sufficiently great to outweigh the offense) by a dollar standard and a rest of the world that could not accept a dollar standard and could afford to do without it.

Thus attention is turned to the first possible outcome, a drastic reduction or even elimination of the reserve currency role of the dollar and a move to a system in which the United States is treated with greater symmetry and must behave more like other countries in the context of international finance. The success of achieving this depends on an agreement that involves four components: (1) restoration of convertibility of the dollar into other reserve assets, (2) an agreement on how to handle the large volume of outstanding official dollar holdings, (3) an improvement in the adjustment process, especially as it affects the United States, and (4) arrangements to deal with the problems arising from extensive private international use of the dollar. Each of these points will be taken up in turn.

As noted above, the simple arithmetic of US liquid assets and liabilities is against undertaking an obligation of convertibility without further changes, especially in view of the suspicion that not all the dollars are willingly held. This limitation also applies to "indirect" convertibility that is brought about by a US obligation to support a given set of exchange rates by market intervention. Without adequate reserves the United States cannot sensibly agree to more than token intervention, no matter how hard French Finance Minister Giscard d'Estaing and other European officials press the point. So discussion shifts at once to the other areas.[4]

Consolidation of Foreign Exchange Reserves

A leading proposal, with numerous variants, is to consolidate all reserve currency holdings by converting them to an international claim of some kind, a special issue of SDRs or a new kind of deposit at the IMF. In the limiting case, the consolidation would be both compulsory and complete and would be accompanied by prohibition on further acquisitions of dollars by official holders. In other words, after the consolidation the dollar would become fully convertible and conversion would always take place. This represents the ideal, fully symmetric world sought by some reformers. Most proposals do not go this far and allow the retention of "working balances" of dollars for exchange market intervention and other limited purposes, but these working balances would be restricted in amount.[5] Still weaker versions call for establishing the possibility of converting out-standing dollars into some special reserve asset but leave the option to the existing holders of dollars. Many outstanding dollars would presumably remain unconverted because of the interest yield they command or because of distrust of, or inconveniences associated with, the new asset. This ver-sion aims to satisfy those who reluctantly hold dollars now, by providing indirectly a form of guarantee on their international reserves. But it would not satisfy those who are concerned with the weaknesses of the present system, for it still leaves the dollar with a substantial reserve currency role and the United States without sufficient discipline on its capacity to run payments deficits.

Still other versions permit consolidation of outstanding dollar balances as of some fixed date but do not prohibit the subsequent acquisition of dollars. This proposal would start with a clean slate but would leave open the possibility of a repetition of the present difficulty in future years.

The link between convertibility of the dollar by the United States and the consolidation of outstanding reserve balances of dollars into some other, possibly new, reserve asset is clear and direct: The United States cannot undertake a convertibility obligation so long as the number of dollars subject to conversion so greatly exceeds the United States' capacity to convert. Moreover, without consolidation the United States might find its own reserves depleted over time even if it maintained balance in its international payments, taking one year with another. This possibility arises because countries in surplus might convert their dollar earnings at the United States Treasury, while countries in deficit would pay with dollars rather than with other reserve assets. The link also cuts the other way: Without convertibility any consolidation is ipso facto only once-for-all, and the United States remains free to run payments deficirs.

The Adjustment Process

Even a strong version of consolidation would not permit the United States to agree to reserve asset convertibility. Convertibility also requires that provision be made for adequate balance-of-payment adjustment and for dealing with large movements of foreign private dollar holdings. Without assurance that it can adjust its own effective exchange rate (that is, actually influence cross rates, not merely alter its parity in terms of gold/SDRs), the United States under convertibility would have to govern its domestic economy by the dictates of balance-of-payments requirements. Yet for the United States that could be exceedingly expensive in terms of underutilized labor and capital, or in terms of inflation, and incurring those costs would be in the interests neither of the United States nor of other countries. Thus, as perceived by the United States, an adequate adjustment mechanism must meet two conditions: (1) Countries with substantial payments surpluses must adjust in one way or another so as to eliminate the surpluses; and (2) when many countries are in surplus, the United States must be able to change the exchange rate between the dollar and other currencies.

The Bretton Woods regime provides assurance on neither of these conditions. Adjustment of exchange rates is considered a last-resort device, with a presumption against it. And given the large and discrete nature of the changes, there are built-in inhibitions to using this device, as noted above. This being so, countries in surplus are under no serious pressure to change their exchange rates. The presumption must be altered so that a country in surplus is assumed to appreciate its currency, unless there are compelling reasons against appreciation.

The present system as it has evolved around the reserve currency role of the dollar also makes difficult an adjustment of the dollar exchange rate with any certainty, for inertial forces are on the side of preserving the exchange rate between other currencies and the dollar no matter what happens to the dollar/gold parity. The tortuous negotiations of December 1971 made clear how difficult an adjustment of the dollar exchange rate can be, even in the face of demonstrable disequilibrium. (The second devaluation of the dollar, in February 1973, in many respects went more smoothly. But even that followed a major and disruptive flow of funds from dollars into other currencies, leading to a closing of the foreign exchange markets.) Again, it is necessary to shift the presumption in favor of a change in the exchange rate of the dollar with respect to other currencies when the United States is in payments deficit and the surpluses are widespread. These presumptions would of course have to follow certain guidelines, to minimize the chance that exchange rate changes take place when they are unnecessary or undesirable. The guidelines should be agreed to and understood by all countries so all countries could be held accountable to them. Such guidelines, or presumptive rules as I have called them elsewhere,[6] would meet both the requirements of the United States.

Unfortunately, resistance to both points remains strong. Many officials do not like the idea of shifting the presumption to greater flexibility of exchange rates, and most financial officials do not at all like the idea of laying down rules, even presumptive rules that could be ignored in good cause, to govern changes in exchange rates. This is regrettable, but it is a present fact. For reasons that are obscure, the developing country members of the Committee of Twenty and the International Monetary Fund Executive Board seem also to have taken a strong stand against greater exchange rate flexibility. Their reluctance is thus added to the reluctance of many Europeans to move in this direction, a reluctance that is fortuitously but unfortunately reinforced at the present time by the assigned but exceedingly difficult task of proceeding toward European monetary unification on a relatively short timetable. Perhaps a few more financial crises will provide the required dose of persuasion. But in the meantime, an honest forecast is that the US requirements for improvements in the adjustment mechanism will not be met.

Private Dollar Holdings

As if there were not enough other difficulties, there remains the problem of foreign private dollar balances. These have become huge: $20 billion in American banks at the end of 1972, augmented by an additional $60 billion or more in the Eurodollar market, net of inter-European bank deposits. Some of the Eurodollar deposits are official rather than private—perhaps as much as $10 billion—but to the extent that is so, the outstanding official claims on the US reserve assets under a regime of convertibility have been understated above.[7] Even after allowing for official balances, the private balances are very substantial. To give some idea of the relative magnitude of these holdings, together they exceed the total domestic money supply of every country except the United States ($253 billion) and Japan ($101 billion). These large balances presumably reflect the need for international money in the world of private transactions, and the advantages of international banking. They may also reflect the competition of unregulated banks with domestic banks which in all countries are subject to numerous government regulations concerning reserve requirements, the payment of interest on demand and time deposits, restrictions on assets, and the like. Whatever the reason, large balances are held for transactions purposes and for short-term investment. These balances are highly mobile in times of impending financial disturbance, which in turn contributes to the disturbance.

How do these balances fit into the plans for international monetary reform? Should they be funded along with the official balances? Should restrictions be placed on the Eurocurrency market so that the balances, once funded, do not simply reappear? Eliminating the private balances and restricting the Eurodollar market could only be done at considerable cost to the efficiency of private international transactions. At least this is the dominant view in international banking circles, and it is probably correct. To the extent that the growth of the Eurodollar market has taken place merely as an evasion of sensible government regulations of domestic banking systems, however, the cost of restricting the market would be lower, and might even turn into a benefit. The weighing of the those costs and benefits will not be considered here. The point is, so long as the Eurodollar market exists, it is a source of potential disturbance, and large movements of private dollars into official hands at some future time could easily undo whatever had been accomplished through consolidation of official dollar holdings.

To appreciate this, suppose that the adjustment process works well, in the sense of keeping payments in balance over a period of time, but that it works slowly. Then if large private dollar balances are converted into other currencies, what happens? Is the United States to be held accountable for converting the resulting official balances into other reserve assets? Unless there is some provision for accommodation of this contingency, the system will break down, that is, a convertible dollar will necessarily be declared inconvertible or be allowed to float freely in the exchange market. There is, to be sure, some self-correction in the Eurodollar market. A large withdrawal of Eurodollars will lead to a sharp increase in Eurodollar interest rates, and this rise will tend to inhibit further withdrawals. But if Eurodollar rates rise far enough, they will attract funds from the United States (or funds that otherwise would have returned to the United States), and this will be so even with restrictions on capital outflows from the United States; for such restrictions, unless they encompass *all* international transactions, that is, unless they represent a full panoply of exchange controls, are bound to be less than fully effective in the postulated circumstance. Thus the corrective adjustment in Eurodollar rates will not be sufficient.

Moreover, the exposure to large movements of capital does not arise only from large private foreign dollar holdings. Other currencies are increasingly held by foreigners as well—the mark has already been mentioned—and these funds will be mobile as well, although their countries of origin are better supplied with reserves to cope with them than is the United States. More significant, *domestic* funds are also increasingly mobile and can be expected to move in ever greater volume across the foreign exchanges when profit-making opportunities present themselves. This is one manifestation of the growing economic interdependence among countries.

Lines of Credit

It is necessary to have large swap facilities or other large lines of credit to cover this contingency. But unfortunately such lines of credit may recreate the situation that consolidation of outstanding official dollar balances was designed to avoid. If the conversion of private dollar balances into other currencies is short-lived, the situation will reverse itself and no problem will arise. But if the conversion turns out not to be reversed then some arrangement will be necessary for additional consolidation. The arrangement in the past to cover such contingencies has been for the United States to draw on its network of swap facilities, amounting now to nearly $12 billion, for credit for ninety days and possibly longer; but if reversal did not occur within a relatively short period of time, then the swaps would be repaid out of a drawing on the IMF, which in effect converted the swaps into a three-to-five year line of credit. But the present swap network and US drawing rights (at $8.4 billion for the gold tranche and four credit tranches combined) at the IMF are totally inadequate for the potential exposure involved in conversions of private dollar balances. Moreover, US drawing rights at the IMF are limited by the probable need for the

IMF itself to borrow in order to honor a large US drawing. This inadequacy has been masked in the past by a totally different mechanism: the willingness (however reluctant) of central banks to acquire and hold dollars without limit. Thus a "dollar standard" automatically provides the required line of credit to the United States: Recycling is built into it. An alternative would be to endow the United States will a large initial allocation of reserves, say, in the form of SDRs, so that it could meet any convertibility obligations arising from massive conversion of private dollar holdings. But such an allocation could also be used to finance payments deficits. It would therefore be difficult to justify, especially in a period in which many developing countries are also laying down special claims for larger allocation of SDRs.

Freely floating exchange rates would of course avoid this whole problem—or, more accurately, they would transform it into a different but no less difficult problem, namely, how to avoid or mitigate the influence of speculative currency movements on exchange rates, which represent too important an economic variable for most countries to allow to move with complete freedom under all circumstances.

The best alternative would be to convert the IMF into a true lender-of-last-resort—a true central bank for central banks in the classic sense—by allowing it to lend any amount of SDRs necessary to permit member countries, and in particular the United States, to maintain their convertibility obligations in the face of large outflows of liquid funds. If currency conversions reversed themselves, the United States would repay the IMF immediately thereafter; if they did not, the United States would be committed to repay the IMF over a long period of years, and the dollar exchange rate would be allowed to adjust enough to permit the United States to run the requisite payments surpluses.

The IMF would have to be released from the present tight constraints both on its capacity to lend and on its authority to create SDRs, and this will of course give central bankers pause. But the lessons we learned to deal with financial crises at the national level years ago must now be applied, with appropriate modification, at the international level. The great and growing mobility of private funds requires it.

In summary, private dollar balances are the *pièce de résistance*: Not to make allowance for them would jeopardize most of the reform plans advanced thus far. But to make allowance for them, for example, by offering a large special allocation of SDRs to the United States or by prohibiting foreign private holdings of dollars or by endowing the IMF with true central bank powers, calls for more drastic changes than have so far been contemplated by officials. This is the basis for my forecast at the outset of this paper: At the end of a decade the position of the dollar will not be very much different from what it is now.

While such a state of affairs may appear to be satisfactory, especially to Americans, that will not be so. For in several senses the system will not be a stable one. Rivals to the dollar, while not displacing it from position, will make possible larger, and more frequent, movement of funds from one currency to another in response to anticipated gains or losses; and these movements will be sufficiently alarming to monetary officials to prompt continuing pressures for tight controls on international transactions. Moreover, an international system that continues to be dependent on a national currency will not be accepted as a durable system, and this lack of acceptance will itself be a source of instability in the system, for attempts, individual and collective, to alter the system will be constantly in the air. The lack of acceptance of a dollar-dominated system can hardly avoid corroding other aspects of international relations as well.

Thus, it is devoutly to be hoped that the forecast proves to be too pessimistic, that those charged with monetary reform will cease dallying and press forward with the complicated and comprehensive changes that are necessary.

Notes

1. There is some ambiguity about how many dollars were held in international reserves at this time, for a substantial discrepancy had developed between liabilities reported by the United Kingdom and the United States, on one hand, and foreign exchange assets reported to the International Monetary Fund (IMF) by all central banks, on the other. The bulk of the discrepancy was presumably dollars held in the Eurodollar market, hence not recorded as liabilities to official holders by the United States. But some of the discrepancy was also explained by official holdings of currencies other than the dollar and the pound.

2. The term "convertibility" is here used to mean convertibility of the dollar into gold at a fixed official price. This is only one of many possible meanings of "convertibility," and one of the least important. The dollar continues to be convertible into other currencies without restriction, either at a relatively fixed price or at a fluctuating price. For various distinctions and their relative importance, see Gottfried Haberler, *Currency Convertibility* (Washington, D.C.: American Enterprise Institute, 1954).

3. See Ronald I. McKinnon, *Private and Official International Money: The Case for the Dollar*, Princeton Essay in International Finance No. 74, April 1969.

4. For a critical review of the conditions for resumption of convertibility of the dollar, with a presumption against it, see William Fellner, "The Dollar's Place in the International System: Suggested Criteria for the Appraisal of Emerging Views," *Journal of Economic Literature*, X, September, 1972, pp. 746–55.

5. Robert Triffin, for example, has proposed that no more than 15 percent of a country's total reserves could be held in the form of national currencies. See his "International Monetary Collapse and Reconstruction in April 1972," *Journal of International Economics*, Vol. 2, September 1972, p. 387.

6. See my "Gliding Parities: The Case for Presumptive Rules," in G. Halm, ed., *Approaches to Greater Flexibility of Exchange Rates: The Burgenstock Papers* (Princeton University Press, 1970). I there suggest that changes in international reserves above some minimum amount would provide the most defensible guideline, but other criteria might also be added. See also C. Fred Bergsten, *Reforming the Dollar: An International Monetary Policy for the United States* (New York: Council on Foreign Relations, September 1972), pp. 48–62.

7. Data on the Eurodollar market, while improving rapidly, are still unsatisfactory. Eight European countries report the Euro-currency claims and liabilities of their banks to the Bank for International Settlements, which in turn publishes summary information in its annual report. But a breakdown between private and official deposits is not available, and extensive activities by banks in other countries are not decomposed into bank and nonbank claims and liabilities, thus preventing a measure of the real size of the Eurodollar market. For example, $11 million of the US bank liabilities were to foreign banks, many of which are undoubtedly in the eurocurrency market. Thus some "double-counting" is involved in simply adding the two totals.

9   Sterling, European Monetary Unification, and the International Monetary System

In mid-August 1971, while most Europeans and many Americans were basking in the summer sun, President Nixon dropped an economic bombshell whose reverberations will be heard for many years to come. On the domestic side, which does not concern us here, it involved measures to expand the American economy, coupled with wage and price controls for the first time since the Korean War of 1950. On the international side, it involved the imposition of an additional 10 percent tariff on all dutiable imports (comprising about two-thirds of total imports) and the relatively esoteric but emotive declaration that the US dollar would no longer be freely convertible into gold by foreign monetary authorities.

These two steps affecting international transactions represented a direct assault on the leading principles that had guided international economic intercourse since the Second World War. Those principles conferred on gold a central, although somewhat concealed, role in the international monetary system, required fixity of foreign-exchange rates at "par values" to be changed only infrequently and under specified circumstances, called for gradual reduction of government-imposed barriers to trade, and, above all, involved a recognition by all major countries of mutual interest in matters affecting international commerce and hence close cooperation in managing the international economic system.

This system, embodied in legal form in the Bretton Woods Agreement and in the General Agreement on Tariffs and Trade (GATT), had become, however, subject to severe tensions arising from developments that had not been fully anticipated when it was laid down, and to which it has been unable fully to adapt. These tensions were bound to cause substantial changes in the system, but few anticipated just how soon and in what dramatic form initiation of the alterations would come.

British North-American Committee, 1972. Reprinted by permission.

The purpose of this paper is not to discuss the whole range of issues concerning the international monetary and trading system, but rather to focus on four narrower problems: (1) the impact of Britain's entry into the European Community (EC) on the external role of sterling, which requires a prior look at (2) the impact of entry on the British balance of payments, (3) the prospects for a unified European currency, and (4) the impact of a unified European currency on the international monetary system. It will, nevertheless, be necessary to make an excursion into the broader framework of the existing monetary system, for the tensions found there will help not only in understanding, even if not approving, the American moves of August 1971 but also in interpreting the possibilities and problems of monetary evolution in an enlarged European Community.

By now, it has become conventional for economists to approach analytical discussion of the international monetary system under three separate headings, each representing a complex set of problems and offering a range of possible solutions that are partially—but only partially—separable from one another. The headings *liquidity, adjustment,* and *confidence* offer a fruitful organizing scheme, around which most issues of practical as well as theoretical importance can be discussed, and an understanding of which is essential background for considering the concrete policy questions that face nations. However, for completeness, I would broaden these topics by adding a further heading—*interdependence*—which covers a range of issues related to but fundamentally different from the first three topics. These four analytical topics will be briefly discussed before returning to the more specific problems listed above.

Four Problems for the International Monetary System

Liquidity

The liquidity problem arises from the alleged need of a growing international economy for a corresponding growth in international reserves to support it, combined with the fact that adequate additions to monetary gold, the traditional reserve asset, are simply not available from extant gold production after deduction for private uses of gold. A rise in the price of gold might solve this problem, both by increasing the value of existing monetary stocks and by enlarging the quantity of gold available for additions to monetary stocks, but it would do so only with costs in terms of potential inflation, maldistribution of the gains (South Africa and Soviet

Russia are the leading producers), and waste of economic resources that are best avoided.

The gap between demand for new reserves and available supply of gold has existed for many years and has been filled by the growing use of the US dollar as a reserve asset, initially "as good as gold" because of the standing commitment of the US Treasury to convert central bank held dollars into gold at a fixed price. But, the Treasury's ability to honor this commitment has become more tenuous over time as the ratio of reserve dollars to the US gold stock has grown, as it inevitably must do under the postulated circumstances, even with US deficits only large enough to satisfy the growth in world demand for reserves. Thus, a "gold-exchange standard," under which most countries hold the national currency of some central country that in turn holds gold, must necessarily evolve into an "exchange standard" as the conversion commitment becomes less plausible and ultimately impossible to honor except for proportionally small amounts. In these limiting circumstances, however, the reserve-providing country is able literally to issue international money, and hence to command resources from the rest of the world at will, a prospect that is politically unacceptable. President Nixon's announcement of August 15, 1971, that the dollar would no longer be freely convertible into gold simply involved formal acknowledgment of the dilemma of a gold-exchange standard, and the subsequent decision by most other major countries to "float" their currencies against the dollar, at least temporarily, reflected their unwillingness to accept the full implications of a dollar standard.[1]

Sterling and the French franc play the role of reserve currency in areas historically associated with Britain and France, respectively, but, in practice, their ability to "exploit" the reserve currency status of their currencies in recent years has been sufficiently limited to place them in a fundamentally different category from the United States.

While the reserve currency status of the dollar may be subject to abuse and hence is politically and economically offensive, it has performed a genuine social function; calls to eliminate this status, therefore, require alternative solutions. It is in this connection that the special drawing rights (SDRs) at the International Monetary Fund (IMF) were developed, for they potentially provide an international solution to the need for growing reserves, eliminating the world's dependence for reserve growth both on gold and on the dollar. They have had an auspicious beginning, but they are still too new and untested to hail as the reserve asset of the future. Their early life has been complicated by US deficits of unprecedented size, which leads to the second major heading, adjustment. But, before we turn to adjustment, it should be noted that the analytical foundation for the dependence of a growing world economy on growing international reserves is a tenuous one; private finance and trade credit certainly must grow, but they are different from reserves, which are used only to finance residual imbalances between countries beyond what can be financed (or beyond what countries desire to finance) through private markets.[2] It has not been established that payments imbalances must increase with the growth in trade and private financial transactions, although there is some presumption that they will do so. In any case, the relationship is not independent of the adjustment process, for rapid adjustment will reduce the need for reserves. But, since governments and central banks often use imports as a guide to their needs, there is at least a psychological link between the growth in trade and the growth in demand for reserves.

Adjustment

The adjustment process concerns the capacity of countries to eliminate imbalances in their international payments. The problem arises because both the "classical" method of deflating the economy of a country in payments deficit and inflating the economy of a country in surplus and the Bretton Woods method (which, in principle, countries today are bound to use) of eliminating "fundamental" imbalances by discrete changes in the exchange rate meet great political resistance. Deflation or inflation frequently conflicts with domestic economic objectives, which in democratic societies are politically dominant. Discrete changes in exchange rates in a world of high capital mobility invite market disruption and huge national losses as a result of anticipatory movements of funds; they jolt the economy more than most other changes in economic policy; and they are politically risky for those who make the decision. Moreover, countries in surplus have a disincentive to up-value their currencies and deliberately weaken the competitiveness of their industries, and, unlike countries in deficit, they face no limit corresponding to the exhaustion of international reserves.

   The adjustment problem is further complicated by the special role that the dollar has come to play in international finance, since it means that the technical solution (currency devaluation for a country in deficit) offered by the IMF is not available to the United States unilaterally in the sense that a successful devaluation of the US dollar against other currencies would require active decisions by other countries to change the rates at which they intervene vis-à-vis the dollar in the exchange markets. Thus, decision-making inertia combines with a fear of becoming less competitive with respect to the world's largest trading nation to favor maintaining existing exchange rates in the case of a US move, which to that extent denies the United States control over its exchange rate, as distinguished from the world price of gold. Hence, the US adoption in August 1971 of a 10 percent surcharge on imports represented an attempt to influence the price at which all (dutiable) imports enter the United States. The reluctance of many other countries to allow their currencies to float freely upward, and France's insistence on pegging its commercial transactions to the dollar at the prevailing exchange rate, illustrated just how little control the United States had over the relation between its currency and others even in the face of strong inducements for others to appreciate. Weeks of difficult and even acrimonious bargaining were required to achieve the parity changes of late 1971, and then only after the United States had taken measures that threatened the international monetary system itself.

Solutions to the adjustment problem have been sought along the lines of introducing greater flexibility into exchange rates, with a view to reducing both the attractions of speculating on a change in parity and the degree of national prestige and political commitment now involved in maintaining existing parties. The parity changes of sterling, the French franc, and the German mark in the late sixties removed the major sources of disequilibrium among European countries and thereby lulled the financial community into a false sense of well-being with regard to the adjustment problem. IMF discussions of the subject, at fever pitch in 1969, became desultory, and a complacent report was issued in 1970. The currency flare-up in May 1971, which led Austria and Switzerland to revalue their currencies and Germany and the Netherlands to "float" theirs, reminded everyone that all was not well. But, the insufficient sense of urgency on the part of most national monetary authorities and the IMF led to the unilateral actions by the United States in August 1971. A recurrence of financial crises can be confidently predicted until the adjustment process is improved.

Confidence

The confidence problem arises from the coexistence of several widely acceptable reserve assets, and hence the possibility of disturbing shifts among them. The emphasis here is on reserve assets, since shifts between financial instruments by private individuals, however massive, can, in principle, be compensated by counteracting shifts among central banks ("recycling"). So long as central banks cooperate, private shifts can disrupt particular markets but they cannot threaten the system as a whole. The possibility of shifts in central bank portfolios, especially shifts out of dollars or sterling, could, in contrast, induce a basic change in the system by compelling the reserve currency countries to declare foreign-held balances henceforth inconvertible (into gold or SDRs in the case of the United States and into dollars, gold or SDRs in the case of Britain) at a fixed price.

The likelihood of such shifts depends in large part on the balance-of-payments positions of the reserve currency countries and the prospect of a change in the value of these currencies against other reserve assets, i.e., a devaluation of sterling or a rise in the dollar price of gold. Thus, it can be argued that the confidence problem is entirely derivative from the adjustment problem, and that a solution to the latter will reduce the former to a problem of negligible importance. If the solution to the adjustment problem encompasses more frequent and possibly continuous changes in the dollar price of sterling or the dollar price of gold, however, the prospect of major shifts between reserve assets remains, for movements in these prices will create incentives to shift from one asset to another, incentives that cannot wholly and continuously be compensated by interest-rate differentials (even if central banks were fully willing to substitute interest earnings for capital losses) without tying domestic monetary policies largely to this objective.

A variety of solutions have been suggested, most having the same central characteristic of involving a conversion of the several reserve assets of today into a single, composite reserve asset—for example, SDRs—which countries would agree to hold exclusively, except for working balances. Thus, the existing reserve assets would be consolidated into a single, central account, subject to international management, and the possibility of speculative shifts among them would be eliminated.

Interdependence

The problem here is that markets for capital, business enterprise and even labor increasingly exceed the span of national control at a time when citizens are making ever more exacting demands on their governments for economic performance. Yet, the national instruments of economic policy, to be effective, usually require that markets for labor and capital be no larger than the nation. The most obvious and topical area in which the loss of control can be observed is monetary policy, where high international capital mobility under a regime of fixed exchange rates increasingly limits central bank control over domestic monetary conditions. With the Eurodollar market linking most domestic money markets directly or indirectly, only the largest countries can influence monetary conditions through their actions, and even they have increasing difficulty in doing so, as the 1970–71 German attempt to maintain monetary conditions tighter than those in the United States testifies—it led to abandonment of the fixed exchange rate. The problem is that as any country attempts to tighten its domestic monetary conditions beyond those prevailing in other major countries, and in particular in the United States, it will find its commercial banks borrowing increasingly from foreigners for conversion into local currency. Under the central banks' obligation to buy foreign currency at a fixed price, this practice will automatically lead to an increase in the money supply no matter how hard the central bank is trying through its other operations to limit such an increase. If domestic banks are prevented from borrowing abroad, firms, local authorities and even individuals will go abroad for funds directly, mainly to the Eurodollar market in London. A world money market under fixed exchange rates requires a world monetary policy, and countries will have to find measures other than monetary action (e.g., tax policy) to stabilize domestic economic activity, to the extent that domestic requirements differ from those in the community of nations at large. The tax and expenditure policies of a government can be used to influence the course of domestic demand, and international capital movements will ensure that the money supply will accommodate the change in demand, at least insofar as confidence in existing exchange-rate parities persists, so that for any single country, monetary policy becomes passive—a point to which we will return in discussing monetary integration in Europe.

Alternatively, in order to reestablish domestic monetary control, steps will have to be taken to fragment the international market, returning it to the national level. In this instance, greater exchange-rate flexibility, in addition to contributing to adjustment, will serve the latter function by introducing greater uncertainty into the earnings on short-term funds shifted between currencies; the temporary German switch to rate flexibility in 1970 represented such an attempt, as does the widening of exchange-rate margins to $2\frac{1}{4}$ percent on either side of the dollar that took place in December 1971.

Many countries have also imposed or tightened controls on movements of financial capital in an attempt to reassert national monetary control. These efforts can work for a while, but improvements in communication and enlargement of contacts between residents of different nations (including business enterprises) augurs against long-run success in fragmenting the international capital market in this way.

Of the various possible forms of interdependence, monetary interdependence is perhaps the furthest advanced at the present time, and certainly poses the most visible problems for preservation of national economic control. But, the pressure of increased interdependence toward coordination of national policies, or even toward supranational control, also exists in other areas, for example, in maintaining competition in the face of transnational mergers and takeovers of business enterprises or in maintaining national influence over the distribution of income in the face of increased international mobility of skilled individuals. These matters will require solutions different from those appropriate to the monetary arena, but they also are less pressing.

It should be noted that while large-scale movements of funds from one country to another in response to divergent interest rates and other monetary conditions do lead to recorded "deficits" or "surpluses" in the balance-of-payments accounts, these imbalances must be carefully distinguished conceptually from imbalances arising from divergences in long-term growth trends or in cost-price competitiveness. The adjustment problem discussed above refers to these longer-term divergences, not, without stretching the term, to large movements of interest-sensitive capital responding to divergent national monetary actions. A change in exchange-rate parities can correct the former problem, but not the latter. Preservation of national monetary autonomy requires either extensive exchange controls or flexible exchange rates to isolate national markets from international flows.

British Entry to the European Community and Sterling

The foregoing analysis sets the stage for discussion of the issues of immediate interest, which will be limited in this chapter to the first two problems noted at the outset—the impact of Britain's entry to the European Community on the external role of sterling, and the prerequisite question of what entry will mean for Britain's payments balance—drawing in other matters as appropriate. But, these two problems cannot be considered sensibly except in some overall framework for analyzing the international monetary system, which the above discussion briefly attempts to provide. Whereas this framework has now become largely conventional, discussions of the economic effects on Britain of its entry to the European Community, of the impact on the role of sterling, and of the prospects for a unified European currency are bound to be more conjectural and hence more tendentious. In addition, the effects of these developments on the monetary system at large are not independent of what is happening elsewhere, especially with respect to the outflow of dollars and the American as well as European response to it.

Britain's Balance of Payments

The first economic question that is usually asked in connection with Britain's entry into the European Community concerns the impact on Britain's balance of payments. This focus has rightly been criticized as ignoring the more fundamental factors affecting economic welfare, but it is relevant to the role of sterling in an enlarged Community, for if sterling is perpetually under a cloud its prospects for providing the basis for a common European currency will be considerably dimmer than if Britain's payments position retains the strength it has shown in the last few years.

The major certain impact of entry on Britain's balance of payments concerns the effect of the common agricultural policy (CAP), which will worsen Britain's current account position by an estimated £300–£400 million (roughly $800–$1,000 million), made up partly of higher prices Britain will have to pay for European agricultural products and partly by Britain's financial contribution to the Community from variable levies collected on imports from outside the Community.

It is not clear which way the net change in trade in manufactures will go. Britain's imports from the rest of the Community will clearly rise more than they otherwise would as a result of the elimination of tariffs, but some of this gain will be at the expense of outsiders. By the same token, however, Britain's exports to the Community will increase, and there is some evidence that the second effect will dominate the first, since European demand for British goods is apparently somewhat more responsive to price changes than is British demand for European goods. On the other hand, Britain's exports to the rest of the world will decline relative to what they would otherwise be, as a result both of the loss of Commonwealth preference and of the loss in income that some other countries will experience because of Britain's switch to the common agricultural policy. Estimated net effects range from a worsening by as much as £200 million a year to an improvement of £100 million annually.

Some hope has been expressed that Britain's entry will lead to a large net inflow of capital, partly in the form of European portfolio investments in

British securities and partly in the form of third country (mainly American) investment in Britain to serve the enlarged Common Market. As to the first, the probability seems low that there would be a *net* inflow of portfolio investment into Britain because British investment in European securities has been under greater restraint in recent years than Continental investment in British securities.

As far as direct investment is concerned, there is evidence, though not decisive, for believing that a net *outflow* from Britain could occur, at least for a number of years. The main reason is that rates of return on real investment seem to be higher in the existing European Community than they are in Britain. The evidence is not conclusive, since reliable figures on rates of return are not available for most European countries. Available data indicate, however, that American investments in manufacturing earned an average of over 15 percent in the European Community in 1969–70, compared with under 10 percent in Britain, both after payment of local profits taxes. Averaging rates of return on American investments over a longer period narrows this gap substantially, for British profits were cyclically depressed in 1969–70 while German profits were cyclically strong. Nevertheless, profits on investments in Britain over the seven years from 1964–70 were still marginally lower than the average for the Community, and profits on investments in Germany during the same period were 40 percent higher than those in Britain.

It must be emphasized that this evidence is only suggestive. Nevertheless, if rates of return prove to be higher in the Community than in Britain, then removal of the restraints on outflow of British direct investment to the Continent, as would be required with entry, would probably lead to a net increase in British investment there, since even the British market could be served duty-free from the Continent. Should this happen, the result would not be merely or even mainly a balance-of-payments problem, for it would also affect the location of new British-owned plant and equipment to serve both foreign and home markets. A possible increased British investment in Europe would very likely involve an outflow of funds, with corresponding pressure on the balance of payments; and any switching of foreign (i.e., American) investment from Britain to the Continent would certainly have that effect. But, even in the improbable event that such British investment were to be financed entirely from outside Britain, giving rise to no net outflow of capital, the prospect that some additional investment in new British productive capacity would be installed in the European Community rather than in Britain would lead to less growth of output in Britain. Thus, it is possible for certain residents of Britain to benefit from entry into the

Common Market even though the economy of the British Isles may not benefit in terms of faster growth for some period of time.[3]

The joining of factor markets requires bringing factor returns into correspondence in the new, enlarged market. Capital is more mobile than labor, and British investors will be given an opportunity for profitable investment that, generally speaking, they do not have today. If there are persisting significant disparities between rates of return in the United Kingdom and on the Continent, the rate of return on investment would have to rise in Britain, which would put restraints on real wages compared to what they might be without the movement of capital. Analytically, the joining of markets leads to a new "equilibrium" distribution of income at the given institutional and tax structure. For Britain, this would require a relative, though not necessarily an absolute, decline in real wages. If it were to occur, such a shift would be in addition to the decline in real wages resulting from adoption of the common agricultural policy. If labor were unwilling to accept the relative decline, the outcome might be a period of industrial unrest and high unemployment in Britain, as British firms increasingly served the British market from outside Britain.

Optimists may hope that continuation of Britain's present payments surplus after repayment of outstanding debt may be sufficient to cover the admitted burden of the CAP, without a devaluation. Pessimists argue that a devaluation will be necessary to cover the CAP burden. The view above is even more pessimistic, for it suggests that one devaluation alone may not be sufficient, for (to put the matter in chronological perspective) a devaluation in the mid-seventies to cover the CAP burden may fail to anticipate adequately (or may not be allowed by EC partners fearful of their own competitive positions to anticipate) the outflow of British investment and consequential return flow of imports that will build up gradually after investment restraints are removed. However, in this case, a new devaluation would only be palliative *unless* it succeeded in reducing real British wages enough (relative to what they would otherwise be) on a lasting basis to make investment in Britain attractive relative to investment on the Continent; and, in any case, tentative EC plans would absolutely bar devaluation after 1981. In short, British entry to the Community, entailing as it would complete removal of restraints on investment in Europe, will alter the required distribution of income in Britain in favor of profit. How far the change in income shares will have to go to equalize profit rates, and how acceptable the change will be, is difficult to say. But, even a small change in income shares—1 or 2 percentage points—is large relative to annual increases in income. It might mean, for example, that wage and salary workers would experience *no* increase in income during a year in which the economy was growing normally, following which wages would resume growth but from the relatively lower level.

This extremely pessimistic outlook is perhaps mitigated by several factors. First, rates of return have gradually been falling in Europe (again based on the same kind of limited evidence mentioned above), and this will go some way toward closing the gap; but the process is a slow one. Second, British firms will not respond to the new opportunities at once, so British investment in Europe may begin modestly and spread over a long period of time. Attachment to established practices and concern for worker goodwill will assure continuing investment in Britain even when higher returns can be achieved elsewhere. Third, profit rates may conceivably rise in Britain as a direct result of entry, either because of economies of scale that can be realized in Britain but not on the European Continent, or because inefficient practices prevailing at present are eliminated in response to the *threat* of competition and, in the case of labor practices, of plant relocation, as distinguished from their actuality.

Finally, joining the Community does not imply that Britain loses complete control over its distribution of income and its level of investment, at least in the medium run. But, it may have to manipulate the effective corporate profits tax, as Belgium has done, to achieve a desired level of investment, and, as a result, either cut government expenditures or impose heavier taxes on those other residents of the Community that are less responsive to higher returns on the Continent.

Sterling Reserves

Next to these issues, the question of the reserve and transaction currency roles of sterling is entirely secondary and much over-rated as a problem either for Britain or for the Community following Britain's entry. In any case, this issue now seems to be resolved with French acceptance of Britain's statement of intention to phase out the sterling balances over an unspecified number of years.

It is not entirely clear what European anxieties were on this score. At times, it has been suggested that the reserve role of sterling gives undue advantage to Britain; at other times, that the large sterling liabilities will place an undue burden on other members of the Community. The first point seems incorrect and the second misplaced. The reserve role of sterling is in secular decline; official sterling balances of the sterling area generally have not risen over time, despite a substantial increase in total reserves of the sterling area countries. To be sure, official sterling balances have recently risen as a result of good export earnings in the overseas sterling area, high British interest rates, and a dollar guarantee; but, most of this increase simply restored their pre-1967 levels. As the trade of sterling area countries diversifies, so will their reserves. Moreover, Britain is not relieved of balance-of-payments "discipline" by virtue of official sterling reserve balances. In recent years, the payments position of the outer sterling area has tended to reinforce that of Britain, so that British reserves tend to rise and fall by more than Britain's own payments position, reinforcing balance-of-payments pressure on Britain. This experience contrasts with the fifties, when the payments positions of the two areas were more complementary, due to proportionately larger trade between them.[4]

In both of these respects, it is an error to link sterling and the dollar together, for the position of the United States in this regard has been entirely different from that of Britain. Dollar balances have risen, and the United States, by virtue of the reserve currency role of the dollar, has been relieved of some balance-of-payments discipline.

Concern about the possible burden of sterling liabilities is misplaced because, as a practical matter, the members of the Community, along with other industrial countries, carry that burden anyway, where "burden" means responsibility to supply the cash in the unlikely event that the official holders of sterling should massively attempt to convert their sterling to something else. Solidarity among the industrial countries is high when it comes to providing short-term credit to finance speculative movements, for the good reason that it would redound to the disadvantage of all of them if a major country were to be forced to take strong unilateral action (a large devaluation or restrictions on trade) in response to speculative movements of this type. "Burden" in this sense is quite different from accepting the liabilities, which will be quite unnecessary when Britain is a full member of the Community. As a potential claim on national resources, the liabilities will remain Britain's.

Sterling continues to play an important role as a currency for private transactions, and this does give rise to speculative movements of funds when the parity of sterling is in doubt. But, the magnitude of the resulting outflows are no greater than they have been for other major countries in similar circumstances today: France lost $2.5 billion in reserves in less than two months in 1968; Germany gained $6 billion in early 1969 and lost the same amount in late 1969 after appreciation of the mark. Two billion dollars moved into Germany in a single 24-hour period in May 1971, and $4 billion moved into Japan in 10 days in August 1971, despite Japan's extensive exchange controls. All countries are subject to large speculative flows when parity changes are in prospect, and the magnitudes are greatly enlarged by the high mobility of liquid funds. Britain is no longer unique in this respect.

Furthermore, even if all sides fully agreed on the desirability of dispensing with the reserve and transactions roles of sterling, it is not clear how that could be done. Triffin[5] and others have suggested that the reserve role could be eliminated by persuading or requiring all official holders to deposit their sterling in a central fund backed by all major countries, and to be issued liquid claims on the fund instead. But, that alone would not suffice; the key to elimination of the reserve role of sterling would be agreement by all countries not to hold sterling assets in their official reserves *in the future*, an unprecedented self-denial. To the extent that they are willing holders now, they would be reluctant to undertake any such agreement; and, in any case, denying asset holders access to one of the world's major financial markets (British treasury bills, etc.) would violate today's financial conventions.[6] Even if such an agreement could be negotiated among monetary authorities—and undoubtedly it could be with sufficient pressure—this would not eliminate the private foreign balances in sterling, many of which are held for transactions purposes and some of which are held for investment purposes. So long as a good market exists, it would be virtually impossible, and certainly undesirable, to prevent foreigners from operating in it; indeed, under existing EC directives, Britain would be obliged to allow other members of the Community to buy and sell British securities. As long as London remains unequalled as a market for short-term investment, and as long as sterling-denominated assets are not threatened by fears of devaluation, large foreign-held sterling balances will persist.

Of course, Britain could greatly reduce the incentives to hold sterling. It could deliberately lower its interest rates, for example. But, such a policy would often run counter to what was required for domestic or balance-of-payments objectives. As long as the institutions of the City of London are efficient and reliable, sterling will be an attractive currency to hold for many purposes. Indeed, it is the strength of the City's institutions that have buoyed the reserve and transaction roles of sterling, rather than vice versa. Britain could also, however, gradually remove the dollar guarantees to officially held sterling introduced in 1968, and that would, no doubt, lead to some reduction in the reserve currency role of sterling.

The contrasting observations on the possible difficulties of entry and the continuing strength of British financial institutions can be summed up by saying that *if* economic adjustment to Britain's entry takes place smoothly, either because the pessimistic prognostication regarding the location of British investment is wrong, or because the British public willingly accepts the necessary realignment of wages and profits and hence the distribution of income, then sterling will be the most attractive European currency, despite the overseas sterling liabilities. If the adjustment proves long and painful, however, it will cast a shadow over sterling for the duration, and the institutions of the City will increasingly turn their talents to other currencies, as they indeed already have. This brings us to consideration of the third problem——that of European monetary unification.

Monetary Unification in Europe

The members of the European Community have expressed "their political will to introduce, in the course of the next 10 years, an economic and monetary union" which *inter alia* will involve the formation of "an individual monetary unit within the international system, characterized by the total and irreversible convertibility of currencies, the elimination of fluctuation margins of rates of exchange and the irrevocable fixing of parity rates"——in short, a single currency in everything except possibly name.[7] Irrevocably fixed exchange rates combined with total and irreversible convertibility imply that balance-of-payments adjustment *within* the Community will be of the same type that prevailed during the gold standard, viz., any net outflow of funds from a region (country) within the Community will automatically result in monetary deflation in that region sufficient to bring the outflow to a halt.

These two conditions also imply a common monetary policy, even if only a passive one, for the Community as a whole, since any attempt by member countries to pursue divergent monetary policies will automatically result in payments imbalances that will, in turn, force countries back into monetary harmony. Thus, national governments will be sharply limited in their ability to finance budget deficits through domestic credit creation; they will have to rely instead on their capacity to raise funds in private markets. The pursuit of a common monetary policy for the Community as a whole raises questions both about the mechanism for accomplishing this and about the political responsibility of those who are entrusted with determining that policy.

Monetary union in Europe does not, however, imply fixity of exchange rates and reliance on gold-standard type monetary adjustment concerning Community-wide payments imbalances with the outside world; these could be handled with the variety of techniques currently available to national governments, such as exchange controls or changes in exchange rates.

Three Approaches to Monetary Unification

If monetary union is the objective, what are the means for achieving it? Three ways to begin have been proposed:

• The official Werner Report on European monetary union at the operational level lays heavy emphasis on narrowing the range of permissible fluctuation in exchange rates among the European currencies, which, because the dollar is used as the intervention currency, can now fluctuate more against one another than they can against the dollar.

• European, and especially German, critics of the Werner Report have argued that monetary union cannot be achieved and exchange rates successfully narrowed without first coordinating economic policies, and especially budgetary policies, among the members of the Community. They therefore urge a concerted effort to coordinate policies, with increasing authority for determining policy guidelines to be centered with the Community in Brussels.

• Third, Robert Triffin has proposed that the first steps toward monetary union should consist of a limited pooling of reserves with joint management, followed by extension of conditional credit among members of the Community, to help finance payments deficits.[8]

These approaches are not, of course, mutually exclusive, and in being cast as alternatives have generated much needless controversy over their relative merits. Triffin's conditional credits, for example, can be linked to some harmonization of policies, and so can the narrowing of exchange-rate movements. Some conscious parallelism in all three approaches is no doubt desirable. Several observations of these current controversies can be made.

First, the strong emphasis placed on the need to coordinate policies, especially by Germany and the European Commission, reflects the dominant European view that government policies are the principal source of disturbance to the balance of payments, and that if only they can be brought into line everything will be all right. It is true that excessively expansionist policies often have been a source of payments difficulty. There are other sources as well, however, and full harmonization of government policies will by no means assure equilibrium in international payments. Cost movements in different national economies may diverge over time for a variety of reasons, including differential strengths and tactics of labor unions, different rates of adoption of new technology, and the like; and demand for foreign products may grow at differential rates as a consequence of the growth in incomes. For all these reasons, and others, a country's balance-of-payments position may gradually slip out of equilibrium under a regime of fixed exchange rates, even when monetary and fiscal policies have been "harmonized" in some conventional sense of the term, e.g., common rates of growth of money stocks. Pointing to the fundamentally monetary character of all payments difficulties is not sufficient to establish that inappropriate monetary policy is the source of the difficulty, except in the trivial, and to policy makers totally uninteresting, sense that sufficiently stringent monetary action can always eliminate a payments deficit. For it may generate a major depression in the process. An implication of monetary union, as noted above, is that monetary adjustments will be relied upon to ensure balance among its constituent parts; but, monetary adjustment may require substantial deflation or expansion in some regions relative to the union as a whole, and, in particular, may cause serious regional unemployment problems in the absence of Community-financed regional policies to mitigate them.

Second, harmonization of national policies within the Community should not be carried too far prematurely. In particular, precisely because of the regional pressures that may be created by a monetary adjustment mechanism, it would be desirable to allow governments considerable latitude to adjust their budgets to their national requirements. The important point is that governments would cease to be able to finance government deficits, beyond specified limits, through domestic credit creation, i.e., at their central banks. Instead, they would have to issue their securities in a Community-wide capital market when they needed to finance a budget deficit, and this would tend to draw funds into the area in question, thus compensating, at least temporarily, for the deflationary pressures of a regional payments deficit. Hence, governments would retain, through the flexible use of fiscal policy, some influence on the level of total demand within each national market. Such flexible use of fiscal policy can be reconciled with tight Community-wide control on monetary policy by the development of an effective and efficient capital market within the Community, so that each region (national member) could, in effect, achieve monetary expansion by selling securities (in the form of government bonds or bills) to residents of other regions, using the proceeds for expansionary policies. Such a program for regional stabilization is not, of course, sufficient for offsetting persistent differences in regional costs; it will work only if the regional imbalance is a temporary one, or if it is one that can be corrected through sufficient capital investment. There are limits to which borrowers, even national governments, can raise funds for nonproductive expenditures.

Third, therefore, exchange rates between members of the Community cannot be fixed irrevocably until the underlying trends of the national economies, not merely the government policies, come into close harmony, or until the Community develops a mechanism for effecting sufficiently large transfers among the regions of the Community to compensate for the depressive effects on some regions of a gold-standard type adjustment mechanism that relies on monetary movements alone. The transfers that take place under the common agricultural policy represent the beginnings of a large intra-Community transfer mechanism, although that particular one may occasionally be perverse from the point of view of cushioning depressed regions by giving rise to transfers from regions of low income and employment to regions of high income and employment (e.g., from Belgium and Italy to France). Movement toward Community-financed unemployment compensation would represent a much more direct and effective step in this direction.

Fourth, the creation of a European Reserve Fund will not in itself help to solve any of the functional problems that will confront national economies during the process of integration. At best, it would permit the conservation of some international reserves, which members of the Community now use (via multilateral clearing through the exchange market) to settle imbalances among members as well as between members and the rest of the world. But, conservation of reserves has hardly been one of the most pressing needs of the Community in recent years, in contrast to the position of some less-developed countries. Creation of a reserve fund would, however, institutionalize concern for the monetary integration of the Community, encourage and accustom national officials to discussion of monetary policies *before* monetary actions are taken, and provide the institutional basis for joint action when other conditions were ripe for it, e.g., for intervention in exchange markets on behalf of the Community as a whole, vis-à-vis the dollar or other outside currencies.

Finally, however, the controversy over transitional tactics really conceals divergent objectives. At least one member of the Community, France, does not accept in principle the desirability of supranational control of monetary policy; but, it is very much interested, for foreign policy reasons, in achieving a concerted position of the Community on alterations in the international monetary system, and, in particular, on the role of the dollar and on the creation of SDRs. After President Nixon's announcement in August 1971, other members of the Community have come increasingly to share this desire, but as much out of concern for the continuing viability of the system as for foreign policy reasons. The Commission, in addition, has an institutional interest in maintaining momentum toward a supranational community and sees the monetary realm as the most promising one for this purpose at present.

Monetary Unification without a Single Currency

The EC Resolution of February 1971 speaks of "an individual monetary unit" but is otherwise vague on the question of a European money. As far as their monetary autonomy is concerned, the position in which member countries will find themselves after monetary union is similar with or without a common currency, but important differences remain between a single currency and several currencies with irrevocably fixed exchange rates. In particular, with several currencies, a mechanism is required to preserve fixity of rates between them, while still maintaining some flexibility, or at least the possibility of movement, with respect to nonmember currencies. A subsidiary problem involves clearing the accounts among the various currency units within the Community.

Broadly speaking, there are three ways in which fixity of exchange rates among a group of currencies can be maintained while preserving flexibility against other currencies. The first involves a direct commitment by each central bank or its agents (e.g., the commercial banks) to buy and sell the currencies of the other member countries at announced buying and selling rates. Net balances accumulated by these transactions would be settled periodically by transfers of some reserve asset directly between the central banks. Central banks would in effect "make the market," and the present practice of relying on a relatively free private market for foreign exchange would be abandoned.

If the advantages of a vigorous, competitive market in foreign exchange are judged too great to abandon, even among member currencies, then fixity of exchange rates must be maintained through official intervention in the private market to prevent exchange rates from straying outside the permitted range. Past practice has been to do this through the intermediary of the US dollar, leaving to private arbitrage the task of keeping exchange rates between any two currencies other than the dollar in line. This practice has the well-known disadvantage, from the viewpoint of the Community, of permitting twice the fluctuation in exchange rates between any two

Community currencies that can take place between any one currency and the dollar. Yet, the objective is, if anything, to *widen* the possible fluctuations against the dollar, white *narrowing* the fluctuations between member currencies. This practice has the further consequence, increasingly resented, of reinforcing the position of the dollar as a reserve currency, for countries routinely deal in dollars and therefore must hold at least working balances in dollars.

External margins can be widened while internal margins are narrowed in two ways consistent with continued reliance on private markets: (1) close coordination of the points of intervention in dollars by all member countries, with a view to assuring that no two member currencies find themselves at sharply different points in the permissible band of variation with respect to the dollar; and (2) substitution of some member currency for the dollar as the intervention currency for all but one of the member countries, calling on the final member to intervene in its markets with respect to the dollar and leaving it to private arbitrage to take care of the rest. The Werner Report adopted the first of these possibilities, giving rise to the "snake in the tunnel" metaphor under which coordinated intervention would hold exchange rates between members' currencies to a narrower band of variation than would be permitted for all member currencies, moving together, with respect to the dollar.[9]

The alternative of a European intervention currency would permit greater institutional autonomy but would also require a sharper break in prevailing practices. Because of the technical facilities available, sterling would be a natural choice for the new intervention currency within the enlarged Community, but any member currency would do. All members would, in practice, define permissible ceilings and floors for the rates of exchange between their currencies and sterling, just as they do now in dollars, and would intervene by buying or selling their currency against sterling to ensure that those limits were not exceeded. Britain, in contrast, would continue to deal in dollars. This arrangement would break the fixed relationship between exchange margins for the dollar and exchange margins between any pair of member currencies, and would permit wider exchange-rate variation for the former and narrower variation for the latter. The choice of sterling need not involve extension of credit to Britain beyond the minimum working balances which other member countries would have to maintain for daily intervention and which, indeed, several of them maintain already; and even this credit could be avoided if the Bank of England would agree to provide sterling whenever needed for such intervention, or to be the sole intervenor in the market. The choice of sterling would have the disadvantage, from Britain's point of view, of denying sterling the slightly enlarged flexibility against the dollar that the other currencies would enjoy. From this point of view, it would be preferable to choose a currency that is not likely to be either very strong or very weak among currencies of the Community, such as the Dutch guilder, which would also have the attraction of being less controversial politically within Europe than would the choice of sterling or the German mark. But, Dutch financial markets are too small relative to the potential size of the reserve movements required, so special provision would have to be made to insulate the Dutch domestic market from reserve flows of other countries.

Creation of a European Currency

The idea of a genuinely new European currency—call it the Europa—is being increasingly bruited about, and, once in place, the separate identities of existing national currencies would presumably disappear over a period of time, thus eliminating the technical problem of maintaining fixed rates among them. A single currency would be necessary, moreover, to make "irrevocability" of parities really credible.

It is not technically difficult to design a new currency and its relationship to existing currencies, although it should be noted that the IMF's SDR is not a precedent in this case because it is a claim held by central banks alone, whereas the Europa would circulate with the public. The problem rather would be to gain public acceptance. The efficient financial services of the City of London would be available for the Europa, provided the basis could be established for its use. To make it work, it would be necessary to create both an adequate supply of Europa-denominated claims and a demand for them. Community governments would almost certainly have to issue debt denominated in Europas (to provide the basis for a secondary market in claims) and to accept it in payment for taxes (to create a demand for Europas). Even then, the Europa would face stiff competition from re-spected national currencies in domestic use, especially under arrangements, such as those described above, that facilitated the easy exchange of one member currency for another at a virtually fixed price. To launch the Europa successfully, it would be necessary not only to solve the problem of basic adjustment within the Community—that would be a political pre-condition for a common monetary policy—but also to denigrate existing national currencies. Thus, public debt denominated in national currencies would gradually have to be retired and, even then, somewhat higher interest rates might have to be offered on Europa securities to encourage the banks and the public to hold them, although the necessary premium would, of course, diminish as Europas became more widely accepted.

In addition to facing stiff competition in domestic economies from national currencies, the Europa would also face stiff competition on the international plane from the US dollar. Unless it is brought under a persistent cloud by prolonged disequilibrium in the US payments position (which is not the same as a recorded deficit on definitions currently employed by the US government), the dollar is likely to retain and indeed to strengthen its position as an international currency for private transactions and short-term investment. There are substantial economies of scale in any financial market, arising from the greater chance of being able to match supplies of and demands for funds on any given maturity without a sharp change in price—in a phrase, the greater the market, the greater the liquidity of the assets that are traded in the market. It will be difficult for a new and untried currency, even when backed by the world's largest trading area, to overcome the leading advantages of the dollar for many years to come.

A new European currency would have a greater chance of success on the international scene—and even possibly within Europe—if it represented an evolution from some existing currency. If one could abstract from political considerations, and from the balance-of-payments difficulties that are likely to attend Britain's entry into the Community, the logical candidate for this enlarged role is sterling. Important technical facilities already exist for dealing in sterling, not the least of which is the large outstanding public debt, which provides the basis for a sizable secondary market in interest-bearing claims, and this is essential if a currency is to be widely held outside its country of issue. The transformation of sterling into this European role would, of course, require placing its management in European hands, on the one side, and having other EC members issue their public debt in Euro-sterling, on the other. The Bank of England would become a Bank of Europe, and under European management would determine the amount of issue of Euro-sterling. There would be no special credit to Britain arising from this role. All governments, including the British government, would be limited in their capacity to finance budget deficits by resort to the central bank. Even the outstanding sterling liabilities would remain fully Britain's liabilities, although, of course, the external reserves of the entire Community would be available to "cover" them against a run.

The only feasible alternative to the pound in this new "European" role would be the German mark, for which the absence of the technical advantages available to sterling might be more than outweighed by the large external savings (attested by the large German current account surplus) of the German public, making the DM an attractive currency in which to borrow. Even after taking this into account, however, sterling is likely to have the edge.

There is, of course, some relationship between the arrangements under which national currencies are linked at fixed and unchanging parities and the possible evolution of a national currency into a supranational one. A currency that is adopted as an intervention currency for purposes of limiting movements in exchange rates is more likely to evolve naturally into a supranational currency than is another, and this may be a consideration that led the Community to reject the use of one European currency by all member countries in favor of the more cumbersome "snake in the tunnel" or "intervention in all currencies" approaches. Indeed, political considerations of national prestige, as well as longstanding suspicion of sterling in European official circles, is likely to militate against what might otherwise be the easiest, the fastest and the most efficient route to the creation of a European currency.

Implications for the International Monetary System

Suppose now that the practical difficulties have been overcome and a new European currency has been successfully brought into existence with the corresponding adjustments in European monetary management. What are the possible implications for the monetary system as a whole? Seven can be mentioned briefly, to conclude this survey of the issues.

First, by internalizing much "foreign" trade into a single monetary area, the demand of the EC members for international reserves would presumably drop substantially because European countries today use international reserves to settle imbalances among themselves, whereas within a monetary union they would not.[10] Unless the European Community willingly held these newly "excess" reserves, its actions could result in world inflationary pressures or could disrupt the international payments system, depending on the composition of its reserve assets, how it chooses to run them down, and how the rest of the world responds.

Second, sterling balances, if not handled by then in some other way, would become Europa balances by virtue of the conversion of British public debt from sterling to Europas and, while they would remain British liabilities, they would clearly and automatically be covered against conversion into other currencies by the reserve assets of the enlarged Community.

Third, the Community would have to agree on a common set of exchange controls, or on their removal, since distinctions between national monetary systems would have been eliminated. Thus, either the Germans will have to abandon their predelection for relatively free capital movements or Britain and France will have to relax substantially their present controls and, as a result, might once again become substantial net lenders to the world.

Fourth, the Europa would willy-nilly become a new reserve currency, at least to a modest degree, because of the overwhelming importance of the enlarged European Community as a trading area, the fact that a large fraction of world trade would be denominated in Europas, and the large market in Europa claims that would have developed for internal use. Stringent steps would have to be taken to prevent the emergence of the Europa as an international currency, if that should be desired (as some Europeans claim), requiring the virtual exclusion of nonmember governments from Europa financial markets.

Fifth, the emergence of a single European currency would create the possibility for easier movement of exchange rates between the United States and Europe as a whole, movements that are now inhibited by a structural situation involving a number of European countries that cannot revalue or devalue without also considering moves of other European countries, but who find it exceedingly difficult to coordinate effectively among themselves a matter as sensitive as parity changes. During the prolonged transition and breaking-in period, however, the formation of a European currency is likely to involve greater rather than less rigidity in exchange rates vis-à-vis the dollar, because interests of the various members of the Community in exchange-rate movements are likely to diverge sharply much of the time; the result will be immobilism.

Sixth, Europe would regain its monetary independence from the United States in the sense that it could more successfully pursue monetary policies at greater variance from those in the United States than is now possible, both because concerted monetary action in Europe would have great influence on world monetary conditions even under a regime of fixed exchange rates, and because greater exchange-rate flexibility would permit somewhat greater monetary autonomy.

Seventh, under a regime of fixed exchange rates, the emergence of a new, major currency with correspondingly strong financial institutions (probably centered in London) will aggravate the problem of large shifts of financial capital between two centers in response to slight interest differentials or slight changes in sentiment regarding exchange rates. These massive shifts of funds will, in turn, complicate greatly the task of monetary management and will occasionally disrupt foreign exchange and money markets. On the other hand, this problem is not unfamiliar even today; and the existence of two strong financial markets both creates the incentive for and holds out the possibility of close and even-sided collaboration between Europe and America in monetary management.

Notes

1. In the exchange-rate settlement of December 1971, it is true, the European countries and Japan agreed to peg their currencies against the dollar again without the *quid pro quo* of a dollar convertible into gold or other assets—in effect, they agreed to a formal dollar standard. But, this agreement occurred on the short-term expectation that agreement itself (at new exchange parities, with a band of variation around parity widened from 2 to $4\frac{1}{2}$ percent) would lead to a large reflow of dollars out of European and Japanese reserves, and on the further expectation that, in the context of longer-range monetary reform to be worked out in 1972, the United States would reestablish some form of official convertibility for the dollar.

2. There is a confusing ambiguity in the term "liquidity" that leads some observers to the view that there is no shortage of liquidity *because* the Eurodollar market and other instruments of private finance have grown so rapidly. The "liquidity problem" discussed here concerns the capacity of monetary authorities to maintain a fixed exchange rate in the face of large swings in private payments and receipts across the foreign exchanges, and, in this sense, the growth of the Eurodollar market, by facilitating movements of short-term funds, may be said to have increased the need for (central bank) liquidity rather than satisfied it.

3. An indication of this possible switching effect was revealed in a poll of 100 large British firms who were asked how Britain's entry into the European Community would affect their investment plans. Fifty-two percent said they would increase their investments on the Continent, compared with only 24 percent increasing their investments in Britain, while only 2 percent indicated that they would reduce their investments on the Continent, compared with 7 percent planning a reduction in Britain. Projected switches in source of procurement were even more striking: 38 percent planned to increase their procurement in the European Community, compared with 1 percent planning a reduction there. This contrasts with 4 percent planning increases in procurement in Britain, compared with 16 percent planning reductions. See *The Guardian*, July 16, 1971, p.15. It would, of course, be useful to have comparable results for Continental European firms.

4. For evidence on this point, see R. E. Caves et al., *Britain's Economic Prospects* (Washington: The Brookings Institution, 1968), pp. 182–84.

5. Robert Triffin, *The Fate of the Pound* (Paris: The Atlantic Institute, 1969).

6. From September to December 1971, however, Britain did prohibit all nonsterling area investors from adding to their holdings of Treasury bills and other short-term securities.

7. EC Resolution of February 9, 1971, reprinted as Annex I in *Economic and Monetary Union* (Werner Report), Supplement to *Bulletin of the European Communities* (1970), No. 11.

8. Robert Triffin, "On the Creation of a European Reserve Fund," *Banca Nazionale Lavoro, Quarterly Review* (December 1969), pp. 327–46.

9. After the currency disruptions of late 1971, the European Commission in Brussels recommended in early 1972 that each member of the community accomplish this objective, not by coordinating their market intervention in dollars as under the Werner Plan, but by intervening in the currencies of *all* other member countries simultaneously. Intervention in dollars would be confined to the vicinity of the borders of the new $4\frac{1}{2}$ percent band in flexibility, whereas exchange variations among member currencies would be held to about half that range by direct intervention. This proposal greatly underestimates the technical difficulties involved in intervening simultaneously in eight currencies at consistent rates in a changing market, of coordinating that intervention with other member countries who might also be intervening in the market in all member currencies, *and* of coordinating intervention in dollars, all of which would be necessary.

10. Under certain patterns of intra- and extra-European transactions, the demand for external reserves following unification could conceivably increase; but these are not likely to prevail in practice.

10 The Future of the SDR

Sixteen years ago, the international community embarked on a bold and dramatic experiment—creation of a world money by fiat. Now, the special drawing right (SDR) is in danger of atrophying into irrelevance. The international community hesitates to create new SDRs (two allocational decisions have been made over the past 14 years), and it even shows some reluctance to use fully the SDRs it has created.

Two questions need to be asked about the present state of affairs: (1) How can the SDRs be made a truly effective international monetary medium? and (2) Is it still worthwhile to continue trying to make the SDR an effective international monetary medium?

With respect to the first question, Professor Kenen has argued in his paper that if the SDR is to have a meaningful future as a reserve asset, other than for use in transactions with the International Monetary Fund, it must be made usable as a means of international payment.[1] That, in turn, will entail allowing the SDR to be used by private holders—at least by commercial banks—so that the SDRs can be used in the international financial system as it actually functions. Central banks must have reserve assets they can use in their everyday transactions with banks and exchange markets; and they are more likely to hold an asset in their reserves, the easier it is to use in such transactions.

If the SDR is successfully modified to make it a means of payment in the world of private finance, then central bank demand for SDRs will increase, and the supply will have to be increased commensurately. To this end, Kenen makes two proposals: (1) that whenever quotas are increased, SDRs be allocated to cover the hard-currency portion of the additional subscriptions; and (2) that a substitution account be created which will permit

International Money and Credit: The Policy Roles, ed. G. von Furstenberg (Washington, D.C.: international Monetary Fund, 1983), 361–367. Reprinted by permission.

central banks to deposit other forms of reserve assets in exchange for SDRs.

I basically agree with Kenen's line of argument. Most "settlements" take place through financial markets, and demand for reserves is strongly linked to their usability for settlements. It is noteworthy that at the end of 1981, about a quarter of cumulative SDR allocations were in the Fund, even though total country reserves grew sharply over the preceding decade. That high proportion reflects the fact that although SDRs could readily be used in settlements with the Fund, they could not be used for other settlements, which take place in the exchange markets.

I also agree that SDR allocations should be made more routine and that a good way to do this would be to link SDR allocations, more or less automatically, to quota increases. This practice would have the disadvantage of removing the last inhibition on most Fund members' desire for quota increases, since these increases would be virtually free. But those inhibitions are not very great now; and, for the reasons to be given below, I believe that the growth of owned reserves is desirable and that, at the margin, it could be provided in large part by SDRs.

I am more doubtful about Kenen's other proposal for increasing the supply of SDRs, through a substitution account. As envisioned here, the account is quite different in form from the proposals for a substitution account made in the late 1970s, which would have created separate entities with no formal link to the Special Drawing Rights Department of the Fund. Kenen's proposal would integrate the substitution account into the Special Drawing Rights Department; it would be voluntary; and it would be a once-for-all undertaking (with a five-year period for action). Why not? What is the harm in that? My answer is that there would still be lengthy and unfruitful argument over who should bear the ultimate exchange risk for an account whose assets and liabilities would not match after the passage of time. More consequentially, the Fund might be obliged for long periods to pay out on its SDR liabilities more than it was earning on its foreign currency (mostly dollar) assets, or vice versa. If payments exceeded earnings, where would the additional resources come from? The obvious answer is that the Fund would simply create sufficient SDRs to make up the difference. But that would be reserve creation unrelated to world liquidity needs and would require possible adjustments to the normal allocations. Alternatively, the Fund could raise charges on its regular loans. In either case, there would be complaints from many Fund members, who would call for redress in other areas of Fund activity. If earnings exceeded payments, the Fund, by the same token, could lower charges on its regular loans. That move would be welcomed by many Fund members, but others would resist on the grounds that such reductions would encourage yield-induced drawings from the Fund.

These are not compelling objections, but they must be set against the alleged gains from the substitution account, which are likely to be small. The use of SDRs in international settlements will increase only gradually, and the resulting increase in demand for SDRs can probably be satisfied, over time, by new allocations. If that judgment proves incorrect, a substitution facility could be created when it was necessary.

Moreover, in the event that the demand for SDRs grows rapidly because of its attractiveness for settlements, the SDR would very likely also be used much more widely in private transactions as well; and central banks would then find it possible to hold SDR-denominated accounts in commercial banks. In other words, supply will grow in step with demand where, as here, the demand is stimulated by increased convenience in use. These private SDRs would be analogous to an increase in deposit money based on "base money" from the bank of issue, in this case the Fund. New SDR allocations would thus be leveraged by financial institutions.

So I agree with Kenen's proposals, except for the substitution account, and my objections to that are not fundamental, but rather reflect a judgment that the benefits will not be commensurate with the considerable costs of putting it in place.

The more fundamental question is why we should attempt to improve the SDR so that it becomes a functioning international money. The Second Amendment stipulates that Fund members will collaborate to make the SDR the principal reserve asset of the international monetary system, but that injunction is vague and needs to be examined in the context of likely developments over the next several decades.

Kenen does not address this question in any depth, but mentions two arguments, which he does not find compelling, for an SDR-based system: (1) that a move to such a system will introduce greater discipline into the system as a whole, by providing greater control over reserve creation; and (2) that an SDR-based system is desirable, since it would avoid the instabilities inherent in a multiple-reserve-currency system, the likely alternative to an SDR-based system. He points out that the correlation between money creation and reserve creation is weak under the present regime of floating exchange rates and highly developed capital markets. And he points out that the alleged instability of a multiple-reserve-currency system is based on a false analogy with bimetallism or other models in which the source of instability is the attempt to maintain fixed prices between two or more assets, not the mere existence of two or more attractive assets. Here again, I agree with Kenen, and, if anything, would be inclined to put his criticisms more strongly.

But if these are not adequate reasons for trying to strengthen the role of the SDR, are there adequate reasons? It is useful to recall the original rationale for SDRs, which, in my view, applies as well today as it did in the late 1960s, even though in two important respects the international financial system is very different: we have an extensive and well-functioning international capital market, and we have flexible exchange rates. The key assumption underlying SDR creation is that there is a governmental demand for *owned* reserves, and that this demand does not have to be satisfied by earning them—that is, the demand for owned reserves is not basically mercantilistic and can be satisfied by direct allocation. The rationale for SDR creation was that this demand for owned reserves could not be satisfied adequately and indefinitely either by gold or by national currencies.

The assumption of a demand for owned reserves is not overturned either by the move to flexible exchange rates or by the tremendous growth of international capital markets since the late 1960s. Most countries are unwilling to let their currencies float freely. In fact, 103 of the 146 members of the Fund formally tie their currencies to something—to another country's currency, to a basket of currencies, to the SDR, or—in the case of several European countries—to the European currency unit. Most of the remaining countries have internal (sometimes undeclared) rules or indicators linking their currencies to something else. There are important exceptions—in particular, Canada, Japan, the United Kingdom, and the United States—but even these countries have occasionally intervened heavily to influence their exchange rates. The demand for reserves remains under a regime of flexible exchange rates.

In normal times, this demand can be satisfied by borrowing; and indeed in the late 1970s, many countries borrowed to add to their reserves of foreign currencies—empirical evidence, if any is needed, for growth in the demand for reserves. But credit-based reserves tend to disappear when a country runs into serious difficulty, as Kenen points out. They do not provide the same security and assurance of availability as do owned reserves.

So there is a demand for owned reserves. Do they have to be earned? I believe not, but that is an empirical question, and the answer may well vary from time to time. Certainly many countries still welcome—and seek—export-led growth, but that by itself does not constitute sufficient evidence that their growing demand for reserves cannot be satisfied by direct allocation; rather, it may be evidence that the most severe constraint on growth is foreign exchange earnings. A demand for earned reserves, of course, poses a serious problem for the international monetary system as a whole if it is entertained by all countries, for all countries cannot earn (net) reserves simultaneously, and the system would be subject to a deflationary bias— something that has not been evident during most of the past decade.

If only high-income countries need to earn their reserves—that is, if their demand for reserves is mercantilistic in character—that demand could be satisfied by allocating SDRs to developing countries and allowing the industrialized countries to earn them through exports. This kind of notion seems to lie behind some of the proposals for an SDR-aid link and other forms of "massive transfer." Apart from a possible error in the underlying assumption (taking a long view, and abstracting from the current state of underemployment in the world economy), the trouble with this proposal is that perceived requirements for foreign aid would inevitably get mixed up with assessments of the need for additional world liquidity when it came to allocation of SDRs. Protestations to the contrary, however honest and well meant, are simply not credible. Once development planning comes to depend in a consequential way on SDR allocation, it is inconceivable that there would not be a major outcry against a Managing Director's proposal for no allocation, no matter what the state of the world economy.[2]

If there is a demand for owned reserves that can be satisfied by allocation, what should be the basis for allocation among countries? The current practice of using Fund quotas is perhaps imperfect, but these quotas at least represent attempts to capture the need for reserves. Perhaps this practice can be improved upon on the basis of future research into the long-run demand for owned reserves; but in the meantime, it seems superior to alternative formulas. Deliberate attempts to transfer resources through SDR allocations are likely to undermine whatever political support there is for SDRs in the industrialized nations.

Of course, SDRs are not necessary to satisfy the demand for owned reserves; this demand has been satisfied by gold in the past, and it has been, and can continue to be, satisfied by national currencies, provided the countries whose currencies are used are relaxed about their growing liquid liabilities to other countries.

Gold was abandoned as a viable reserve medium when the Second Amendment entered into force, and for good reasons. Gold remains a nonferrous metal with many private uses, and it must be extracted from mines. On both counts, the price of gold has consequences on the real side

of the world economy which, over time, would interfere, as it has historically, with gold's playing the role of a monetary medium conducive to
economic stability. Furthermore, gold has the same disability as the current
SDR: it is not a means of payment, and therefore must be mediated by
currencies.

National currencies have emerged as the international means of payment
and, consequently, as reserves—first the pound sterling; then the U.S.
dollar and (in a limited realm) the French franc; and more recently the
deutsche mark, the Swiss franc, and the Japanese yen. A currency-based
system can work provided, as noted above, the reserve-currency centers
are not excessively anxious about the steady growth in their liquid liabilities. It is not intrinsically unstable, as is sometimes contended; and
periods of currency turbulence can, if necessary, be dealt with through
close cooperation between the central banks concerned.

On the other hand, large external holdings of a country's currency can
make its monetary policy hostage to sentiment about the currency. The
United States has avoided this so far by virtue of the large size of the US
economy and the scale of the US financial markets relative to world
holdings of dollars. The Federal Reserve System has sometimes adjusted
monetary policy because of exchange rate developments. (In my view, it
should pay more attention to exchange rate movements than it has in
recent years.) But those adjustments were not mainly motivated by concern
for the reserve-currency role of the dollar. Despite some selective diversification of reserve holdings by currency that have taken place in recent
years, especially in 1977–79, the reserve-currency role of the dollar has, on
the whole, helped to stabilize, rather than to destabilize, exchange rates vis-
à-vis the dollar. In particular, in 1977–79, the European authorities added
$40 billion to their dollar holdings. Other monetary authorities also added
approximately $15 billion to their dollar reserves during this period. If
other authorities had added more dollars and fewer marks to their reserves
during this period, there would have been less pressure on the dollar-mark
rate than there was, but that does not entitle one to characterize the
reserve-currency role of the dollar as "destabilizing."

Still, over time, the relative position of the United States in the world
economy will continue to decline as other countries develop, yet it will not
yield primacy of place to any other single economy. So if world reserve
needs are going to continue being satisfied by the dollar (supplemented by
some other currencies) while growing at a rate faster than the nominal
growth rate of the US economy, external dollar holdings sooner or later
will surpass domestic holdings of dollar assets; and long before that time,

concern about shifts of dollar holdings will place constraints on, and then perhaps dominate, US monetary policy. Some might welcome the discipline that this would impose on national monetary policy. I would consider this an undesirable development, however, not least because the "discipline" imposed would sometimes be of the wrong kind, motivated by desires for glory or other political considerations, such as wishes to influence foreign policies unrelated to economic policy, and sometimes it would conflict with the exercise of consistent national economic preferences, reached democratically.

These developments will take many years to mature. The development of an international money will also take a long time. I believe, therefore, that it is prudent to continue to improve and to allocate the SDR.

Notes

1. Peter B. Kenen, "The Use of the SDR to Supplement or Substitute for Other Means of Finance," in *International Money and Credit: The Policy Roles*, George von Furstenberg, ed. (Washington, D.C.: International Monetary Fund, 1983).

2. When, in 1969, I raised an objection to the generalized system of tariff preferences on the grounds that they would create a vested interest by developing countries against the further liberalization of world trade on a most-favored-nation basis, the then Secretary General of the United Nations Conference on Trade and Development assured me that this was not so; developing countries would always see their interests lying in a general lowering of trade barriers by the industrialized countries, and consequently developing countries would not oppose further trade liberalization. During the Tokyo Round of General Agreement on Tariffs and Trade (GATT) negotiations, however, a number of developing countries objected to deep cuts in tariffs on the grounds that such cuts would dilute the tariff preferences they received under the Generalized System of Preferences (GSP). Officials and international civil servants cannot bind their successors when they are pleading current self-interest.

11   The International Monetary System in the 1980s

The international monetary system can be defined as the formal rules, informal conventions, and practices governing official international financial transactions. The international monetary system can be subdivided into two broad headings: its adjustment process and its provision of international liquidity. The confidence that the relevant publics of the world hold in the adjustment process and the provisions for liquidity are also important. In this paper I consider the likely prospects for the international monetary system along with some leading alternative arrangements over the decade of the 1980s. The principal focus is on provisions for international liquidity, for that is thought to have a great bearing on the prospects for controlling inflation in the world economy. In section 1 I review the objectives of the international monetary system; in section 2 I offer a brief discussion of the adjustment process; in section 3 I discuss international liquidity, and in sections 4 and 5 I touch on the question of external indebtedness and the institutional role of the International Monetary Fund (IMF).

1   Objectives of the International Monetary System

What do we want the international monetary system to do? First, it should promote a productive international division of labor, including productive disposition of the world's savings. In that fashion, incomes in all countries can be increased. The most productive division of labor and savings can generally be achieved if barriers to trade and to long-term capital movements are low and predictable, and that in turn implies that the adjustment mechanism should not, except in extremis, rely on the imposition and removal of selective barriers to trade and to long-term capital movements or on varying the amounts or quality of foreign assistance.

March 1982.

Second, the international monetary system should contribute to macro-economic stability, or at a minimum it should not itself be the source of inflationary or contractionary pressures on the world economy. This objective requires that the extent of international liquidity should neither be so great that countries do not feel themselves under any constraint in terms of the growth in their imports nor so scarce that countries collectively need to retrench economically in order to protect their balance-of-payments positions, because not all countries can have balance-of-payments problems at the same time.

Third, the international monetary system should be resilient rather than brittle in the sense that it should be able to survive well the variety of shocks to international transactions that are bound to occur from time to time. We might even expect the international monetary system to reduce shocks and to disperse those shocks that do take place in order to minimize the impact on individual countries. Reducing shocks implies discouraging them at the source, and that in turn implies a system that provides individual countries some disincentive to export their internal disturbances.

Fourth, the international monetary system should preserve as much autonomy as possible for nations, so that each can define and pursue its own national economic objectives in its own way, so long as that pursuit does not create burdensome problems for other countries and for the international system as a whole.

There is obviously some potential conflict among these objectives. National choices among economic policies may not be conducive to maximium gains from an international division of labor and savings, for instance, or with the objective of minimizing shocks to other countries. In these instances, as always in politics, mechanisms are necessary for consultation and for resolution of disputes. Sovereign nations are sovereign, and in the end they can act as they choose. But the response of the international community can influence the costs and benefits that flow from national choices.

2 The Adjustment Process

The adjustment process refers to the various methods countries use to ensure balance in their international payments beyond the period in which short-term borrowing or a draw-down of reserves can cover a payments deficit.

Today the adjustment mechanism for all major countries consists in allowing their exchange rates to change so as to ensure balance, combined

with changes in domestic economic policy that may be necessary to complement the changes in exchange rates or to keep them from going too far.
Because exchange rates are floating rather than fixed, the effects of monetary and fiscal actions are "internalized," so that countries experience more
directly the consequences of their actions and are thus likely to correct
them more quickly if the consequences are unacceptable.

Most other countries also rely on these two elements, with perhaps
somewhat less weight on changes in exchange rates. In addition, they often
rely on changes in selective controls on international transactions (e.g., on
exports of financial capital by residents or import licensing provisions) and
changes in selective incentives designed to attract funds from abroad (e.g.,
tax incentives for direct investment or subsidies to exports).

As countries become more extensively integrated into the international
financial system, they typically enlarge their capability for borrowing from
abroad in the long-term and to cover prospective imbalances in payments.
By the same token, however, their ability to rely on exchange controls is
circumscribed, for tightening them substantially would jeopardize continued access to financial markets.

Selective incentives to foreign investment do not suffer from this disability and indeed derive some of their attraction from the high mobility of
capital and its response to sure reward. Such incentives, however, are often
difficult to alter quickly; thus they tend to become part of the economic
structure and less a part of the adjustment mechanism.

There has been considerable dissatisfaction with the functioning of floating exchange rates since they became general in 1973. I have argued
elsewhere[1] that when we abstract from week-to-week movements, floating
exchange rates among major currencies have performed quite well, indeed
along lines that would be predicted by standard theory on the subject, and
that they have served as an important shock absorber during a period of
extraordinary turbulence in the world economy. Newspapers routinely
report the maximum swings in exchange rates, but that is not what is
economically relevant to any country. Rather, it should be interested in
some average of exchange rates between its currency and other currencies,
weighted in proportion to their economic importance for the country in
question. Moveover, some movement in exchange rates is necessary over
time to correct for the differences in inflation between countries. Allowing
for both these points produces a "real effective exchange rate." A series of
real effective exchange rates for December of each year for several of the
major industrial countries is reported in table 11.1. It can be seen there that
these rates moved considerably over the period of floating exchange rates

Table 11.1
Real Effective Exchange Rates and Current Account Balances, 1973–1981.

December of	Exchange Rates (March 1973 = 100)			Current Account ($ billion)		
	USA	Japan	Germany	USA	Japan	Germany
1973	95	107	106	7.1	−0.1	4.7
1974	98	90	105	4.9	−4.7	10.3
1975	103	85	97	18.1	−0.7	4.1
1976	101	88	104	4.2	3.7	4.0
1977	98	99	105	−14.5	10.9	4.1
1978	95	108	105	−15.5	17.5	9.2
1979	97	87	106	−1.0	−8.7	−6.3
1980	100	101	99	1.9	−10.8	−16.0
1981	109	93	99	6.6	4.8	−5.4
1982	119	85	98	−9.2	6.8	3.1
1983	123	89	95	−40.9	20.8	4.2
1984	132	86	92	−101.6	35.0	6.3
1985	119	94	95	−117.7	49.3	13.1

Note. Real effective exchange rate is the own trade-weighted average of bilateral exchange rates with fifteen other industrial countries, adjusted by the wholesale price of nonfood manufactured goods.
Sources: Morgan Guaranty Trust Co.; Internation Financial Statistics.

from 1973 through 1980, but they did not move wildly. Furthermore, the movements were closely related to the balance-of-payments positions (as measured by the current account) of each country. The real effective exchange rate of the US dollar, for instance, tended to depreciate between two Decembers when the US current account for the intervening year was in heavy deficit and to appreciate when it was in surplus. This pattern, which can also be observed for other major countries, is just what "textbook theory" should lead us to expect, provided that the current account is an appropriate measure of payments imbalance, or is thought to be by financial institutions and others who engage in foreign investment.[2] The years after 1980 were an exception to this pattern: The US dollar appreciated sharply, apparently unrelated to the US current account position, and other leading currencies depreciated more than would be expected on the basis of their countries' current account positions. The difference can be explained by tight monetary policy in the United States, leading to exceptionally high real interest rates, which induced investors to move their funds from assets in other currencies into dollar-denominated assets. This pull of funds into dollars also inhibited a fall in interest rates in other countries, despite a decline in economic activity in those countries.

It is true that daily and weekly movements of exchange rates have sometimes been disconcertingly large for an economic variable as important for most national economies as the exchange rate. This may reflect the facts that the system is relatively new and that public confidence in it and corresponding institutional arrangements have not been sufficiently established to provide the arbitiage that should smooth out such sharp peaks and valleys.

Alternatively (on the theory that movements in exchange rates reflect movements in underlying portfolio preferences and have to adjust sharply in the short-run), such sharp short-run changes in spot rates may become tolerable once traders learn (and the institutional mechanisms are established) to hedge through forward or financial markets. Major residual disturbances can be reduced through official intervention in exchange markets if the social gains are thought to be great, even though this may involve some losses to the monetary authorities. To the extent that the sharp movements are due to too hasty (mis)interpretation of new information or simply psychological bandwagon effects, the authorities may of course make money by stabilizing the market.

If such "managed floating" proves to be too difficult and if, despite a sound underlying adjustment mechanism, we cannot live with the short-run alternative, we may seem to have two choices: We can severely curtail capital movements, or we can return to fixed exchange rates in one fashion or another. Unfortunately, the first is economically impossible, for it would require a movement toward economic autarky that modern industrial economies could not tolerate. The reason is that capital movements, even if they could be controlled in principle, cannot be effectively separated from trade transactions, which typically move on credit. Swings in "leads and lags" of trade credit are effectively capital movements, and they can be enormous.

The second alternative, fixing exchange rates, is politically impossible at the present time and for the immediate future because it would imply a strong harmonization of national monetary policies and effective abandonment of national monetary policies as an instrument of domestic economic policy. This is something democratic governments cannot do for any sustained period of time and particularly in a period in which national inflation rates diverge so sharply that harmonizing monetary policies at low inflation rates would greatly depress economic activity in the high-inflation countries.

A third alternative, which has not received much attention, would be to introduce a small transactions tax on all purchases or sales of foreign currency, say 0.25 percent. The purpose of this tax would be to reduce the financial incentives to move funds across the foreign exchanges for purely short-term gain, for example, placing funds in the Eurodollar market because of higher interest rates prevailing there. Insofar as sharp day-to-day and week-to-week movements in exchange rates are due to the movement of short-term funds and insofar as expectations about what longer-term exchange rates should be are not deeply rooted, the discouragement of international movement of footloose financial capital would be a stabilizing element. Such a transactions tax would not eliminate longer-term movements in exchange rates and indeed would not eliminate all sharp short-term movements in exchange rates, but it might represent an improvement over current arrangements. It should be supplemented by cooperative intervention in exchange markets to smooth movements in exchange rates. A transactions tax would of course discourage foreign trade to some extent; and to work fully it would have to be applied by agreement among all countries with major financial centers, because transactions wholly outside the jurisdiction of the countries whose currencies were being traded should also be taxed.

3   Provision of International Liquidity

International liquidity, as used here, includes all measures available to monetary authorities to help finance payments deficits, including not only official reserves but also access to funds from other governments (e.g., swaps), from international institutions (e.g., IMF drawing rights), and from private financial markets. The need for international liquidity would not arise if exchange rates floated freely, without official concern leading to intervention, or if domestic money were effectively the same as international money, as under the gold standard, so that monetary adjustments between any economy and the rest of the world would take place without official mediation.

In the past three decades, reserves have been considered the most important component of international liquidity, although experience in the late 1970s suggests that for many individual countries that is not the case. Two questions arise in connection with international reserves: (1) How is the world total determined? and (2) how do additions to reserves get allocated among countries?

Historically, gold provided the main component of reserves, supplemented in important ways by the British pound and later by the US dollar. The supply of new gold to reserves was determined by production less disappearance into private use, and that in turn depended on the costs of mining, on the various factors that determine private demand for gold, and in more recent years on the export policies of the main gold-producing countries of the world, South Africa and the Soviet Union. Gold production was distributed by nature, so to speak, and unsatisfied demands for monetary gold had to be met by importing it.

Since World War I and especially since World War II, gold reserves have been supplemented by sterling and dollars. For a period total sterling issue was limited by the Bank of England's gold reserves and was distributed according to the willingness of countries to borrow or earn it. But the major official sterling balances were built during World War II, mainly by Commonwealth countries selling war material and facilities to Britain against IOUs in sterling. These were later redistributed among countries through payments imbalances.

Dollar balances have been built up largely since the 1940s, with countries earning dollars (sometimes through the sale of assets) and holding on to them. There were no effective limits on the issuance of dollars, and when conversion of dollars into gold at the US Treasury became intolerable, the United States in 1971 ceased to commit itself to make such conversions on demand. It is important to keep in mind, however, that the large build-up of dollar reserves represents the *combined* effect of foreign demand for them and US willingness to supply them. They do not simply represent a foisting of unwanted dollars on the rest of the world by a guileful United States.

Starting in the early 1970s, a new international reserve asset, the SDR, was created by a vote in the IMF and distributed directly to countries on an agreed formula, IMF quotas. During the 1970s countries also began to add other national currencies to their official reserves, notably the German mark and the Japanese yen. Table 11.2 gives a rough picture of the evolution of international reserves from 1945 to 1985.

Several points should be made about the data shown in table 11.2. First, foreign exchange has provided the bulk of growth in reserves. Second, reserve growth in the 1970s shows roughly the same relationship to the growth in world trade as in the 1960s, viz., for every percentage point growth in the value of world trade, official reserves grew by about two-thirds of 1 percent.

Third, in 1980, gold at $42 per ounce was valued well below market values of about $500 per ounce. The temptation to revalue gold at market prices should be resisted, however, because the market price of gold has proved highly volatile and the market is thin. Between 1978 and 1980, gold prices more than doubled; between 1980 and 1982 they fell by one-

Table 11.2
End of Year International Reserves ($ Billion Equivalent).

Holdings	1945	1960	1970	1980	1985
Gold[1]	33.3	38.0	37.2	41.8	40.1
US gold holdings	20.1	17.8	11.1	11.2	11.1
Foreign Exchange[2]	14.3	18.6	44.6	370.8	378.7
US liabilities	4.2	11.1	23.8	157.1	172.8
Other[3]	–	3.6	10.8	36.5	62.5
Total Reserves	47.6	60.2	92.5	449.1	477.7
Addendum: World exports	34.2	113.4	280.3	1844.6	1783.

1. At official prices of $35/oz before 1980 and $42/oz in 1980 and 1985.
2. Reported assets differ from US reported liabilities by minor differences in concept, by measurement error, by official holdings of foreign exchange other than dollars, and by official deposits in the eurocurrency market.
3. Special Drawing Rights (SDRs) and reserve positions in the IMF.
Sources: Federal Reserve Bulletin; International Financial Statistics

third. Official sales of gold into the market would rapidly depress the price, except insofar as South Africa and the Soviet Union withheld sales to prevent the decline. So long as official gold is valued well below market price, on the other hand, gold is not likely to be mobilized as reserves except as a last resort and then probably only as collateral for borrowing.

This brief history of reserves, however, ignores the tremendous growth in funds available to many individual countries through the so-called eurocurrency market (which is lively in Asia and the Western Hemisphere as well), such that after the oil shock of 1973–74 many countries were able to cover unexpectedly large payments deficits by borrowing rather than drawing down their reserves. The IMF also played a quantitatively important role as a source of liquidity to member countries.

Proposals for Reform

The somewhat ad hoc character of the growth in international liquidity has at times left some observers uneasy about the adequacy of liquidity and other observers uneasy about its superabundance. Both schools worry about the lack of systematic control over the growth of international liquidity. SDRs were created to introduce a controlled element into the growth of reserves, one that held out the possibility over time of substituting for foreign exchange (largely US dollars) in the future growth of reserves.

It should be noted that the "need" or "demand" for international reserves is not a well-defined concept, especially in a world of managed floating. Many countries may have some notion—it is unlikely to be more than that—of what level its reserves should be and, more important, how rapidly they should grow. But many other countries will have no such idea. And because only a relatively small number of countries account for the bulk of international reserves, unclarity in these countries gives a fairly wide latitude for what the level of world reserves should be. New circumstances (such as the large oil price increases or newly acquired access to international financial markets) may cause substantial revisions in national notions of reserve adequacy. For all these reasons, considerable elasticity should be allowed for in the provision of international reserves.

The Dollar

It is not a mere coincidence that the US dollar came to dominate the provision of international reserves. There are sound reasons, apart from gold convertibility, why, in a world of many currencies, one currency should come to dominate the others. It provides efficiency in the formation of markets to have a hub with spokes, and perhaps a few regional centers, rather than bilateral markets between numerous individual currencies. And it is also natural that the currency selected should be that of the dominant trading nation and financial center if, as was the case, they are the same country. The financial center provides abundant investment possibilities with high liquidity (so nations need not fear their transactions will dominate the market) and with relative anonymity (a quality prized by central bankers).

Once such a currency *cum* financial market has been established, its advantages of scale will not be easy to overcome. Thus, even though the United States has declined steadily in relative terms in the world economy and in world trade, the advantages of the dollar as an international currency and hence as a reserve currency remain overwhelming. Only a major relative inflation in the United States, uncompensated by market interest rates, is likely to diminish the international role of the dollar rapidly.

Gold

It is not possible to return to the use of gold as the principal reserve asset, even though at $400 per ounce the value of official gold reserves would be about $375 billion. New supply is erratic, and is largely controlled by two nations, South Africa and the Soviet Union, having dubious political relations with the rest of the world. The great volatility of the price of gold in recent years demonstrates, if it needs demonstrating, that until the late 1960s the US dollar was supporting the price of gold and not other way around. Finally, we have learned that, if gold becomes an unacceptable constraint, we can always change the price of gold. This lesson is irreversible. Hence a regime based on gold at a fixed price in terms of one of more currencies is not credible.

SDRs

When it was first created, the SDR was dubbed "paper gold" in the financial press, and in certain respects the appellation was apt. But creation of SDRs could represent a much more orderly process than that provided by the new supplies of gold, and the price was *defined* in terms of a basket of currencies, currently the currencies of the five largest trading nations. It represented a useful if still quantitatively minor supplement to other forms of reserves. But it will not be able to *substitute* for national currencies in international reserves until it can compete fully with the advantages of national currencies and especially with the US dollar. SDRs have the advantage over the dollar and indeed over any single currency of being a composite of currencies and thus of providing some diversification against the risk of exchange rate movements. Since 1980, SDRs also command a weighted average market rate of interest. But its use, through the IMF, is still a bit cumbersome and lacks the speed and the anonymity that characterize use of dollar reserves. Moreover, so long as SDRs can be held only by monetary authorities, they cannot readily serve as collateral for private loans, as foreign exchange reserves can.

The SDR could in principle enjoy these wider advantages, provided that they could be traded in private markets. (The SDR can now be and to some extent is used as a unit of account in private markets. But here we are speaking of official SDR assets.) Private market trade in SDRs would require a change in the IMF agreement, and it would further require the development of an active private market in SDRs in competition with markets in US Treasury bills and other short-term dollar and foreign-currency denominated claims and indeed in SDR deposits. Then countries could intervene in exchange markets in SDRs and could move the proceeds in and out of interest-bearing assets at low cost.

What would all of this accomplish? First, it would establish the *basis* for limiting (by agreement) the accumulation of national currency denominated assets as international reserves. Outstanding dollar and other foreign currency balances could be converted once-for-all into SDR obligations at a substitution account, the exchange risk on which to be shared in some equitable way (a difficult but not insoluble problem). These actions in turn would accomplish the dual purpose of permitting control over the total amount of international reserves (provided that official gold could not be valued or used at market prices) and of exerting some restraint on the policies of the countries whose currencies are used as reserve currencies, because they would no longer be able to finance their payments deficits by issuing internationally acceptable money.

The difficulty with accomplishing these aims is the large amount of privately held dollar and other foreign currency balances that now exist in the world market. The amounts are so large that huge amounts of SDRs would have to be issued to the United States if a major depreciation of the dollar as a consequence of large-scale conversion was to be avoided. Or other special provisions would have to be made to respond to such a crisis. The United States would be ill-advised to agree to any scheme limiting international use of the dollar without ample provision for support on virtually unconditional terms. But to give the United States such a special issue to be held in reserve against a possibly remote contingency would make nonsense of the notion of controlling the level of international reserves.

I conclude from this cursory discussion that the problems of finding a functional substitute for the dollar as international reserves are at best formidable and often are conceptually flawed. In time, a new European currency, the ECU, might come to substitute for the dollar. But before that state is reached, the ECU would have to develop along the lines discussed for the SDR. Of course, if Europe did eventually succeed in developing an effective European currency, it would pose the same difficulties for the international monetary system that the dollar poses today.

Thus the dollar is likely to remain the principal source of international reserves through the 1980s, with some contributions from other currencies, such as the deutsche mark and the yen, but not on such a scale as to challenge the dollar in a serious way.

If this is so, can improvements be made in present arrangements? Basically, the need is to inhibit major shifts of official reserves from one currency to another. This will require some coordination of monetary policies among the reserve centers, but the prospects for close coordination will remain limited for domestic reasons. If shifts cannot be avoided, the reserve centers must be prepared to intervene in exchange markets to block major disturbing movements in currency values, and they must be prepared to provide adequate financial support to make the required intervention possible. With such close cooperation, the "dollar plus" reserve system should be manageable.

4   External Indebtedness

A point of major concern in the present international economy is the huge
external debt that has accumulated over the past decade, mainly by developing countries. Long-term external indebtedness (maturities over one
year) by nonoil developing countries had reached $425 billion by the end
of 1981, up from $97 billion in 1973. Service payments on this debt
amounted to 21 percent of export earnings, up from 14 percent in 1973.

To what extent is this debt a problem for the international economy as a
whole? It is certainly a problem for some individual countries. That is not
the focus of this paper, although it is noteworthy that many countries—
including the United States in the nineteenth century—have been heavy
borrowers abroad without running into serious difficulty; properly used,
external resources can contribute substantially to economic development.
Canada has been a net borrower throughout most of the 115 years of its
existence.

There are two possible problems for the international economy as a
whole; in practice they are likely to be inseparable, but they are analytically
distinct and require somewhat different approaches to protect against. The
first is a banking crisis, whereby many banks become insolvent due to, say,
default by a major foreign borrower. The second is a foreign exchange
crisis, whereby banks or countries have difficulty getting enough foreign
exchange to sustain existing arrangements. The first could lead to a "collapse" of some part of the banking system and of international lending and
no doubt would lead to a foreign exchange crisis. The second would lead
countries to adopt restrictions on trade and payments and perhaps also to
deflate their economies. A banking crisis can be prevented by appropriate
support to the banks; a foreign exchange crisis can be prevented through
appropriate support to central banks or governments.

The mechanism for supporting banks lies with *national* central banks.
With the strong internationalization of banking, association of commercial
banks with particular national authorities has some ambiguities. Central
banks have discussed this question and have worked out a rough division
of responsibility among national banking authorities: Host countries to
international banks are responsible for the liquidity of banks on their
territory, and home countries are responsible for the solvency of all banks
owned by resident banks. The understanding is not tight, but it establishes
a framework for cooperation if a banking crisis were to arise.

In addition, the practice of debt rescheduling has evolved from a series
of particular cases. Where the debt is government owned or government

guaranteed by the creditor countries, rescheduling of the debt of countries in serious financial trouble is now routine. Private creditors are expected to follow with a similar rescheduling. The rescheduling permits borrowers to spread their obligations over a longer period of time, usually with a generous grace period in the near future, and it permits the lending institutions to keep the loans on their books, that is, it reduces their liquidity for the sake of their solvency. Debt rescheduling is typically arranged in the context of an IMF program that the debtor country agrees to.

With floating exchange rates and with extensive international borrowing facilities, the problem of supporting countries against a foreign exchange crisis is somewhat less acute now than it used to be. A currency under pressure can depreciate, and that sets in motion some corrective responses. However, sharp depreciation of a currency can create serious problems of macroeconomic management, and international lending facilities may dry up in the hypothesized global exchange crisis. In that case, the countries in question will have to borrow from other countries or from the IMF. World Bank structural adjustment loans and bilateral foreign assistance might be available, but within the time dimension of a true crisis the main bilateral support would have to be from central banks in the countries to which funds were fleeing. Swap agreements between the US Federal Reserve System and other central banks exceed $30 billion in total, and extensive short-term credit facilities also exist within Europe, especially the European Community's European Support Fund.

5 The International Monetary Fund

The International Monetary Fund has already been mentioned several times. It is the principal institutional embodiment of the international monetary system. It was established in 1947 to oversee the rules of financial cooperation among member countries and to lend to countries to help them adhere to the rules. More recently it has taken on responsibility for the creation of Special Drawing Rights (SDRs), a new form of international money. The key rules that the IMF was to support and enforce were fixed (but changeable) exchange rates between member countries and convertibility of currencies for all international transactions in goods, services, and private remittances. The first of these rules has now been transformed into a more general surveillance over exchange rate policies of member countries, to ensure that they are consistent with a well-functioning international monetary system. In practice, convertibility has been increasingly extended to international capital transactions as well, largely because of the difficulty of distinguishing them from current account transactions, but formally the distinction remains.

The most visible role of the IMF is lending to countries. When countries run into balance-of-payment difficulties, they turn (usually too late) to the IMF for support. The IMF works out a one- to three-year economic program with the country before making the full loan. Increasingly, private lenders also hold back new loans to a country in difficulty until agreement on a program has been reached with the IMF. Although it has been controversial with some developing countries, this "conditionality" of IMF lending is essential if the IMF is to perform its proper functions. The IMF is not and was never intended to be an agency to deliver foreign aid. Its purpose is to permit countries to adhere to international rules of behavior and to avoid major retrenchment of their economies during periods of *temporary* balance-of-payments difficulty. In that event, there must be some assurance that the difficulties are indeed temporary; a bridging loan has to have an abutment on the other side. This leaves plenty of room for judgment about what exactly the conditions should be but not about the principle of conditions. The IMF usually focuses on exchange rate and credit policy in the borrowing country and also on the overall government budget and on new external borrowing, insofar as they have an important bearing on credit policy.

The IMF lends through a separate facility, the compensatory financing facility, in those cases where there is a shortfall of export earnings from the recent past and those expected to prevail in the near future (two years back and projections two years forward, centered on the current year). In this case, virtually no conditions are attached, because the temporary nature of the imbalance lies in the character of the projections, provided that the country does not falsify them through a change in policy. Recently, exceptional expenditures on food imports have been made to qualify for use of this facility.

IMF lending commitments rose sharply in 1981 to $14.6 billion, up from $8.5 billion in 1980 and $2.0 billion in 1979. This reflects partly an augmentation of resources that countries are allowed to borrow from the IMF and partly a sharp increase in need during the recessionary conditions of the past two years and following the oil price increases of 1979–80.

One unresolved issue is the possible role that the IMF might play as a lender of last resort, that is, an agency that could lend without limit if necessary to prevent collapse of the international financial system. At present the IMF lending capacity is sharply limited by the resources made available to it by member countries. In addition, it lends at the initiative of member countries, not at its own intitiative. To move the IMF toward the position of a true world central bank would require relaxing sharply its own lending limits and would allow it to lend at its own initiative (e.g., by buying securities in the open market).

Notes

1. "Flexible Exchange Rates, 1973–1981: How Bad Have They Really Been?" in *The International Monetary System under Flexible Exchange Rates*, R. N. Cooper, J. de Macedo, P. Kenen, and J. Van Ypersele, eds. Ballinger, 1982, 3–16. [Chapter 4 in this book.]

2. In more normal times one would expect the major industrial countries of the world to run current account surpluses, that is, to be net exporters of capital. But in a period of large OPEC surpluses, which the last nine years has generally been, this normal expectation must be altered.

12

The Evolution of the International Monetary Fund toward a World Central Bank

Sooner or later one country after another developed or created a national central bank to preside over its national monetary system. As the world becomes more interdependent, are we likely to see a similar evolution at the global level? Should we encourage it? In this paper I try to address the parallelism between central banking at the national level and at the global level and also the differences, focusing on the International Monetary Fund (IMF). I outline the incipient characteristics of a world central bank in the IMF as it is currently constituted and suggest how these characteristics might be developed to transform the IMF into a full-fledged central bank.

In section 1 I sketch the principal characteristics and objectives of national central banks. This is followed by a discussion of the IMF as it is currently constituted. In section 3 I then draw a number of parallels between the present IMF and central banks. In section 4 I consider the possible evolution of the IMF into a full-fledged central bank along several different dimensions.

1 National Central Banks

The notion of a central bank has evolved over time, and it is still not completely well defined. Some central banks emerged from leading commercial banks, like the Bank of England. Others, such as the Federal Reserve System, were brought into existence by statute with a central banking role in mind. But even in the latter case the actual functioning of the central banks has evolved extensively with the passage of time.

We must look at the structure, objectives, instruments, and governance of national central banks. The structure of most central banks is like a

Towards a New Bretton Woods, vol. 1, Commonwealth Economic Papers 18 (London: Commonwealth Secretariat, April 1983). Reprinted by permission.

commercial bank, from which many evolved. Like a bank but unlike a business enterprise, the activities of central banks revolve around their balance sheets. On the asset side are its financial investments—typically of short maturity—allocated among domestic assets, claims on government, and claims on foreign countries (its international reserves). The liabilities of a central bank are typically deposits of commercial banks and the government plus currency issued to the public. The core of central banking is the manipulation of these assets and liabilities. Central banks have other functions as well, however, notably regulation of commerical banks to ensure their soundness.

The instruments used by a typical bank include buying and selling securities against its own liabilities, in the process of which it creates money. This can be done at the initiative of the central bank, as in open market operations, or at the initiative of the seller of the securities under rules and conditions laid down by the central bank, as in rediscount operations. The central bank may change the conditions and especially the interest rate under which it rediscounts. It may also commit itself to a regular pattern of purchases or sales of securities. It implicity does this when it adopts a fixed exchange rate between its currency and that of some other country, implying that it will buy or sell foreign exchange against its liabilities to limit movements in the exchange rate. Or it may engage in steady predetermined purchases of some assets to provide for a steady growth in the domestic money supply.

Under the laws of many countries the central bank can also instruct commercial banks or other regulated financial institutions on their portfolios, for example, as regards their foreign exchange holdings (as under exchange control regulations) or credits to private businesses.

It took about two centuries for the Bank of England to evolve from a commercial bank with special responsibility for financing the government to the exclusive issuer of notes to the public (except for the Bank of Scotland), holder of the nation's gold reserves, and lender of last resort to the banking system. The last function involves a willingness to buy high-quality assets from commercial banks against its own deposits—at a penalty interest rate. John Maynard Keynes complained in the 1920s of the *limited* role of the Bank of England and urged it to manipulate its balance sheet so as to stabilize the price level rather than focusing exclusively on the exchange rate.[1]

The Federal Reserve System came into existence in 1913 as a consequence of the banking panics of the 1890s and of 1907. It was designed to provide an efficient clearing system, to regulate the commerical banks, and to provide a lender of last resort. The note issue in the United States had in practice already been taken over from commercial banks by the US Treasury, but the Federal Reserve System was given that function for large denominations as well. As early as the 1920s the Federal Reserve System adopted practices different from those that had guided the Bank of England: It "sterilized" the impact on the domestic money supply of the inflow of gold from abroad to prevent excessive monetary growth from raising prices and destabilizing the economy. Thus it began the process of economic stabilization.

By the mid-1960s modern central banking seemed to have settled down into a pattern. The main instrument of policy was open market operations, although central banks had other instruments as well. Part of the art of central banking has been to maintain an aura of mystery around its objectives and how it pursues them. Most central banks have succeeded in creating a certain ambiguity about their objectives and weights they attach to them. Nonetheless, based on testimony before the Radcliffe Committee, Richard Sayers could describe the objectives for the open market operations of the Bank of England in the following way:[2] (1) The Bank seeks to protect the discount market and the banks from violent oscillation between stringency and glut of cash; (2) the Bank seeks a certain level of treasury bill rates, primarily in the interest of influencing international short-term capital movement so as to maintain the gold and the foreign reserves at an adequate level; (3) the Bank seeks to influence the liquidity of the commerical banks; (4) the Bank has to manage the national debt in the sense that it has to arrange for issue and redemption of government securities and maturity distribution of the debt in such a way as to ensure that the government can always meet its obligations, and [it has] to do this in such a way as to avoid an unnecessarily high burden of interest rates; (5) the Bank encourages an upward or downward movement in long-term interest rates according to which direction it considers appropriate to the underlying investment/saving propensities in the economy, although this is still probably a subordinate aim.

Notice that the focus here is on stability of interest rates, both short- and long-term, an objective that in recent years has yielded to much more focus on steadiness of growth in some variant of the money supply. The third objective stated by Sayers is ambiguous as regards the focus on long-term secular growth of bank liquidity as opposed to relatively short-run variation in liquidity to counter business cycle tendencies in the private economy. The emphasis on managing the public debt is also noteworthy; it is the traditional function of the Bank of England but one that is not shared by the Federal Reserve System.

The objectives of the Federal Reserve System are basically similar except regarding management of the government debt, for which it has accepted no responsibility since 1951 beyond the maintenance of orderly financial markets that make possible Treasury management of the public debt.

The Federal Reserve System is of special interest in the current context, because its creation entailed much controversy over the role of the federal government in banking in the United States. The resulting structure of the Federal Reserve System reflects a compromise: It is composed of twelve regional reserve banks whose stockholders are the commercial banks subject to regulation. In the early years of the Federal Reserve System, these regional banks even maintained separate rediscount policies and rates. A seven-member board sits in Washington, appointed by the president for fourteen-year terms but responsible only to congress. Key monetary decisions are made by the Open Market Committee, which consists of the board augmented by five of the twelve presidents of the regional reserve banks on a rotating basis. The Open Market Committee meets every three weeks. Regulations governing the commercial banks are promulgated by the board but executed by the regional banks. Unlike in some other countries, foreign exchange operations are under the control of the US Treasury, but the Treasury has no decision-making powers with respect to monetary policy (except insofar as it can influence new legislation).

In contrast, the Bank of England is formally responsible to the British Treasury, although by tradition it has much autonomy. Central banks around the world run the spectrum in independence from the sitting government. In many cases central banks are merely the agent of the Minister of Finance. At the other extreme, the German Bundesbank is fully independent of the government in power, as regards both monetary policy and foreign exchange rate operations, although of course it is sometimes in consultation with the government.

2   The International Monetary Fund

Although the IMF has sometimes been called a central bank for central banks and although it does perform that function to a limited extent, its role both in conception and today is much more limited than is the role of a national central bank. It is worth stating in full the formal objectives of the International Monetary Fund as stated in Article 1 of its Articles of Agreement:

The purposes of the International Monetary Fund are:

(i) To promote international monetary cooperation through a permanent institution which provides the machinery for consultation and collaboration on international monetary problems.

(ii) To facilitate the expansion and balanced growth of international trade, and to contribute thereby to the the promotion and maintenance of high levels of employment and real income and to the development of the productive resourses of all members as primary objectives of economic policy.

(iii) To promote exchange stability, to maintain orderly exchange arrangements among members, and to avoid competitive exchange depreciation.

(iv) To assist in the establishment of a multilateral system of payments in respect of current transactions between members and in the elimination of foreign exchange restrictions which hamper the growth of world trade.

(v) To give confidence to members by making the general resources of the Fund temporarily available to them under adequate safeguards, thus providing them with opportunity to correct maladjustments in their balance of payments without resorting to measures destructive of national or international prosperity.

(vi) In accordance with the above, to shorten the duration and lessen the degree of disequilibrium in the international balances of payments of members.

Four features of the operation of the International Monetary Fund are noteworthy. First, member countries, which now number 146, including virtually all countries apart from the Soviet Union and some of its satellites, Switzerland, and Taiwan, deposit their currencies in the IMF in an amount defined by *quota*, which also defines each countries' voting rights. By agreement in 1983, total quotas have been increased to 90 billion SDRs, just short of 100 billion US dollars. Second, member countries can draw on the currencies of other countries when they have a balance-of-payments problem. Allowable drawings are linked to quotas, with a current limit of 150 percent of a country's quota per year and a maximum normal drawing of 450 percent of quota. For extensive drawings, a country must work out a balance-of-payments adjustment program acceptable to the IMF. Third, the IMF has general responsibility for "surveillance" over the rules and functioning of the International Monetary System. The rules involve inter alia convertibility of currencies for current account transactions. Originally the rules also required that exchange rates be relatively fixed, but now they require only that national exchange rate policy be consonant with smooth functioning of the international monetary system. More generally, in accordance with its charter, the IMF is concerned with ensuring relatively smooth balance-of-payments adjustments to avoid persistent disequilibria in international payments. And finally, since 1969, the IMF has been empowered to create a new international money, the SDR, for transactions among official monetary institutions and has actually created SDRs on two occasions, 1970–1972 and 1979–1981, to the total extent of about 24 billion US dollars.

The governance of the IMF is unique among international organizations, along with its sister institution the World Bank, in having a representative form of government. Day-to-day management of the IMF is in the hands of a managing director, who reports to a board of twenty-two executive directors that meet three times a week. The executive directors represent all the members of the IMF. The managing director is formally responsible to the Board of Governors, which meets once a year and whose votes in the ultimate decisions governing management of the IMF are weighted according to a formula (embodied in each country's quota) that is designed to reflect roughly both the importance of each country in the world economy and the importance of world trade for each economy.

3   Parallels between the IMF and a National Central Bank

One can see in the structure of the IMF faint glimmerings of a world central bank, but on close examination it falls far short of the role played by central banks in national economies. Like a national central bank, the IMF can effectively create international money in two ways: (1) through its lending operations at the initiative of a borrowing country, because the IMF's use of currencies creates a "reserve position in the Fund" for the country whose currency has been drawn, and this reserve position in turn can be freely drawn on by that country when it needs to; or (2) through the allocation of SDRs, at its own initiative (i.e., following a vote of its members). In this sense the IMF is already a bank of issue. But in the case of the first channel of money creation, roughly analogous to the rediscount facility in a national central bank, the IMF's medium is national currencies. It issues its own liabilities not to the borrowing country but to the country whose currency has been borrowed. Polak has argued that the IMF could function with considerably greater simplicity, both of mechanism and of language to describe what is happening, by consolidating its general account, which is available for normal drawings, and the SDR account, which deals with creation of SDRs.[3] This would avoid the intermediating use of national currencies in IMF operations. I return to this possibility later.

The IMF can even perform the lender-of-last-resort function as that term has been used historically. In particular, it can lend large amounts to a particular country that is in balance-of-payments trouble. True, normal borrowing is limited by each country's quota. But in extreme circumstances these limits can be waived by a vote by the Executive Board. Then the limit is simply total available IMF resources (that is, its usuable currencies) for these purposes.

The SDR creation mechanism cannot be used for such emergency lending because the decision-making process for creating SDRs is a complicated and prolonged one. And SDRs must be allocated to all member countries, not selectively. But we should recall that, although the Bank of England and other central banks historically could issue their own liabilities as lender of last resort, they could not do so without limit. In some cases there were legal limits on the creation of their liabilities; but even when there were no such limits, they feared the loss of gold or of other reserves, which were held in limited supply. Thus the IMF in this regard stands at a certain point in the historical evolution of national central banks, but it has not reached the present state of national central banks where there is in principle no limit to the support that they can give to their banking systems. I return to this point to clarify certain misunderstandings about the lender-of-last-resort function.

On the regulatory side, the IMF also performs the function of a rudimentary central bank, but here its authority is even more limited than it is as a bank of issue. Its members are sovereign states, bound in principle by the Articles of Agreement but with no enforcing authority. The IMF can enforce the Articles to a limited degree by making its loans conditional on specified changes in behavior by the borrowing countries. This practice, known as conditionality, is resented around the world, but it follows closely, mutatis mutandis, the behavior of national central banks. National central banks universally set down the ground rules on which they will lend to commercial banks. Often they designate certain high-quality paper as "rediscountable" without question—the analogue to low conditionality lending by the IMF, although without the collateral that the rediscountable paper offers—but even those·designations can be altered. Beyond that a central bank will examine the portfolio of a commercial bank that desires to borrow and perhaps will require alterations in it. In addition, central banks have the authority to direct portfolio changes by commercial banks even when they do not come to the central bank to borrow—by changing reserve requirements (in the United States), by requiring special deposits, by placing ceilings on certain kinds of credit, and so on. The legal setup within nations requires compliance by the banks if they want to continue to operate. The IMF has no analogous authority at the international level. Its Articles do, however, decree certain general norms of behavior that members are expected to follow, and it does have the authority to designate national currencies for its own use in its lending operations.

There has been a debate from the beginning over the balance to be struck in the IMF over the degree of IMF guidance on economic policies appropriate for member states. The original (1943) American plan for what later became the IMF, proposed by Harry Dexter White, the chief American delegate, gave the proposed new institution wide supervisory powers over domestic economic policy, even the power to alter exchange rates. Writing in January 1944, J. M. Keynes described the then US views:

In their eyes (the new Institution) should have wide discretionary and policing powers and should exercise something of the same measure of grandmotherly influence and control over the central banks of the member countries, that these central banks in turn are accustomed to exercise over the other banks within their own countries.[4]

Keynes's reference to "grandmotherly" was no doubt a gentle allusion to the role that the Bank of England, the "old lady of Threadneedle Street," played with respect to the British banks; and on occasion "grandmother" was more like a stern father. What actually emerged in the IMF involved a good deal less discretion and power than White had originally proposed—on reflection Americans could not accept the wide powers involved in his plan either—but a good deal more than Keynes would then have preferred and White thought he had negotiated. Some form of conditionality, that is, tightening down on the economic policies of countries that borrowed from the IMF, was necessary because the IMF resources were much more limited than Keynes had proposed. Moreover, even Keynes was prepared to see quite strong IMF discretionary powers with respect to borrowing countries once they had drawn more than 50 percent of their large quotas under his plan.[5]

4   Possible Evolution of the IMF toward a World Central Bank

In speculating on how the IMF might evolve further toward a world central bank, it is necessary to specify the institutional setting in which this is to take place and the motivations for economic behavior that can possibly be influenced by an XIMF—an expanded IMF.

The relevant time horizon is taken to be roughly the next twenty years. In this period the world will continue to be made up of sovereign nation states with autonomous national monetary policies. Exchange rates among currencies will in principle float against one another, but there will be increased perception of economic interdependence and the need to coordinate various aspects of economic policy. This perception will lead inter alia to heavy management of exchange rates and acceptance of the implied restraints on the exercise of full monetary autonomy.

The key behavioral assumption is that world reserves can influence world economic activity, at least for a time. The mechanism operates through national government policy rather than directly through private transactions, although if the SDR's use is broadened to include private holding, there might also be some influence directly on commercial bank lending and hence on private economic activity.[6] We will return to this latter point. A more generous level of world reserves will result in less restrictive economic policy by member countries, and vice versa. The process is limited in time, however, because of the presence of "reserve sinks," that is, large countries that determine their policies more or less independently of reserve levels and who, if necessary, are willing to accumulate reserves without relaxing their economic policies.[7] Most countries, however, are assumed to be constrained by foreign exchange, so that an augmentation of reserves will permit relaxation of trade controls and/or macroeconomic restraints. By the same token, a reserve contraction will have the opposite effect, where "contraction" need not mean a literal decline in world reserves but only reserve growth less than the normal growth in demand for reserves.

So long as the IMF does not have a monopoly on international liquidity, however, its influence will be heavily conditioned by what is happening in private financial markets as well, because most countries can add national currencies—mainly the US dollar but also other currencies, such as the German mark, the British pound, the Japanese yen, the Swiss franc—to their reserves by borrowing or by earning them from other countries that have borrowed them. This possibility raises the interesting question of whether there is an asymmetry in influence. Perhaps the IMF can stimulate world demand but cannot restrain it when private markets are ebullient. This would reverse the British economist Dennis Robertson's dictum concerning national monetary policy that "you cannot push on a string." He thought monetary policy could restrain demand but could not stimulate it.

The exact role of the SDR is crucial in assessing potential IMF influence on world monetary conditions. At present it is only a minor supplement to international reserves, amounting to less than 5 percent of world reserves even if gold is valued at (artifically low) official prices—and considerably less if monetary gold is valued at (artifically high) market prices. Nor is it used extensively except in transactions with the IMF itself. Indeed, by late 1981, a quarter of total SDRs created were in the IMF's own general account. There is no general disposition at present to increase vastly the role of the SDR.

Kenen has correctly pointed out that the SDR is not likely to be wanted extensively by central banks until it is integrated into the actual method by which international settlements take place, that is, through intervention in foreign exchange markets. Kenen would have the IMF encourage more extensive private use of SDRs. To this end he proposes setting up a new clearinghouse to which central banks could transfer SDRs in exchange for deposits of national currencies by their commercial banks with each central bank.[8] In this way commercial banks would effectively have access to SDRs and could begin to deal in them. Once private use of SDRs was widespread, central banks could intervene in foreign exchange markets through the medium of SDRs, and demand for SDRs as reserves would rise relative to the desire to hold national currencies as reserves. Kenen's proposal is ingeniously designed to avoid an amendment to the Articles of Agreement, which now limits holdings of SDRs proper to ófficial institutions, of which the clearinghouse would be one. If the commercial banks began to trade extensively in SDR-denominated claims, based on their SDR claims on the clearinghouse, that would represent the beginnings of fractional reserve-based deposit banking on a world scale, and IMF issuance of new SDRs (or transfers into the clearinghouse by other official holders) could then influence bank credit and hence economic activity directly rather than only indirectly through alterations in government policies.

As noted, Polak has sketched a revised IMF that integrates the general account and the SDR account, basing both on SDRs. He shows that this could simplify the IMF considerably without changing fundamentally its mode of operation. SDRs would replace the current reliance on national currencies. This change would, however, require an amendment to the Articles of Agreement, and if that were done, the amendment could be extended to allow private holders, in particular, commercial banks, to hold SDRs directly in the IMF, rendering Kenen's clearinghouse unnecessary as a device to avoid amendment. The implied division of labor between the IMF, dealing with official institutions, and the clearinghouse, which would deal with commercial banks and other private financial institutions, might still be desirable even if the Articles of Amendment could be altered to permit private holdings of SDRs.

Polak's scheme does entail one important substantive change: The IMF would no longer depend on contributions of national currencies to support increases in quotas. It could simply, under the amended Articles, create SDRs in order to meet calls on it by would-be borrowers. In this respect it would represent a strong move closer to a true central bank. Its ability to create SDRs in this way, however, would (under Polak's scheme) still be limited by the quotas of the member countries, which would be added to their acceptance limits under the current provisions for SDR creation.

I turn now to five central bank functions and ask how the IMF might evolve during the next ten to twenty years into a world central bank with respect to each of them. Some have already been covered implicitly in the preceding discussion; others involve new elements.

Lender of Last Resort

As noted above, in important ways the IMF already performs the function of lender of last resort. It cannot, however, create its own liabilities without limit under emergency circumstances, as a national central bank can. The scheme outlined by Polak would effectively permit it to do this, although full freedom to do so would also require elimination of acceptance limits on SDRs. But a word should be said about this central bank function, for it has been used too loosely in much recent discussion. The phrase arose, and is still used, in the context of meeting a liquidity crisis in a commercial bank, whose liabilities are more liquid than its assets and may be called faster than the bank can mobilize its assets to meet the calls. The central bank then steps in and "liquifies" the bank's assets by making a market for them, perhaps at a penalty interest rate. The function is not designed to bail out an insolvent bank, where liabilities exceed assets in value. Different remedies are necessary for that. In macroeconomic terms, applying the lender-of-last-resort function to the entire banking system, it is designed to accommodate a shift by the public in its demand for money, typically toward money issued by the central bank (e.g., currency). It is not designed to finance a run from all financial assets, including money, into goods.

The distinction between liquidity and solvency does not apply cleanly to countries. A country can find itself illiquid in the sense that it is short of ready-at-hand cash to meet its pressing obligations. But how is a country insolvent? The natural extension of this concept, which is not without its problems, is that the country has borrowed abroad more than it can service in the long run. That is, national solvency involves maintaining some maximum relationship of external debt to GNP, properly measured; in terms of growth, debt should not grow more rapidly than the capacity of the borrowing country to service it.

By analogy with national central banking, the lender-of-last-resort function of the IMF should be to meet liquidity needs that arise in some context other than external borrowing in excess of what a country can service in the long run. The IMF is not designed to finance an excessive demand for foreign goods over the long period. In playing its role of lender of last resort today, the IMF does not make this distinction explicitly, but presumably it is reflected in the adjustment program worked out with each particular borrowing country. The main limitation on the IMF's ability to function today as a lender of last resort is its limited resources; it is simply not large enough to handle the United States as a borrower or several medium-sized countries that need to borrow at the same time. The General Arrangements to Borrow had to be created in the 1960s to deal with the possibility of a US borrowing; and in some of its recent programs the IMF has made going ahead with many debt-ridden countries conditional on substantial additional lending also by commercial banks.

A final remark is desirable to clear up a misunderstanding. The term "lender of last resort" has never meant *only* lender of last resort." Central banks have often lent funds, directly or through the market, to the commercial banking system before it encountered a liquidity crisis. Similarly, the IMF can and should be able to lend well before a country reaches a liquidity crisis. The term simply conveys the notion that, if a country has a liquidity crisis, an institution is available to lend what is necessary to see the country through a difficult period.

Secular Growth in International Liquidity

With a mechanism in place for creating the SDR, the IMF is able to add to international liquidity on a secular basis. Indeed, that was the rationale for the creation of SDRs in the first place, to supplement and ultimately perhaps to substitute for gold and national currencies in the growth of international reserves. Being able to influence international liquidity, however, it not the same as being able to control it. Control is impossible so long as countries are free to add national currencies to their reserves, as they are likely to be able to do for a long time. Within the 10–20-year time horizon of this paper, a prohibition on increments to foreign currency reserves is highly improbable. A more likely development is that countries whose currencies are used as foreign exchange reserves will come increasingly to appreciate the cost of this role for their currencies, especially in terms of their own loss of national monetary autonomy. They may even take steps to discourage expanded use of their currency abroad. But return to a one-reserve world, even if an extensive private use of SDRs is encouraged, is unlikely in the remainder of this century. The IMF can thus contribute to the growth of international reserves, and because it generates a claim that is no country's liability, it can control the growth of *net* reserves. But it will not in this period be able to control the growth of gross reserves without major and probably undesirable changes in the ways nations interact with financial markets.

Stabilizing the World Economy

As noted above, the role of central banks in stabilizing economic activity, as opposed to financial markets, came relatively late in their evolution. And even today it is not fully accepted as a legitimate function. Indeed, monetarists contend that central bank efforts to "fine tune" their actions in the interests of economic stabilization are more likely to be a destabilizing influence than a stabilizing one, because of lags and uncertainties in the economy's response to a given monetary action. Be that as it may, the IMF could play a modest role in global economic stabilization within the framework described earlier, of nation states constrained by external payments. In particular, three mechanisms for helping to stabilize the world economy are possible with only modest extensions of the present IMF.

First, the IMF could consciously vary the conditions on which it lends according to the state of the world economy. In times of world economic boom, the IMF could somewhat tighten its conditions to all borrowers on the twofold grounds of helping to cool the world boom and encouraging the borrowing country to adopt a stabilization program that does not rely for its effectiveness on a continuing world boom. By the same token, in periods of world economic slack the IMF would ease up on the conditions it imposes on all borrowers, compared with what otherwise would be imposed, thus helping to cushion or reverse the world recession. Such adaptation of IMF conditionality to world economic conditions might also include the interest rate charged on loans, although that would be less important than the stabilization targets agreed with the borrowing countries. This kind of adaptation to world economic conditions would be analogous to a central bank's altering the conditions for rediscounting in response to the business cycle. Those adjustments have historically focused on the rediscount rate of interest, but other conditions, particularly as regards the quality of rediscountable paper, have also been altered as well.

Such behavior by the IMF could not eliminate booms and recessions in world economic activity, for IMF lending would not be large enough in the foreseeable future to do that. But it could help to damp down fluctuations.

There are practical difficulties with this proposal. Countries would have to understand that, depending on world economic conditions, they might be required to undertake stiffer actions than they did on some past borrowings or than another otherwise comparable country did in the previous year. Acceptance of this variation would require exceptional understanding on the part of high turnover ministers in the borrowing countries. Similarly, it is not easy to induce a bureaucracy of country desk officers to alter their criteria in a more or less uniform way according to general instructions from top management based on world economic conditions. But these are difficulties, not insuperable obstacles, and such variations in conditionality would be well worth introducing.

One feature of the present IMF does automatically alter lending conditions with world economic conditions: the compensatory financing facility. In a world slump, if export earnings fall below the projected level, as defined by a five-year moving average, countries can borrow under the compensatory financing facility with little or no conditionality. Recently this facility has been extended to cover increases in the prices of imported cereals. The facility has worked well, and over $11 billion had been borrowed under it by early 1983. But many countries exhausted their borrowing rights, which are limited in relation to quota, during the 1981–82 world depression. The compensatory financing facility should be enlarged to deal with such severe recessions. As the IMF is presently constituted, its resources ultimately pose a limit to the degree of liberality of the compensatory facility, along with other IMF lending. Adoption of the Polak scheme would deal with that. The IMF could lend SDRs through the compensatory financing facility as well as in its normal lending operations, and its total lending capacity would then be limited only by the willingness of member countries to accept SDRs in payment for their goods, a limit that is not likely to be binding during periods of world recession.

A number of proposals have been made for extending further the coverage of the compensatory financing facility. These include measuring export earnings, for purposes of drawing from the compensatory financing facility, in real rather than nomimal terms.[9] Whatever the merits of this idea purely in terms of stabilization, extension of the compensatory financing facility in this direction would be incompatible with the evolution of the IMF toward a world central bank. Banks of issue must deal in nominal, not real, values. Automatic unlimited financing of export shortfalls in real terms could lead to an acceleration of world inflation, with the IMF financing an ever increasing world price level in an attempt to compensate for a change in relative prices. This particular reform is therefore undesirable in a setting in which evolution of the IMF toward a world central bank is considered desirable.

Third, the XIMF could issue SDRs in a countercyclical way, providing more in periods of slump and fewer or none in periods of world economic boom. If commercial deposits are developed in SDRs, along the lines discussed, such variation in SDR issues could influence economic activity not only through its influence on government policies but also by making the commercial banking system more or less liquid in terms of SDRs and thus by influencing private bank lending.

Moving in this direction would require streamlining the procedures for SDR allocation to allow for year-to-year variations and to permit relatively quick decisions, instead of the prolonged process of bilateral consultation that now occurs for allocations that are to cover a period of five years.

Regulating National Economies

An important role for national central banks is regulating the behavior of the commercial banks under their jurisdiction. The extent and visibility of this regulation varies greatly from country to country. The analogous role for the XIMF would be to regulate the economic, or at least the monetary, policies of its member states—in Keynes's words, to exercise "a measure of grandmotherly influence and control over the central banks of member countries." As discussed, the degree of this control has been a source of controversy and disagreement from the inception of the IMF. Yet it is not conceivable to have a central bank that lends to its members, and creates money in the process, at the member's initiative, without some degree of control over the policy actions that influence the need for member borrowing and ability to repay. If this is granted, then the discussion must focus on the practical and detailed implementation of this general authority, and it is difficult to do so intelligently at a high level of generality. The particulars of the individual cases are decisively important. Given the strong resentment that exists, wrongly, in many parts of the world concerning IMF conditionality, however, it is difficult to imagine a consensus developing that would endow the IMF with more direct authority than it now has over national economic policies, which in their totality strongly influence world economic conditions. This means that the IMF's influence over world economic conditions is likely to remain relatively indirect, exercised along the lines already sketched, through alterations in conditionality and variations in SDR allocations. Direct coordination of national macroeconomic policy by the IMF, as Harry Dexter White once envisaged, does not seem likely in the foreseeable future.

There is one dimension of policy coordination in which the IMF could perhaps play a more active role: management of exchange rates. There is widespread dissatisfaction with the last ten years of floating rates. Much of this dissatisfaction is misplaced, in that it attributes to floating exchange rates difficulties in the world economy that were quite different in their origin. A return to fixed (adjustable peg) exchange rates among all major currencies is neither feasible nor desirable in the near future. At the same time, there is little doubt that some international cooperation in the management of exchange rates is desirable, and indeed it has already occurred among some countries on occasion. The IMF is charged with the responsibility of exercising firm surveillance over the exchange rate policies of its members to ensure that they are consistent with the purposes of the IMF set out in Article 1. The IMF could move more aggressively than it has to identify inappropriate exchange rates and even to define target zones or reference rates for member currencies. These designations would have operational significance insofar as they guide exchange market intervention by member states and influence market perception of where exchange rates ought to lie. The IMF could identify publicly exchange rates that were out of line, whether or not it had specified reference rates, with a view to influencing both government and market behavior.

The focus on exchange rates is not so narrow as it at first may seem, because the level (in a market system) and sustainability of any particular exchange rate depends inter alia on the entire array of member country economic policies but especially on monetary policies. Thus a surveillance mechanism that narrows variations in exchange rates would do so by implicitly coordinating national monetary policies.

Stabilizing Markets

A final function of national central banks has been to help to maintain orderly markets. By analogy, in respect to member nation policies this issue has already been covered in section 3. But one might go further and ask whether the IMF should not intervene *directly* in currency and/or short-term financial markets when necessary to help maintain orderly markets. This activity would require a major institutional overhaul of the existing IMF, which is not set up either for direct market intervention or to select and handle the financial assets that it would have to hold in its portfolio if it were to be a regular participant in financial markets. In a run longer than that under consideration here, such direct intervention might be something to keep in view as a future step in the evolutionary process toward a world central bank, but it goes even further than allowing the SDR to be held by private banks and will not be considered further here.

Governance

If the IMF is to be moved toward a world central bank, with greater authority and operational flexibility than it now exercises, who is the IMF to be responsible to for its actions? Under its present structure, it is responsible to its member governments as embodied in their finance ministers meeting annually. No doubt that could remain the basic arrangement for some time to come. But if the IMF is to be more actively involved in global economic management, judgments on the state of the world economy will have to be made more often than once a year, and ministers are not likely to be willing (or politically able) to delegate responsibility for decisions on such weighty matters to the managing director or the Board of Executive Directors. It will probably be necessary to institute some intermediating arrangement for making key economic decisions. Adaptation of the Interim Committee of Governors, sitting on a representative basis, would be a natural way to accomplish this, although it is by no means the only possible way. The Interim Committee could extend its meeting times from two to three or even four times a year and sit as a kind of open market committee to guide the XIMF in its enlarged responsibilities.

5   Concluding Observations

The IMF has already evolved extensively and in general toward an international central bank during the first thirty-five years of its existence. Its creators would be surprised at the authority it has developed during this period, especially as regards conditionality, and its ability, albeit limited, to create reserves through its lending operations and through the allocation of SDRs. (They would probably be astonished, however, given its general success, to discover how small its resources have become relative to the value of world trade and other international transactions.)

By the mid-1970s, the IMF was beginning to take a global view of its lending activities rather than simply viewing them as a series of individual country problems. And by 1982 the IMF was insisting successfully that commercial banks increase their lending to particular countries in support of IMF lending and stabilization programs if they were to be effective. By the year 2003 the IMF might advance much beyond this in its authority, unless its evolution is stunted by sharp disagreements over the basic philosophy that is to guide IMF actions and over how it is to be governed.

Notes

1. See his *Tract on Monetary Reform*, 1923, written during the period of floating exchange rates following World War I.

2. From Sayers, *Modern Banking*, 7th edition, Clarendon Press, 1967, pp. 112, 113. Perhaps more than any other, this text helped to train banking officials throughout the British Commonwealth.

3. See J. J. Polak, *Thoughts on an International Monetary Fund Based Fully on the SDR*, pamphlet no. 28, International Monetary Fund, 1979.

4. Quoted in Sydney Dell, *On Being Grandmotherly: The Evolution of IMF Conditionality*, Princeton Essays in International Finance, October 1981. Dell offers an excellent review of the evolution of conditionality in the IMF.

5. For discussion of the relationship between adjustment and liquidity in the early IMF plans, see Richard N. Cooper, *The Economics of Interdependence*, 1968, chapter 2.

6. The behavioral assumptions here differ sharply from those put forward by Stanley Fischer in his "The SDR and the IMF: Towards a World Central Bank?" in George von Furstenberg, ed., *International Money and Credit. The Policy Roles*, International Monetary Fund, 1983. Fischer postulates the establishment of a true world money, something that is not contemplated here within the relevant time horizon.

7. For discussion of the role of reserve sinks, having in mind the United States and West Germany, see R. N. Cooper, "International Liquidity and Balance of Payments Adjustment," and H. G. Johnson's skeptical comment, in *International Reserves: Needs and Availability*, International Monetary Fund, 1970.

8. Peter B. Kenen, "The Use of the SDR to Supplement or Substitute for Other Means of Finance," in George von Furstenberg, ed., *International Money and Credit: The Policy Roles*, International Monetary Fund, 1983.

9. See, e.g., Carlos F. Diaz Alejandro, "International Financial and Goods Markets in 1982–83 and Beyond," March 1983 (unpublished).

13   A Monetary System for the Future

In this fortieth anniversary year of the international monetary conference at Bretton Woods, New Hampshire, there have been numerous but vague calls for a new Bretton Woods conference to improve our international monetary system which, if not actually ailing, at least leaves many participants uneasy and discomfited. Much of the discomfort relates to the large and burdensome external debt that has accumulated around the world, but much also goes beyond debt to the underlying monetary arrangements among countries.

Are international monetary arrangements stable? Are they likely to survive over a considerable period of time, such as a couple of decades? My answer is negative. Dissatisfaction with the very short-run and year-to-year movements in real exchange rates, combined with technological developments which will lead to further integration of the world economy, will sooner or later force a change in existing arrangements. Unless that alteration is carefully managed, it will take the form of defensive, insulating measures involving restrictions on international transactions, both trade and finance. That would be politically divisive and economically costly.

A new Bretton Woods conference is wholly premature. But it is not premature to begin thinking about how we would like international monetary arrangements to evolve in the remainder of this century. With this in mind, I suggest a radical alternative scheme for the next century: *the creation of a common currency for all of the industrial democracies, with a common monetary policy and a joint Bank of Issue to determine that monetary policy.* Individual countries would be free to determine their fiscal policy actions, but those would be constrained by the need to borrow in the international

Foreign Affairs 63, no. 1 (1984): 166–184. Reprinted by permission. Copyright 1984 by the Council on Foreign Relations, Inc.

capital market. Free trade is a natural but not entirely necessary complement to these macroeconomic arrangements.

This suggestion, outlined in the following pages, is far too radical for the near future. It could, however, provide a "vision" or goal that can guide interim steps in improving international monetary arrangements, and by which we can judge the evolution of national economic policy.

The plan of the article is as follows. Section 1 offers a brief sketch of the main features of the Bretton Woods system and why it failed, drawing attention to two intrinsic flaws in the original conception. Section 2 briefly characterizes the present system and suggests that it is workable and even useful, but unstable in the long run—again, it suffers from two fundamental weaknesses. Section 3 offers a technically workable scheme for the twenty-first century which, however, calls for major political commitments to international collaboration by the key countries, commitments which are much too ambitious for the present time. Section 4 brings us back to the present and suggests what steps we might take in the near future with a view to reaching the longer-term objective as it becomes politically possible.

1 Bretton Woods

The system that emerged from the Bretton Woods Conference 40 years ago had five key structural features:

First, it consciously provided a great deal of freedom for national economic policy to pursue national economic objectives, with the objective of assuring full employment, price stability, economic growth, and so forth. The Bretton Woods agreement was produced in the same climate of opinion which resulted in the White Paper on Employment Policy in the United Kingdom, the Employment Act of 1946 in the United States, and comparable legislation or statements of national policy in other countries, deriving directly from the experience of the 1930s and from a determination that that experience should never be repeated.

Second, the Bretton Woods system stipulated that exchange rates between currencies should be fixed. It was taken for granted that fixed exchange rates were desirable against the turbulent background of flexible exchange rates that prevailed in the early 1920s and again briefly in the early 1930s.

Third, currencies should be convertible one into another for international trade in goods and services, including travel. Again, that stipulation was against the background of extensive use of exchange controls by Nazi Germany during the 1930s and the tight wartime restrictions on trade and payments levied by many countries, which the Bretton Woods architects considered desirable to end as quickly as possible.

These three features taken together—autonomy of national policies, fixed exchange rates, and convertibility of currencies—were in conflict with one another. Countries could not frame their national economic policies independently and still maintain fixed exchange rates and currency convertibility except by luck and coincidence. That potential conflict was recognized by the Bretton Woods architects, who therefore added two further features.

Fourth, provision was made for medium-term international lending to cover balance-of-payments deficits that might result temporarily from the combination of the first three features. A new institution, the International Monetary Fund (IMF), was created as a channel for this new lending.

Fifth, countries were allowed, and in time came to be encouraged, to alter their exchange rates if it became clear that imbalances in payments were not temporary in nature. In other words, if a "fundamental dis-equilibrium" emerged, the exchange rate was to be changed by a discrete amount, with international agreement, in recognition that such imbalances would be inappropriate to finance indefinitely.

These then were the basic features of the Bretton Woods system. Inter-estingly, there was no provision in the system for secular growth in international reserves beyond a somewhat ambiguous provision permitting what was called a "uniform change in par values," that is to say, a deliberate rise in the price of gold. It was implicitly assumed that new gold production taken into monetary reserves would be sufficient to provide for adequate growth. In the event, the US dollar came to provide for the needed liquidity, as well as emerging as the currency of intervention in a regime in which some operating medium was necessary to ensure that exchange rates remained fixed.

During the quarter century between 1945 and 1970, world monetary reserves outside the United States grew by $54 billion, averaging 4.5 percent per year. Gold provided $13 billion of this increase, of which $9 billion was transferred from the high gold reserves of the United States (which reached 70 percent of total world monetary gold reserves in the late 1940s), and $4 billion came from new gold production. Foreign exchange, which was overwhelmingly in dollars, provided $30 billion of the growth in reserves. The IMF provided $11 billion, including $3 billion of the new

Special Drawing Rights (SDRs) in 1970. US reserves, of course, declined during this period because a substantial part of its gold stock was lost to other countries.

As it emerged—though not as it was designed—the Bretton Woods system might be said to have involved a bargain between the United States and the rest of the world: the United States would maintain domestic economic stability, and other countries would fix their currencies to the dollar and would accumulate their reserves in gold-convertible dollars. After a relatively brief period of postwar redistribution of the world's monetary gold stock, they would not actually convert their dollars into gold. Under this bargain, other countries would import economic stability from the United States. If a country got out of line with the world norm, it would have to change the par value of its currency. In turn, the United States did not have to be as concerned as other countries about how it financed a balance-of-payments deficit. Indeed, the very notion of a balance-of-payments deficit was an ambiguous one for the United States under these circumstances, although that did not keep the Commerce Department from publishing figures which it called the "deficit" for many years.

A second characteristic of this arrangement was that the dollar was overvalued relative to what it would have been without steady accretion of dollars in the reserves of other countries. That feature permitted some export-led growth by the rest of the world that would not have taken place under different monetary arrangements, under which American products would have been somewhat more competitive in world markets.

In this view of the world, the United States broke its part of the bargain in the late 1960s by inflating too much in connection with the Vietnam War and the Great Society programs. Some Europeans thought that the United States was inflating too much even in the early 1960s. On this point, they would not have found much agreement from Americans. Indeed, disagreement over US policy in the early 1960s indicated one of the weaknesses of the supposed bargain, namely dispute around the world over what exactly represented economically stabilizing behavior by the United States.

The structure of the Bretton Woods system had two intrinsic flaws in it, so that it would have broken down sooner or later even without the burst of US inflation in the late 1960s. First, the gold convertibility of the dollar was bound to become increasingly doubtful as dollar liabilities rose over time relative to the US gold stock. To halt the accumulation of foreign-held dollar reserves would have stifled growth of the world economy. Yet to allow the accumulation to continue would have gradually undermined the foundation of the system. Professor Robert Triffin of Yale University pointed out this dilemma as early as 1959. A new international reserve asset, IMF-issued Special Drawing Rights—aptly described as paper gold at the time—was finally created in the late 1960s as a long-run substitute for the dollar, thus offering a solution to the dilemma. But the solution came too late. This part of the system broke down in 1971, when President Nixon indefinitely suspended gold convertibility of the dollar. Two points are worth noting in passing. The first is that the US dollar was the only currency that was convertible into gold, even though the Bretton Woods agreement was formally symmetrical with regard to all currencies. The second is that countries continued to accumulate dollars in their international reserves even after gold convertibility of the dollar was suspended.

The second flaw in the Bretton Woods system was its reliance on discrete changes in exchange rates to correct imbalances in payments. Once a disequilibrium persisted long enough to be "fundamental" rather than temporary in nature, it was clear to everyone and the system thus produced the celebrated one-way option for currency speculation. Since the remedy to a fundamental disequilibrium was a jump in the value of the currency, speculators could move into or out of the currency at relatively low cost when they thought the jump would occur and take their gains after it occurred. It is interesting to note that the Bretton Woods architects had appreciated this problem, at least in principle, and to remedy it had stipulated that currencies should be convertible for current account transactions, but not for capital account transactions. The possibility was envisioned that countries might maintain controls on capital flows, and indeed countries were even enjoined to help other countries maintain and enforce their capital controls. So capital controls were in principle allowed under the Bretton Woods system, and indeed in a certain sense they were required by the internal logic of the system.

This feature of the system did not anticipate the enormous changes both in the nature of trade and in international capital movements that would take place over time. With improved and cheaper communications, it became easy to move capital through telegraphic transfers around the world at relatively low cost. In addition, many firms, especially American firms, began to invest heavily abroad in the 1950s and 1960s, so that many intracorporate transactions became international in nature. Finally, international trade gradually evolved away from traditional commodity trade toward special order and long-lead-time manufactures in which payments for trade and credit terms become inextricably mixed. For all of these reasons, it became increasingly difficult to separate capital from current account transactions and to maintain control on capital transactions.

The movement of funds that was associated with anticipated discrete changes in exchange rates became quite enormous and greatly complicated the management of domestic economic policies. In many countries, they threatened the autonomy of domestic national policy which was to have been preserved by the Bretton Woods system. For example, Germany in 1969 experienced a 25-percent increase in its money supply in a single week due to the inflow of speculative funds across the foreign exchanges and to the requirement that Germany maintain a fixed exchange rate for the mark in terms of other currencies.

In truth, the free movement of capital is incompatible with a system of exchange rates that are occasionally changed by consequential amounts and in a predictable direction. This part of the Bretton Woods system broke down definitively in 1973, although the breakdown started in 1970 when Canada allowed its currency to float.

The US inflation of the late 1960s resulted in large dollar outflows in the early 1970s that strained the Bretton Woods system to the breaking point. But it should be clear by now that this was only the proximate cause of the breakdown of the Bretton Woods system. The intrinsic flaws in the system would have come to the surface sooner or later, in response to one strain or another. They happened to come to the fore in 1971–73.

It is worth remarking that the breakdown of the Bretton Woods system was only partial. The International Monetary Fund is an important survivor, both as a lender and as a forum for managing the international monetary system. The convertibility of currencies and the continuing autonomy of national economic policies—both features of the Bretton Woods architecture—are still taken as desiderata in a well-functioning international monetary system. It is a measure of the success of that system that we take them for granted. It was the exchange rate features of the system that broke down, and the psychologically important but technically tenuous link to the historic gold standard via the gold convertibility of the leading currency.

2 Present Arrangements

For the past decade, the world has permitted a variety of exchange rate arrangements, but in practice with a much higher degree of flexibility than prevailed under the Bretton Woods system. This "nonsystem" has served the world economy rather well during a turbulent decade. It is true that the overall economic performance during the past decade, whether measured in terms of inflation rates or growth rates or unemployment rates, has been far inferior to what it was during the 1950s and 1960s. But it probably would have been even worse if governments had tried to maintain the Bretton Woods system through the period. In view of the large disturbances which the world economy has undergone, an attempt to maintain fixed but adjustable exchange rates would almost certainly have required a much higher degree of restrictions over both capital and current transactions than in fact prevailed. Thus exchange rate flexibility helped to preserve a relatively open trading and financial system.

During the decade, movable exchange rates have generally corrected for differences in national inflation rates, as economists predicted they would. But the movements in exchange rates have gone beyond that and affected "real" exchange rates as well—that is, competitiveness as measured by the relative prices at which the goods of one country on the average trade against the goods of another.

An evaluation of the period as a whole is complicated and difficult. Many of the movements in real exchange rates followed textbook predictions, responding to imbalances in current accounts, or to dramatic changes in resource endowments (such as the discovery of North Sea oil), or they followed divergent movements in aggregate demand. But some of the movements in real exchange rates have not followed textbook patterns, and even when they have, they have often been viewed as unwelcome disturbances by some countries, especially following the sharp depreciation of the US dollar in 1978, and again following the sharp appreciation of the dollar in 1981 and 1982. Perhaps for this reason, most countries of the world in fact have not allowed their currencies to float. Rather, they have fixed the value of their currencies against something—against another currency, or a basket of currencies, or, in the case of the European Monetary System, against one another. Thus it is not entirely accurate to characterize current arrangements as involving floating exchange rates. In practice, the exchange rates of several major currencies—the US dollar, the Japanese yen, the British pound, the Canadian dollar—do float more or less freely, but other currencies do not float, although they have shown greater flexibility than they would have under a Bretton Woods regime.

Movements in some key bilateral exchange rates, such as the dollar-deutsche mark rate, have shown sharp short-run variations on occasion during the past decade, which were not keyed to fundamental economic developments in any obvious way. There have been occasional weeks of average daily variations in excess of three percent. Why such great variability? In some respects foreign currency holdings are like any other financial asset, whose current price reflects all the information available that may have a bearing on its future value. New information may then affect market prices (in this instance exchange rates) sharply as the "market" reappraises the future in the light of new information.

This analogy to stock prices helps to explain the abruptness of some movements in exchange rates. But it hardly helps to explain month after month of sharp variability, up and down. Much "new" information, in a longer perspective, is in fact only noise, whose bearing on the price in question can reasonably be expected to be reversed in the near if not immediate future, especially since trade can eventually be expected to respond to persistent movements in exchange rates.

Abrupt up-and-down shifts in exchange rates may not, by themselves, greatly affect trade and production, since they should reasonably be expected to be reversed soon if they are not clearly linked to more fundamental economic developments. The added uncertainty about what an exchange rate will be when a transaction is completed will, however, undoubtedly discourage trade and investment for export to some extent.

The main difficulty with flexible exchange rates is that another influence is also at work, which can transmute the influence of noisy news into larger changes in exchange rates than otherwise would take place. It is the presence of crowd or bandwagon effects in the financial community. Few know how to interpret the news. Many use a movement in the exchange rate itself as a source of information about market sentiment. To avoid being left behind, dealers jump on the bandwagon, thus pushing the exchange rate further in the direction it tended to go initially. Expectations feed on expectations.

When this process is operating, even those who suspect the exchange rate has gone too far still have an interest in holding their investments so long as the prospect for further gain outweighs the probability of reversal. Thus a secondary judgment, oriented toward market dynamics, is superimposed on the reassessment based on the new information, and may come to dominate the movement in exchange rates for a time. This would not be troublesome if there were no real economic consequences. But in some periods expectations about the "fundamentals" may be so weakly held that the rate can be dominated by purely market dynamics for periods measured in weeks or months. When that is so, the exchange rate may in turn affect new information, such as price indexes, increases in which the public interprets as "inflation." Or it may set in motion urgent steps to avoid risks, as when multinational firms move to protect their quarterly balance sheets (at the expense of the operating earnings of the firms). So a vicious circle may temporarily be set in motion. And this vicious circle may aggravate inflation rates and hence inflationary expectations, or it may divert management attention away from real long-term investment to short-term balance-sheet considerations. In either case an unnecessary and avoidable element of instability is introduced into national economies.

Two features of present exchange rate arrangements will not be satisfactory over the long run. First, movements in real exchange rates have major effects on national economies, effects which are often unwelcome. Yet movements in real exchange rates cannot be easily controlled by use of the usual instruments of national economic policy because the determinants of exchange rates are diverse and complex. The result is that at any moment the influence of policy actions on exchange rates is uncertain. Portfolio decisions with respect to financial assets play a key role in the short-run determination of exchange rates, yet the influence of policy actions on portfolio decisions, via expectations, is uncertain. This marks a substantial contrast with the influence of policy actions on the aggregate demand for goods and services, where the linkages with policy are clearer. Despite this, we have not to date been able to eliminate the so-called business cycle. Unpredictable movements in real exchange rates, and unpredictable responses of real exchange rates to government action, greatly aggravate the problem of macroeconomic management.

Second, under a regime of flexible exchange rates there is a temptation, hence some tendency, to manipulate the exchange rate for national purposes. This can be done either to fight inflation, since monetary tightening produces an immediate reward—at the expense of other countries, so long as others do not respond in kind—in terms of a reduced inflation rate brought about by an appreciated currency. Or it can be used to combat unemployment, when expansionary monetary policy depreciates the currency—again, in general, at the expense of other countries. Of course, the new configuration of exchange rates may be satisfactory to all or most countries, but that would be a coincidence. Ordinarily these represent self-centered national actions which simply pass the problem either of inflation or of unemployment to other countries. Members of the IMF have a general responsibility to avoid such manipulation of exchange rates, and the IMF has a general responsibility for surveillance over exchange rate practices, with the aim of preventing such practices. But surveillance really

has not gotten off the ground, and it is not clear under today's arrangements what the IMF can really do, for example, when a Sweden deliberately depreciates its currency in order to increase output and employment,
or when a United States achieves a substantial reduction in its inflation rate
through a policy of tight money which has greatly appreciated the dollar
against other currencies.

Just as present exchange rate arrangements are not really sustainable
over the long run, neither are present arrangements for the creation of
reserves. The principal reserve medium today is a national currency, the
US dollar, dependent in large part for its supply on the policies of the
United States. This has been accepted, more or less grudgingly, because it
has worked reasonably well and there is no clear feasible alternative. But it
leaves a deep sense of uneasiness around the world, even when the United
States in the judgment of others is relatively well behaved; and the uneasiness grows dramatically when in such periods as 1970–71 and 1978 and
1981–82 the rest of the world, or parts of it, believe the United States is
not well behaved.

Moreover, as the United States shrinks in relation to the rest of the
world, as it is bound to do, the intrinsic weaknesses of reliance on the US
dollar will become more apparent, especially in the United States, where
the possible reaction of foreign dollar-holders will become an ever greater
constraint on US monetary policy. The United States is bound to shrink
relative to the rest of the world, not because it is doing badly, but because
the rest of the world may be expected to do well. The natural growth in the
labor force and the rate of capital accumulation are both higher in many
parts of the world than they are in the United States. Furthermore, tech-
nologically lagging countries can reduce the technological gap between
themselves and the United States, which operates on the frontiers of
modern technology. Thus the simple arithmetic of economic growth will
ensure a gradual relative decline of the United States, for instance from
about one-fourth of gross world product at present to around one-sixth 25
years from now if the United States grows on average at 3 percent a year
and the rest of the world grows on average at 5 percent a year, both
plausible numbers.

In short, the present set of monetary arrangements, while not in any
immediate danger of collapse from its intrinsic features, as distinguished
from some external event, is not stable in the long run. It is not a durable
system. It must evolve into something else.

But what will or should it evolve into? One possibility is that the
frustrations arising from the sense of loss of national control will lead to

significant attempts to reassert national control by sharply reducing the openness and permeability of national economies to external influences. The move to flexible exchange rates can itself be interpreted as such a response, since countries enjoyed even less control, especially as regards monetary policy, under a system of fixed exchange rates with high capital mobility. But we have now learned that flexible exchange rates, while they offer some degree of greater national autonomy, do not effectively insulate national economies from external influences, and indeed in some instances may even exacerbate the impact of external influences on national economic developments. So the frustrations at loss of national control continue, and alleviating them requires much stronger insulating material than flexible exchange rates alone provide. It would probably involve a reversion to extensive use of restrictions over capital movements. And since capital transactions cannot be effectively separated from current transactions, there would be a tendency to extend restrictions to current transactions as well.

3 Future Arrangements

I suggest a different possible evolution of international monetary arrangements that attempts to deal with the intrinsic problems with present arrangements that render them unstable in the long run. First, let us go forward 25 years, to the year 2010. That is far enough ahead so that developments that are completely unrealistic in the next five or ten years can be contemplated. But it is not so far ahead that we cannot really contemplate them at all.

By 2010 the populations and labor forces of the modern industrial economies will of course be larger than they are today, but the labor force engaged in manufacturing production in today's OECD (Organization for Economic Cooperation and Development) countries will probably have declined. Manufacturing is likely to go the way that agriculture has already gone, with a declining share of the labor force able to produce all of the material goods that the rest of society needs. Real incomes per capita will be over 50 percent higher than they are today. The world will be very electronic. Thus not only will large-scale financial transactions take place virtually instantaneously to any part of the world—we are close to that situation today—but even retail transactions in financial services and in goods can take place electronically. That is, householders will be able to purchase information regarding taxation, investments, retirement possibilities, or education by consulting electronic catalogues and information sources in their own homes. Even goods will be able to be purchased by inspecting them on a television screen, placing the order electronically, and having them delivered in a relatively short period of time. English will become even more widespread as the language of commerce.

With higher real incomes and lower relative prices for long-distance transportation, much more travel will take place than occurs today. Reliable, high-speed and low-cost communications over the globe will permit management control of production locations in many places. Lower transportation costs (relative to the price of other goods and services) will encourage trade. These factors taken together are likely to result in greater possibilities for substitution of geographic locations, not only in manufacturing production but also in many services. Thus, real movements in exchange rates will be highly disruptive of profits, production and employment in any particular location.

Yet financial factors will still dominate the determination of exchange rates in the short run. In view of the greater sensitivity of production to changes in real exchange rates, governments must reduce arbitrary movements in real exchange rates in order to maintain an open trading system. With widespread information and low transaction costs, an adjustable peg system of exchange rates that requires occasional discretionary movements in market exchange rates is not likely to be tenable—indeed, did not prove to be tenable even under the technological conditions prevailing in the 1960s.

These various considerations lead me to conclude that *we will need a system of credibly fixed exchange rates* by that time if we are to preserve an open trading and financial system. Exchange rates can be most credibly fixed if they are eliminated altogether, that is, if international transactions take place with a single currency. But a single currency is possible only if there is in effect a single monetary policy, and a single authority issuing the currency and directing the monetary policy. How can independent states accomplish that? They need to turn over the determination of monetary policy to a supranational body, but one which is responsible collectively to the governments of the independent states. There is some precedent for parts of this type of arrangement in the origins of the US Federal Reserve System, which blended quite separate regions of the country, and banks subject to diverse state banking jurisdictions, into a single system, paralleling the increasingly national financial market. Similarly, we will need a world monetary system that parallels the increasingly global financial market. It will probably not be possible, even within the time scale envisaged here, to have a truly global Bank of Issue. But that will not be necessary either, and it may be possible to have a Bank of Issue which serves a more limited group of democratic countries, and which can serve as the core of an international system.

The Monetary Authority

The tasks, the instruments, and the decision-making structure of the Bank of Issue could look something like the following:

The governing board would be made up of representatives of national governments, whose votes would be weighted according to the share of the national GNP in the total gross product of the community of participating nations. This weighting could be altered at five-year intervals to allow for differences in growth rates.

The task of the monetary authority would be to stabilize the macroeconomic environment and to avoid or mitigate liquidity crises by acting as a lender of last resort, just as national central banks do today. The debate on the relative weights to be attached to output and employment as opposed to price stabilization, and on how monetary policy should actually be managed, could continue just as it does at present, without prejudice.

The Bank of Issue would accomplish its tasks by engaging in open market operations in which it issued the new currency for the securities of member countries. It could also engage in rediscount operations, whereby it extended claims against itself in exchange for acceptable paper at the initiative of banks within the system, subject to its own acquiescence in those initiatives.

The Bank of Issue need not engage in detailed regulation of the banks throughout the system covered by the new currency. That could be left in the hands of national regulators. It would, however, probably want to issue guidelines—minimum standards—to be followed by national regulators, and to maintain enough surveillance over banks to be sure of itself when it was called upon to act as a lender of last resort.

In the first instance, open market operations by the Bank of Issue could be distributed among the securities of national governments in proportion to their voting weight (i.e., their GNP share), but over time this limitation would probably cease to be necessary as financial markets evolved and securities issued by many national governments became virtually perfect substitutes one for another. In any case, the Bank of Issue's holdings of national government securities could be altered from GNP shares via the rediscounting facility, as needed.

Seigniorage in this system would automatically be distributed to national governments as their securities were purchased by the Bank of Issue, thereby giving them the purchasing power to buy goods and services. In addition, the Bank of Issue would run profits from its interest earnings, and those could be distributed from time to time to national governments on the basis of their voting shares.

The currency of the Bank of Issue could be practically anything. Most natural would be an evolution from the present US dollar, making use of the extensive dollar-based worldwide markets. But if that were not politically acceptable, it could be a synthetic unit that the public would have to get used to, just as it had to get used to the metric system when that replaced numerous national systems. The key point is that monetary control—the issuance of currency and of reserve credit—would be in the hands of the new Bank of Issue, not in the hands of any national government, no matter what the historical origin of the new currency happened to be.

National Economic Policy

The publics of the industrial democracies have placed high expectations on their national governments for economic management. Here governments are being asked to pass monetary policy to a supranational agency, the actions of which they can influence but not determine, taken one by one. Would national governments be giving up all of their macroeconomic control? The answer to this question is negative, since they could still pursue fiscal policy at the national level. What they would be giving up is monetary financing of budget deficits beyond their prorated allocation from jointly agreed open market operations. In particular, they could not engage in inflationary finance to reduce the real value of outstanding currency and debt at the national level, although the requisite majority could do so at the international level. To finance budget deficits, therefore, it would be necessary to go to the capital market. But under the envisaged circumstances there would no doubt be a very high degree of capital mobility among participants, since all securities would be denominated in a single, widely used currency. Of course, the influence of national fiscal actions on national aggregate demand would be limited by leakages abroad through demand for imports, and at the outer limits by the extent to which individual governments could borrow in the capital market.

Governments could also use their fiscal powers to attract internationally mobile firms by means of tax holidays or other fiscal incentives. These practices have already emerged as a new form of fiscal action both within countries (e.g., industrial development bonds issued by individual states within the United States) and between countries. With internationally mobile capital, these practices may indeed succeed in generating local employment in "depressed" areas without necessarily resulting in a misallocation of resources, as the burden of taxation is shifted to relatively immobile residents. Nonetheless, if these practices became too competitive among nations, they might want to put some collectively agreed limits on them, and even allow special differentiation under some circumstances, e.g., when unemployment rates were higher than some agreed norm.

One old-fashioned policy instrument for encouraging local investment and employment is the use of tariffs to discriminate against foreign goods. It would be logical if this single currency regime were accompanied by free trade, just as the dollar area within the United States is accompanied by free trade. That would also be consistent with the collaborative political spirit that would be required for the single currency regime to be established. Free trade would ensure one market in goods as well as in financial instruments. The scheme would be quite workable also with modest tariffs, at or below the levels that now generally prevail among industrialized countries. But the exact nature of the commercial regime is beyond the scope of this article.

How the Regime Would Work

Governments could determine the balance between their expenditures and taxes as they do now, but beyond their pro-rated share of the Bank of Issue's open market purchases and profits they would have to borrow on the capital market to cover any budget deficits. Market access would be determined by a market assessment of the probability of repayment, which would assuredly be high within a plausible range of budgetary behavior. Both receipts and expenditures would be made in the common currency, as would the borrowing. Each country could set its own course independently, with no need for formal coordination of fiscal policy. Financial markets would "coordinate" to some extent, via interest rates, since if all governments decided to borrow heavily at once, in a period in which private demands for credit were also high, interest rates would rise and that would induce greater caution in borrowing. But the larger countries would certainly find it useful to exchange information on intentions with respect to future actions, so that each of them could take the prospective actions of others into account. This exchange would no doubt evolve over time into an iterative process that was hardly distinguishable from coordination, although in the end each country would be free to act as it saw fit.

Monetary policy would be set for the community as a whole by a board of governors, who in practice would probably be finance ministers. No single country would be in control. A weighted majority of the governors would decide the principles both to govern monetary policy (e.g., how much weight to give to monetary magnitudes as opposed to other economic variables in framing monetary policy) and with respect to actual operations. The governors in turn would be accountable to legislatures. The Bank of Issue would have a certain autonomy by virtue of not being beholden to any single legislative or executive authority. Thus it could not be manipulated for particular electoral reasons. On the other hand, its actions would be determined by a majority of officials who would be individually accountable to legislatures or executives, so that if a (weighted) majority of them desired a shift in policy, it would occur.

Balance-of-payments adjustment within this regime would be as easy, or as difficult, as it is between regions of the United States or any other large country today. The adjustment would be automatic, except insofar as it was cushioned by capital inflows induced by fiscal actions. Automatic balance-of-payments adjustment sometimes leads to unemployment, as following a shift in demand away from the products of a particular region or country. Fiscal policy in its various forms could be used to cushion such unemployment. In addition, my guess is that there would be considerable net immigration into the present industrial democracies by early in the next century, and the distribution of that flow of migrants would provide considerable flexibility to the labor force in the region as a whole.

This one-currency regime is much too radical to envisage in the near future. But it is not too radical to envisage 25 years from now, and indeed some such scheme, or its functional equivalent, will be necessary to avoid retrogression into greater reliance on barriers to international trade and financial transactions. Moreover, it is useful to have a vision to provide guidance for the steps that may be feasible in the near future. Some idea of where we would like to get to provides a sense of direction for the next steps.

4 Next Steps

The idea of a single currency is so far from being politically feasible at present—in its call for a pooling of monetary sovereignty—that it will require many years of consideration before people become accustomed to the idea. But the economic effect can be gradually approximated by giving greater weight to exchange rates in framing national monetary policy. Many countries—all those with fixed or semifixed rates—of course already do this. This injunction therefore applies mainly to the United States, Canada, Japan, the United Kingdom, and the members of the European Monetary System taken as a group. If monetary policy were governed in such a way as to limit wide swings in key exchange rates, this would tend also to reduce fluctuations in real exchange rates. This result could be accomplished by adoption of one or another of the formal schemes that have been proposed from time to time, such as the target zone, whereby countries undertake to confine market movements of the exchange rate within a specified band centered on a target rate, which target can if necessary be altered from time to time. The European Monetary System is a variant of such a scheme, with central rates being subject to periodic renegotiation as they become questionable. Seven changes in central rates have been made in the period since 1979, and generally the changes have been sufficiently small so that market exchange rates were not immediately affected, or were affected only modestly.

It may not be possible to reach international agreement on a formal scheme for exchange rate management. But the process of official discussion of such schemes, each particular one of which is subject to defects under some circumstances, will apprise officials of the possibilities for accomplishing the principal objective, viz. to reduce undue fluctuations in real exchange rates. Thus launching a move toward "reform" of exchange rate arrangements may fail in the sense that no formal scheme is agreed on, but still succeed in its underlying purpose of establishing a more or less shared view of what exchange rates should be at a given time and a consensus to work toward keeping market rates within the neighborhood of the consensus rates.

What is also necessary is some consultation among major countries on the overall "tone" of monetary policy. This is a politically difficult step and cannot be taken overtly any time soon, since each nation has its formal system of decision making and channels of responsibilities for determining monetary policy. However, the same result can be accomplished informally, centered around discussion of exchange rate management, for which there seems to be a widespread desire, especially in business circles.

It was suggested in the previous section that the choice of a currency for a one-currency regime is open and in a sense is arbitrary. It could be anything that is agreed, since money is above all a social convention. In fact the choice would be a politically charged issue, with strong if irrational objections to the choice of any national currency. If national currencies are ruled out, that leaves the European currency unit (ECU) and SDR in today's world. The ECU might meet the same objections in the United States and Japan as the US dollar would meet in Europe. That in turn leaves only the SDR, which is now defined as a weighted average of five leading national currencies: the US dollar, the Japanese yen, the German mark, the French franc and the British pound. The new Bank of Issue could not issue IMF-SDRs unless the Bank were the IMF itself. But the Bank could use the SDR as its measuring unit, and issue both currency notes and reserve bank credit in that unit.

The future of the SDR as a currency would be immeasurably enhanced if private parties could conduct transactions in SDRs; indeed, that would be a necessary condition. It would also greatly facilitate the use of the SDR as a central bank currency, since the modus operandi of central banks in most cases is through private markets, and they need a medium which can be used in private markets. Thus the IMF-SDR would be enhanced if some mechanism could be found to make this possible. The IMF Articles would have to be amended to make it possible for private parties and commercial banks to hold the IMF-SDR directly. Professor Peter Kenen of Princeton University has recently made an ingenious proposal which would accomplish much the same result without formally amending the Articles.[1] This is not an urgent step, but it should be done if the role of SDRs is to be strengthened. Also, it would be desirable to issue more IMF-SDRs to keep that asset alive and in use. We will want it sometime in the future. The British economist John Williamson, of the Institute for International Economics, has recently shown that an issue of SDR 43 billion over the next two years, while at first glance a large figure, could easily be justified.[2]

A key question concerning the new Bank of Issue is what countries should participate in its management, use its currency, and forswear national monetary policy. We have come to think of the international monetary system, centered on the IMF with its 146 members, as a global system, albeit excluding most communist countries and Switzerland. That was certainly the conception at Bretton Woods, even though most of the early negotiation had been between the Americans and the British. That was also the spirit of the times at Bretton Woods, when the wartime allies placed their hopes for a better world in the United Nations Organization and its functional affiliates.

But there is serious question about whether one world money is either necessary or desirable. And it is certainly not feasible, even within our generous 25-year time frame. It is not feasible for two reasons. First, it is highly doubtful whether the American public, to take just one example, could ever accept that countries with oppressive autocratic regimes should vote on the monetary policy that would affect monetary conditions in the United States. I believe that the same reservations would obtain in other democratic societies. For such a bold step to work at all, it presupposes a certain convergence of political values as reflected in the nature of political decision making, and the basic trust and confidence to which those give rise.

Second, countries with different values, circumstances, and systems of governance are bound to introduce into negotiations leading toward a common Bank of Issue elements which are of greater interest to them, thus broadening the agenda for negotiation and rendering impossible an already difficult negotiation. For both reasons the proposal should be undertaken in the first instance by the United States, Japan, and the members of the European Community. This group represents the core of the monetary system at present and for some time to come. Other democracies would be free to join if they wished, and if they were willing to undertake the commitments involved, but no one should be obliged to join. Very likely many countries would find it attractive in the early stages not to join, but nonetheless to peg their currencies to the SDR or whatever was the unit of account of the Bank of Issue. They would retain some monetary freedom, however, which members had given up. Some countries would also be reluctant to give up the seigniorage from currency issue, which can be consequential where currency still bears a high ratio to GNP.

In short, there would be an inner club accepting higher responsibilities, but open to additional members who met the requirements, and of value even to nonmembers by providing a stable monetary environment against which to frame their economic policies. But this arrangement would mark a formal break with the universalism that governs the de jure if not the de facto structure of the Bretton Woods system today.

Notes

1. See Peter B. Kenen, "Use of the SDR to Supplement or Substitute for Other Means of Finance," in George M. von Furstenberg, ed., *International Money and Credit: The Policy Roles*, Washington: IMF, 1983.

2. See John Williamson, *A New SDR Allocation?* Washington: Institute for International Economics, March 1984.

Acknowledgments of Sources

"Prolegomena to the Choice of an International Monetary System," *International Organization*, Vol. 29, Winter 1975. Reprinted by permission.

"The Gold Standard: Historical Facts and Future Prospects," *Brookings Papers on Economic Activity*, 1982, No. 1. Reprinted by permission.

"Flexing the International Monetary System: The Case for Gliding Parities," Federal Reserve Bank of Boston, *The International Adjustment Mechanism*, 1970. Reprinted by permission.

"Flexible Exchange Rates: How Bad Have They Really Been?" Reprinted with permission from R. N. Cooper, J. de Macedo, P. Kenen, and J. Van Ypersele (eds.), *The International Monetary System Under Flexible Exchange Rates: Global, Regional and National* (essays in honor of Robert Triffin), copyright 1982, Ballinger Publishing Company.

"The Balance-of-Payments Adjustment Process," Committee for Economic Development, 1973.

"IMF Surveillance over Floating Exchange Rates" in Robert A. Mundell and Jacques J. Polak (eds.) *The New International Monetary System*, New York: Columbia University Press, 1977. Reprinted by permission.

"Eurodollars, Reserve Dollars, and Asymmetries in the International Monetary System," *Journal of International Economics II*, (September 1972) pp. 325–44. Reprinted by permission.

"The Future of the Dollar," *Foreign Policy*, No. 11, Summer 1973. Reprinted with permission. Copyright 1973 by the Carnegie Endowment for International Peace.

"Sterling, European Monetary Unification, and the International Monetary System," British North-American Committee, 1972. Reprinted by permission.

"The Future of the SDR," a comment on a paper by Peter Kenen in George von Furstenberg (ed.), *International Money and Credit: The Policy Roles*, Washington: IMF, 1983. Reprinted by permission.

"The International Monetary System in the 1980s," a paper presented at the Lehrman Institute, May 1981, extended in March 1982 for presentation to the Chinese Academy of Social Sciences.

"The Evolution of the International Monetary Fund Towards a World Central Bank," Commonwealth Economic Papers No. 18: *Towards a New Bretton Woods*, vol. I, London: Commonwealth Secretariat, 1983. Reprinted by permission.

"A Monetary System for the Future", *Foreign Affairs*, October 1984. Reprinted by permission. Copyright 1984 by the Council on Foreign Relations, Inc.

Subject Index

Name Index